Michel de Montaigne

Michel de Montaigne

SELECTED ESSAYS

TRANSLATED, AND WITH
INTRODUCTION AND NOTES
BY DONALD M. FRAME

Published for the Classics Club ® by

WALTER J. BLACK, INC. · ROSLYN, N. Y.

Contents

Essays

BOOK I

BOOK II

BOOK III

Contents

Translator's Note

THE translation and selection are my own. They are based on the conviction that the average reader of today can find enjoyment and profit in a faithful English version of Montaigne; that the complete *Essays* are long enough to give pause to any but the most determined reader; and that the freshest and most important part of Montaigne, certainly for our time and probably for all time, is his pursuit of moral independence and a reasonable, happy way of life. I have included only complete essays, which means omitting some that are important (like the "Apology for Raymond Sebond," a book in itself), but which gives a more faithful impression of his writings and of the leisurely, digressive method that is a part of his charm. My aim in selecting the fourteen essays that follow has been to present as full a picture of the man and his ideas as is possible in a volume of this size.

A new translation seems to require some justification. Five English translations already exist, and some revisions. That of Florio (1603), though picturesque, is too much Florio: often inaccurate, often wordy, often flowery. Cotton (1685-1693) and his revisers, though clearer, are still inaccurate, and too abstract to do justice to Montaigne's vivid concreteness. While the translation of Ives (1925) has many merits, it is sometimes stiff. His refusal to put some of Montaigne's coarse passages into English is regrettable, for a healthy coarseness is a significant aspect of the essayist's mistrust of convention. Two recent translations, by Trechmann (1927) and Zeitlin (1934-1936), seem to me far the best. Trechmann puts Montaigne into fine, straightforward, readable English. However, he is not always perfectly dependable for the meaning; and sometimes he translates freely when I think a more literal rendering would have been just as good English and better Montaigne. My criticism of Zeitlin is just the opposite. His scholarly translation, which is the best for the meaning, sometimes makes awkward English out of everyday French. He makes no effort to reproduce Montaigne's playful puns, and is often academically explicit where Montaigne is cavalierly laconic. However, these two are excellent translations, and I am much indebted to them.

My aim in this translation, which is based primarily on Villey's edition of 1922-1923, has been to reproduce Montaigne's meaning clearly and faithfully in an English as living as his French. To me the great qualities of Montaigne's style are concreteness and naturalness. His ideas are expressed in images, often bold, that move and walk and breathe before us; they must do so in English as in French. His pet dislike in style is pedantry; his avowed aim, directness, pungency, expressiveness: "a simple, natural speech, the same on paper as in the mouth; a speech succulent and sinewy, brief and compressed, not so much dainty and well-combed as vehement and brisk." If Montaigne, who favored the speech of the Paris markets, had been writing in twentieth-century English, he might have drawn frequently upon the lively, careless, pithy language of America. I have therefore felt free in using it myself.

I have made my own translation of nearly all the Latin

quotations—a hazardous undertaking. The English version of course represents the form that Montaigne quotes, even when he misquotes. Since the form inevitably suffers in such fragments, I have tried above all to keep the meaning and the concision, depending on rhyme to remind the reader that, in the original at least, this was poetry.

D. M. F.

Montaigne

In 1940 many Frenchmen turned for consolation from the ordeal of their oppression to a man who kept up his courage and poise through other bitter years—that "wisest Frenchman who ever existed," Michel de Montaigne, whose *Essays* have been reported as a best seller among unbanned books in Nazi-dominated Paris. Ever a favorite in England and America, Montaigne's stature has grown throughout the world with the passing years. "If people realized," writes Christopher Morley, "that almost everything conceivably sayable had been said in Montaigne, why should they ever buy another book?" Every age has found something—and something new—in the *Essays*.

Furthermore, successive ages have seemed, in a sense, to grow up with Montaigne. The earliest trend of his thought was a sort of stoicism, and it was for this that he was most admired by his sixteenth-century contemporaries. Later in his life came his most skeptical period; and later admirers, from Pascal to Emerson, saw the core of his thought in his famous motto, "What do I know?" The idea of writing quite frankly about himself came slowly to Montaigne; likewise his readers were prone to ignore this side of him until the eighteenth century, when Rousseau, who owed much to him, brought the ego into good repute. Finally, the more

Montaigne wrote, the more he came to have faith in following one's nature; and since a century ago when Sainte-Beuve proclaimed that Montaigne was not so much a skeptic or a systematic philosopher as "Nature entire, without divine grace," many readers, like Gide, have found in him a lesson of naturalness and tolerant individualism. Future ages, having digested these lessons and carried them further than Montaigne's fifty-nine years of life allowed him to do, will doubtless exploit new veins of ore in the apparently inexhaustible mine of the *Essays*.

For as a French critic, Emile Faguet, has well said, Montaigne rivals his hero Socrates as a mental midwife, who brings his own ideas into the world of consciousness and teaches his reader to do the same. Writers have been learning and borrowing from him—with and without credit—ever since the first publication of the *Essays:* Shakespeare, Bacon, Locke, Emerson, Thackeray, to mention but a few. An educator in the truest sense of the word, he never imposes his stamp on his students, but brings out the stuff that is already latent in them. Consequently his disciples have been as varied in thought and temperament as those of any great thinker. Yet all have recognized themselves in his self-portrait. "It seemed to me," wrote Emerson of his first reading of Montaigne, "as if I had myself written the book in some former life, so sincerely it spoke to my thought and experience." For in his portrait Montaigne reveals not only his own thoroughly individual self, but the very essence of man.

Montaigne's lifetime (1533-1592) was a period of transition, of contrasts, and of strife. In the early years of the sixteenth century two powerful new trends arose and struggled with the old: the expansive humanism of the Renaissance,

thirsting for knowledge and beauty, and finding them in the works of ancient Greece and Rome and modern Italy, supplanted the waning culture of the Middle Ages; while the Protestant Reformation attacked not only the abuses within the Church, but also, by its insistence on going back to the Bible itself, the tremendous authority that the Church had enjoyed during the Middle Ages. Presently the two new currents of Renaissance and Reformation came into conflict with each other; but the great conflict was between Catholics and Protestants, and culminated in the bloody religious civil wars of the later years of the century.

Michel Eyquem de Montaigne was born in the year when Rabelais published the first book of *Pantagruel,* and was three years old when Erasmus died and Calvin's *Institutes* appeared. He lived through the religious wars and died before Henry IV had even conquered his own kingdom. He was born on the rolling estate of Montaigne in the valley of the Dordogne in southwestern France. His great-grandfather, Ramon Eyquem, of Bordeaux, had bought it fifty-six years before with money earned in his business of salt fish and wine, and had taken the name of the property for his title as a nobleman. Montaigne's father, Pierre Eyquem de Montaigne, was a remarkable man, vigorous in mind and body. After fighting in the Italian wars under Francis I, he married, improved the family fortunes, and served two terms as Mayor of Bordeaux. Young Michel grew up in a family where different creeds lived together in peace. His mother, by descent a Spanish Jewess, was a Protestant, as was one brother and one sister; he himself, his father, two sisters, and three brothers were Catholics. His skeptical tolerance in a time when intolerance was rife, his concern with

conduct rather than dogma, may well have their source in the atmosphere of his childhood.

Pierre Eyquem de Montaigne helped make his eldest surviving son natural and independent by the education he contrived for him. Alert and hungry for new ideas, he studied the most advanced views of his time in Italy and France, and concluded that guidance yielded better results than compulsion. Young Montaigne was never treated severely; he was even awakened every morning by music. To bring him close to the humble people, he had peasants for godfather, godmother, and nurse. To teach him Latin easily and well, he was given a German tutor who knew no French. Young Montaigne neither heard nor spoke his own language until he was six; but throughout his life Latin was a sort of native tongue to him, and the Romans were his dearest friends in literature. The contrast between his early training and his later formal schooling, at the Collège de Guienne in Bordeaux, gave Montaigne strong feelings, which he expresses in his essay "Of the Education of Children," about the importance of proper education and the viciousness of the systems current in his time.

After studying law, probably at Toulouse, he was set up, in the manner of his day, as a counselor in the Cour des Aides of Périgueux. Three years later, in 1557, this group was incorporated into the Parlement (a sort of Supreme Court) of Bordeaux. Law made relatively little impression on Montaigne, and he on it; he cared only for equity. However, in the Bordeaux court he met a serious, noble young lawyer, a little older than himself, Etienne de la Boétie, poet and author of a treatise against tyranny. For four or five years these two enjoyed a deep friendship, the strongest relationship of Montaigne's life, which he commemorates glowingly in his

book. Then in 1563 La Boétie fell ill of dysentery. Montaigne visited him regularly; and when La Boétie told him that his illness was contagious and that he should come less often, Montaigne's answer was to stay by his friend day and night until he died. He never ceased regretting him.

Two years later, without great enthusiasm, he married the daughter of a colleague, Françoise de la Chassaigne, to whom he was a dutiful if not a loving husband. His father died in 1568, leaving him the estate and the château. He had asked his son to translate the *Theologia Naturalis* of Raymond Sebond, and a year later this translation appeared—Montaigne's first publication. By 1571, Montaigne had retired from the court, published La Boétie's Latin verses, and withdrawn to his manor, solemnizing this event by inscribing in Latin on his study wall his intention to leave the weary slavery of the courts for freedom and calm in the bosom of the learned muses. Disappointed ambition may have been a motive of this retirement at thirty-eight; more important were Montaigne's longing for a quiet life in the country with his books, and his distaste for red tape, judicial injustice, and the hypocrisy of public life.

Henceforth Montaigne's life and his book—"a book consubstantial with its author," as he calls it—are as one. In his essay "Of Three Kinds of Association" he tells of the tower in the château which he reserved for himself, with its study and its thousand-volume library, where he loved to read, meditate—and look out the window at the outdoor life that shapes his style. He had seen much of the world, met and observed great men at Bordeaux and on his frequent trips to Paris. He loved to read, and books aroused his thoughts. As he read, he made notes; as the notes grew, he compared

them—from the first with an inborn interest in contradictions
—and drew conclusions.

The earliest *Essays*—the first essays ever written—are col-
lections of stories with brief morals, which Montaigne
started in 1572. In them he rarely ventures to express his
own philosophical ideas; when he does, he follows Seneca's
rigid stoicism. Later Plutarch, put into French by Amyot,
offers him a gentler code which he finds better suited to
him; under this influence he expands, and dares express himself more freely. Sextus Empiricus, with his account of
Pyrrho's magisterial skepticism, confirms Montaigne's own
penchant for doubt, giving him a clean slate and confidence
to write on it words of his own. More and more he seeks
factual certainty in the knowledge of himself. And when in
1580 he publishes the first two books of the *Essays* (in
shorter form than they are now), Montaigne dares to tell
his reader at the outset what is less true at that date than it
will be later: that he himself is the matter of his book.

Meanwhile his life was not all spent in his tower. All over
France intermittent civil wars were raging. While the main
struggle was between Catholics and Protestants, a powerful
third party of ambitious Catholic noblemen, the Ligue, led
by the Guises, finally brought the other two factions into
temporary alliance against them. The year Montaigne started
to write his essays was that of the bloody massacre of Saint
Bartholomew's Day, in which 8,000 Protestants were slaugh-
tered by order of Catherine de Medici, the queen mother,
and Henry of Guise. The province in which he lived was
split between Catholics loyal to Charles IX and later Henry
III of the reigning house of Valois, and Protestants who followed Henry of Navarre, founder of the house of Bourbon
as Henry IV.

Montaigne himself was torn by divided loyalty. Equally respected by both sides, he had been given the order of Saint Michel by Charles IX and made a chamberlain by Henry of Navarre; in 1574 he had been selected to try to negotiate an agreement between the latter and the Duke of Guise. While he admired the Protestant leader, Henry of Navarre, and despised the effeminate and prodigal Henry III, civil war confirmed his conservatism as a faithful subject and a Catholic. Convinced that a man must uphold his king, he fought for Henry III; loyal and clear-sighted, he remained friends with Henry of Navarre and entertained him twice at his manor during this critical period.

After publishing his *Essays* at Bordeaux in 1580 and presenting a copy to the king in Paris, Montaigne set out with a few friends on a trip to Rome via the mineral baths of Switzerland, Germany, and Italy. For three years he had been suffering from gall-stones, the disease that had killed his father and was to afflict and shorten his own life. Now he was traveling for pleasure, to cure his illness, and to see the city he most admired. As he went his cheerful way, he kept an interesting diary, not intended for publication but discovered and printed in 1774, of the sights and people he saw and the 'case history' of his treatments. His stay in his beloved Rome won him an honorary patent of Roman citizenship which he proudly reproduced in full in his essay "Of Vanity," and a polite request from the Papal authorities, who had examined his book, to change certain passages —which Montaigne somehow neglected to do. He was still in Italy when in September, 1581, he was notified that he had been elected Mayor of Bordeaux. Feeling himself neither fitted nor eager for the job, he declined; but two months later, on his return home, he found a request from King

Henry that he accept. It was polite but insistent. Montaigne was mayor.

The office of Mayor of Bordeaux in 1581 was not as exacting as we of today might suppose. Most of the power and responsibility lay with the Jurats, a sort of municipal council. Montaigne had not sought election—indeed he had done his best to avoid it—and he did not hesitate to tell the Jurats just what they might expect of him. He would lend himself, not give himself, to his office; Montaigne and the mayor would always be two. Nevertheless he did a vigilant and efficient job in a trying time when civil war raged in the vicinity. In 1583 he was re-elected. Two years later, as he was resting at home from his labors, the plague broke out in Bordeaux. The Jurats were in charge, but the mayor would normally have been expected to return into the city for the election of his successor. Montaigne asked to be excused from the needless risk. His request was granted, and he remained outside Bordeaux, where indeed his family soon needed him when the plague spread to his home. His admirers have often regretted that he thus sacrificed heroism to prudence; but it is significant that his contemporaries never thought to reproach him for it.

After Montaigne had guided his family for six months in their flight from the plague, he was at last able to return, at fifty-three, to his *Essays*. The success of the first two books had given him confidence, so that in the new third book and in countless additions to the first two, he dared be more completely and frankly himself. His travels had unquestionably broadened him. So in a different way had his experiences during the plague, which showed him that neither learned men nor ancients nor noblemen have any monopoly on the philosophy which consists in learning to die like a man, and that mother Nature takes care of those things better than book-learned precepts.

From his broadened experience came the dominant trends of his maturity: greater concern with himself, whom he portrayed with disarming frankness and detachment ("Of Vanity"); greater freedom from confirmed doubt, greater faith in common sense and experience ("Of Experience"); most of all, greater suspicion of moral codes made to fit all men, greater faith in the right and duty of the individual to find his own way ("Of Repentance"). Two examples show the change wrought in him since his early years. Death, which had so worried him at first that he proclaimed it the goal of life, became now merely a part of the order of nature, the inevitable end which must not spoil life itself. His idol, formerly the austere Cato, became the eminently human, moderate, and versatile Socrates. Montaigne did not change utterly, but he let life teach him, and made its wisdom a part of him. His late writings, Book III of the *Essays* in particular, are his mellowest, his most individual, and his most thoroughly human. In them above all we find the real, the living Montaigne.

The last years of his life were not wholly uneventful. While staying in Paris in 1588 to supervise publication of his new three-book edition of the *Essays*, Montaigne was imprisoned in the Bastille for a few hours by the Ligue, as a sort of hostage, until Catherine de Medici arranged his release. On the same trip he came to know his warm admirer and future editor, the learned young Marie de Gournay, whom he called his "covenant daughter" and made his literary executor. He went with the court to Chartres and Rouen, and mingled with the great men of his time at the States General in Blois. After his return home, Henry IV urged him more than once to come to Paris, and only the essayist's declining health denied him the joy of helping his hero in the way he felt he best could do it.

Montaigne died of quinsy on September 13, 1592. His was a peaceful and Christian death.

What makes Montaigne so interesting to all types of men is his concern with our most immediate and universal problem: what is man, and how is he to live? If above all Montaigne studies himself, that is largely because he is the handiest example of man and life, and can be known most surely. If he spends much time and attention on skepticism, he does not remain completely skeptical; he is wary of the lessons of books, but never of the lessons of life. His ultimate concern, since all we can surely know is that we are alive, is learning to enjoy life as best we can by adapting ourselves to it in human fashion.

The history of Montaigne's thought is one of growth from cautious conventionality to thorough independence and to the conviction that all men should learn to think independently. His early "stoicism" is more an admiration than a conviction, and soon gives place to a more natural ethical ideal. His skepticism is not a halt, but a step forward. It is an attempt to clear the ground of the stumps and stones of fallible authority and verbal logic, so that thinking may rest upon a foundation of solid fact. It is true that he does a thorough job of clearing, notably in his longest chapter, the "Apology for Raymond Sebond," which starts as a defense of the fifteenth-century Spaniard whose *Theologia Naturalis* Montaigne had translated. Finding Sebond attacked for basing religion on human proofs, Montaigne begins by showing briefly that reason is entitled to do its share. Then, in reply to the rationalists who consider Sebond's proofs invalid, Montaigne embarks on a trenchant critique of human knowledge.

In the first place, he says, man is not intrinsically different from the animals; his advantages are only of degree, and at that they are doubtful; numberless tales, which Montaigne gleefully relates, show that the animals can rival man in intelligence and conduct. Man is proud of his knowledge, but it is more harmful than helpful to his happiness and virtue. Worse yet, it is vain. There is nothing about which men really agree, nothing so absurd that some sage has not said it. And no wonder; for man's reason, the instrument of his knowledge, is defective. Powerless to determine his moral life, it is so variable and contradictory that it cannot even determine truth; for all our knowledge depends on our senses, and our senses are imperfect and incomplete. Inevitably we distort whatever we perceive. Perhaps if we had eight or ten senses instead of five, there might be hope; as it is, there is none. For there is yet a final handicap: we are ever changing, and therefore we have no contact with the world of real truth, which is eternal and immutable. Unless God lends us his help by divine revelation, we must remain forever ignorant.

There is more than this to Montaigne's skepticism. This is but the framework of reasoning he erected to support views he already had long held; deeper down lies the skepticism of temperament and experience that Emerson saw so clearly and admired. Naturally hard to convince, and finding that great men disagree as completely as anyone else, Montaigne wonders whether any of them—or himself either—knows the whole truth. Furthermore, he is very much aware that words are not things, but labels pinned on things; that systems of thought are constructed more often of words than of things; that say what the systems will, life will always have the last word. All men know this, but to some it is more important than to others; it was all-important to Montaigne.

Montaigne's religion was probably sincere. Though his notion of faith based on human ignorance may seem strange today, it was not exceptional in his time. What may seem more surprising is that a professed believer should leave Christianity out of virtually all his thoughts. Montaigne's reason is this. Since mortal man unaided has no contact with eternal truth, he should look to human behavior, the proper object of human knowledge, and to common sense and experience, the instruments of that knowledge. This human knowledge, to be sure, is fallible; our results cannot be perfect; still, let us do what we can.

What then can we do with our imperfect tools? We can enjoy life, if we learn how to live; we can learn how to live, if only we learn enough about life, our fellow men, and in particular ourselves. These are not three separate studies. We cannot study ourselves without studying man in general and the part of life that concerns us. For life and man are our terms of comparison: whenever a man says he is good or bad, wise or ignorant, he is comparing himself with others. Furthermore, we humans are enough alike so that each of us, with practice and observation, can find in himself the characteristics of all of us. "Each man bears the entire form of human nature."

So we shall study life in general, the outer circle of our environment; man in general, the inner circle; above all, the center to which all questions return, ourselves. And this study of ourselves need not be merely a means; it may be an end in itself as well. So it was to Montaigne. So it has been to others; yet Montaigne is still unique. He was that rare bird, a happy introvert. Or perhaps we should say a happy introspective; for introversion may suggest a morbid lack of interest in the outer world that would have been abhorrent to the balanced, healthy Montaigne.

The reason for his contentment was his detachment, which allowed him to consider himself as what he was—a man: the center of his own universe, but no more the center of *the* universe than any other of the billions of humans alive. This is a great achievement; it is the key to humor, perspective, justice in thought, contentment in self-contemplation, avoidance of much of the pain of life. But it carries with it a great danger, that of drying up the emotions until joy, like pain, is "sicklied o'er with the pale cast of thought." Montaigne fights this danger with might and main; he even increases his happiness by his consciousness of it. He does not believe in a science of living—man is too variable for that—but in an art of living. It is our most important work here on earth. Hear the triumphant note of Montaigne's last essay, "Of Experience": " 'He has spent his life in idleness,' we say; 'I have done nothing today.' What, have you not lived? That is not only the fundamental but the most illustrious of your occupations . . . It is an absolute perfection and virtually divine to know how to enjoy our being lawfully."

To live happily—to be a real success, that is—we must not only know ourselves, but by knowing ourselves become ourselves. We all think and live at second hand, letting others tell us how, never finding our own way. This is all wrong. It is wrong because it is unnatural. It is unnatural because, all men being made differently, all men are meant by nature to live differently. Montaigne himself does not tell us how to live, but how we ourselves may learn to live. It is true that he would like to see everyone, against their natural bent if necessary, strive to follow certain principles such as truthfulness (the core of morality), kindness, and wisdom. But the first two are easy virtues; and the third is the very principle of self-determination, since wisdom lies in obedience to nature.

Nature is Montaigne's divinity. Everywhere he sees men making themselves unhappy, ridiculous, and even wicked by departing from nature's precepts. The reader will note in his essay "Of Cannibals" that he does not take the paradox of the noble savage seriously, as did Rousseau later; he does not believe we are worse, or worse off, than the cannibals; but he does suggest that we ponder whether we are as much better than they, or better off, as we like to think. For nature to Montaigne is not necessarily primitivism; it is not the romantic nature, compounded largely of instinct and emotion. Nature to Montaigne, human nature in this case, consists of instinct and emotion not suppressed, but controlled as far as possible by reason (or judgment) and conscience, concepts closely allied in Montaigne's thought. Here as elsewhere, harmonious balance is wanted: balance of judgment and spontaneity, balance of soul and body, balance of the qualities and abilities that constitute an all-round man. Reason and conscience will teach us to know our inmost nature, to guide it and improve it when we know it by forming the all-important habits that are a second nature. We need not expect miracles of ourselves—miracles are not *natural*—but we can be happy only if we make a real effort to obey our reason and our conscience. How much we must expect of ourselves, it is for each of us to decide. We must be ever balancing our duty to ourselves—a duty people fulfill admirably but recognize rarely—with our duty to others. This is not easy. It is a perpetual task. But it is also a fascinating task. For in its demands as well as in its satisfactions, it is the way to better, richer, happier living. It is an art, the art of life, the greatest calling in the world.

This then is Montaigne's doctrine; but there is far more in the *Essays* than doctrine. An *essai* in French means an attempt or a trial; and these essays are, as Montaigne says, the trials or tests of his judgment and his natural faculties. Both his inclination and his convictions led him to make himself the subject of his test—himself, not as a nobleman or a mayor or a widely-read thinker, but as a representative human being. The result is a remarkable portrait. The man Montaigne describes is a skeptic, sympathetic with the views of others; a moderate in all things, seeking balance and the golden mean; a conservative in religion and politics, but a warm admirer of the simple courage and good sense of humble people; attentive to his conscience, but rather easy-going; and willing to keep in step with the world, since it may be himself and not the world that is out of step. His is by no means the first autobiography, if we may loosely call it that; but certainly never before, and rarely if ever since, has a man been portrayed with such clinical care and detachment, and at the same time with such humor and urbanity.

The scientist—Montaigne might have smiled at the name, but he might also have been proud of it—tells us the characteristics of the subject that is himself: his inherited traits, his environment, his likes and dislikes, his habits, his thoughts, his observations on his own subconscious, above all his foibles and inconsistencies, of which he speaks with humorous modesty but obvious enjoyment, partly because they are his and partly because man is ever a "marvelously vain, fickle and unstable creature." The artist and man of the world, supervising the writing of the book, contrives to tell of himself in such a way that the individual not only appears clearly, but appears in his most universally human light. The ability to do this is not a literary device. It is not a tool of Montaigne, but a part of him. It is like another sense, a habit of thought, a perpetual awareness of others and insight into their minds.

This is why nearly every reader finds in Montaigne a friend. Like a painted portrait whose eyes seem to follow the spectator wherever he goes, Montaigne's written portrait seems to each reader to be addressed especially to him. Those who call Montaigne an egoist use the word loosely; for he does not obtain his charming illusion by any trick; it springs from sympathy, insight, and a genuine interest in others.

Montaigne tells his story in a style expressive of the man. It is marked principally by concreteness and by lack of apparent order. The lack of order comes partly from Montaigne's countless insertions into his original work, which often break up the movement of his thought. It springs also from his method. Unlike Bacon, who borrowed his title and his medium, Montaigne does not consider a rigorously logical order quite natural. The most natural and therefore the best method is to set down his thoughts in the order in which they come to him. "I go out of my way," he says, "but rather by licentiousness than carelessness." As a result, the *Essays* are anything but a work of reference; in few books is it harder to find what you are looking for. Yet few books reserve more delightful surprises for the reader.

Montaigne's concreteness comes likewise from his principles, from the feeling that style as well as thought should express not the incomplete thinker or the specialist, but the entire man. Even when he writes about abstract matters, his ideas come to him in vivifying images so appropriate, so spontaneous, that they add to the thought and are inseparable from it. "The sincerity and marrow of the man reaches to his sentences," writes Emerson. "Cut these words, and they would bleed; they are vascular and alive." For abstract notions such a form is not only the most palatable, but perhaps also the most profitable; for like the parables of the Bible, ideas so expressed are not put away in mental cold storage, but live, grow, spread, and form a real part, not merely a possession, of their owner.

Montaigne's style, the essay style, was not immediately admired. It was original, casual, colloquial, and personal, in an age of literary imitation, formality, pedantry, and impersonality. Not until the nineteenth-century Romanticist movement did Montaigne receive general acclaim in his own country as a stylist. Since then, however, he has been fully enjoyed in France as he always has been in England, where from his time on the essay has been a respected and treasured literary form.

So cosmopolitan and up-to-date is Montaigne that few books are as close to his in spirit as one by a twentieth-century Chinese that was a best seller in America a few years ago: *The Importance of Living*, by Dr. Lin Yutang. The author reminded us above all that possessions are only a means, not an end in themselves, and that happiness is after all the important thing:

> *The enjoyment of an idle life doesn't cost any money. . . It must come from an inner richness of the soul. . . A man may own a thousand acres of land, and yet he still sleeps upon a bed of five feet. . . Human life can be lived like a poem. . . The greatest ideal that man can aspire to is*

not to be a show-case of virtue, but just to be a genial, likable and reasonable human being.

This is Montaigne's greatest lesson. There is much else in the *Essays*, as we have seen: skepticism, moderation, love of nature, a self-portrait, a treasury of observations about human nature, and directions for achieving moral dignity and independence by studying our own souls and making ourselves at home in them. But the ultimate goal is wiser, happier living:

> *Our good and our ill depend on ourselves alone. . . The poverty of goods is easily cured; the poverty of the soul is incurable. . . It is the enjoyment, not the possessing, that makes us happy. . . There is no use our mounting on stilts, for on stilts we must still walk with our legs. And on the loftiest throne in the world we are still sitting only on our own rear. . . Our great and glorious masterpiece is to live appropriately.*

In time of war, Montaigne still has much to say. Himself a soldier, he knew the virile joys and hardships of military life. Living for years on end in the midst of strife and bloodshed, he went through the strain of wondering every night in his own home whether he would be murdered before he woke. Determined to keep his peace of mind in time of war, he found the way to that inner harmony that is so hard to destroy. If we wonder whether the cause is worth the cost, he is there to remind us that cruelty is the most hateful of vices, that freedom is the dearest need of man; and that humanity, loyalty, truth, and justice are worth a sacrifice. "There is nothing so beautiful and legitimate as to play the man well and properly."

DONALD MURDOCH FRAME

To the Reader

THIS is an honest book, reader. It warns you from the outset that in it I have set myself no goal but a domestic and private one. I have had no thought of serving either you or my own glory. My powers are inadequate for such a purpose. I have dedicated it to the private convenience of my relatives and friends, so that when they have lost me (as they must do soon), they may recover here some traits of my habits and humors, and by this means keep the knowledge they have had of me more complete and alive.

If I had written to seek the world's favor, I should have bedecked myself better, and should present myself in a studied posture. I want to be seen here in my simple, natural, ordinary fashion, without pose or artifice; for it is myself that I portray. My defects will here be read to the life, and my natural form, as far as respect for the public has allowed. If I had belonged to one of those nations which are said to live still in the sweet freedom of Nature's first laws, I assure you I should most gladly have portrayed myself here entire and wholly naked.

Thus, reader, I am myself the matter of my book; you would be unreasonable to spend your leisure on so frivolous and vain a subject.

So farewell from Montaigne, this first day of March, fifteen hundred and eighty.

BOOK I

Of Idleness[*]

Just as we see that fallow land, if rich and fertile, teems with a hundred thousand wild and useless weeds, and that to set it to work we must subject it and sow it with certain seeds for our service; and as we see that women, all alone, produce shapeless masses and lumps of flesh, but that to create a good and natural offspring they must be made fertile with a different kind of seed; so it is with minds. Unless you keep them busy with some definite subject that will bridle and control them, they will throw themselves in disorder hither and yon in the vague field of imagination.

> *As when the light of waters in an urn,*
> *Trembling, reflects the sun or moon, in turn*
> *It flickers round the room, and darts its rays*
> *Aloft, and on the panelled ceiling plays.*
> > [Virgil]

And there is no mad or idle fancy that they will not bring forth in this agitation:

> *They form vain visions, like a sick man's dreams.*
> > [Horace]

¹ Chapter 8.

3

The soul that has no fixed goal loses itself; for as they say, to be everywhere is to be nowhere:

> *He who dwells everywhere, Maximus, nowhere dwells.*
> [Martial]

Lately when I retired to my home, determined so far as possible to bother about nothing except spending the little life I have left in rest and privacy, it seemed to me I could do my mind no greater favor than to let it entertain itself in idleness and stay and settle in itself, which I hoped it might do more easily now, having become heavier and more mature with time. But I find—

> *Ever idle hours breed wandering thoughts*
> [Lucan]

—that, on the contrary, like a runaway horse, it gives itself a hundred times more trouble than it took for others, and gives birth to so many chimeras and fantastic monsters, one after another, without order or purpose, that in order to contemplate their strangeness and foolishness at my pleasure, I have begun to put them in writing, hoping in time to make even my mind ashamed of them.

Of the Education of Children

To Madame Diane de Foix, Comtesse de Gurson

I HAVE never seen a father who failed to claim his son, however mangy or hunchbacked he was. Not that he does not perceive his defect, unless he is utterly intoxicated by his affection; but the fact remains, the boy is his. And so I myself see better than anyone else that these are nothing but reveries of a man who has tasted only the outer crust of sciences in his childhood, and has retained only a vague general picture of them: a little of everything and nothing thoroughly, French style. To sum up, I know that there is such a thing as medicine, jurisprudence, four parts in mathematics, and roughly what they aim at. And perhaps I also know the service that the sciences in general aim to contribute to our life. But as for plunging in deeper, or gnawing my nails over the study of Aristotle, monarch of modern science, or stubbornly pursuing some part of knowledge, I have never done it; nor is there an art of which I could sketch even the outlines. There is not a child halfway through school who cannot claim to be more learned than I, who have not even the learning to examine him on his first lesson, at least according

---

[1] Chapter 26.

to that lesson. And if they force me to, I am constrained, rather ineptly, to draw from it some matter of universal interest, on which I test the boy's natural judgment: a lesson as strange to them as theirs is to me.

I have not had regular dealings with any solid book, except Plutarch and Seneca, from whom I draw like the Danaïds, incessantly filling up and pouring out. Some of this sticks to this paper; to myself, little or nothing.

History is more my quarry, or poetry, which I love with particular affection. For as Cleanthes said, just as sound, pent up in the narrow channel of a trumpet, comes out sharper and stronger, so it seems to me that thought, compressed into the numbered feet of poetry, springs forth much more violently and strikes me a much stiffer jolt. As for the natural faculties that are in me, of which this book is the essay, I feel them bending under the load. My conceptions and my judgment move only by groping, staggering, stumbling, and blundering; and when I have gone ahead as far as I can, still I am not at all satisfied: I can still see country beyond, but with a dim and clouded vision, so that I cannot clearly distinguish it. And when I undertake to speak indiscriminately of everything that comes to my fancy without using any but my own natural resources, if I come across by chance in the good authors, as I often do, those same subjects I have attempted to treat—as in Plutarch I have just this very moment come across his discourse on the power of imagination—seeing myself so weak and puny, so heavy and sluggish, in comparison with those men, I hold myself in pity and disdain.

Still I am pleased at this, that my opinions have the honor of often coinciding with theirs, and that at least I go the same way, though far behind them, saying, "How true!"

Also that I have this, which not everyone has, that I know the vast difference between them and me. And nonetheless I let my thoughts run on, weak and lowly as they are, as I have produced them, without plastering and sewing up the flaws that this comparison has revealed to me. One needs very strong loins to undertake to march abreast of those men. The undiscerning writers of our century who amid their non-existent works scatter whole passages of the ancient authors to do themselves honor, do just the opposite. For this infinite difference in brilliance gives so pale, tarnished, and ugly an aspect to the part that is their own that they lose in this way much more than they gain.

There were two contrasting fancies. The philosopher Chrysippus mixed into his books, not merely passages, but entire works of other authors, and in one the *Medea* of Euripides; and Apollodorus said that if you cut out of them all the foreign matter, the paper he used would be left blank. Epicurus, on the contrary, in three hundred volumes that he left had not put in a single borrowed quotation.

I happened the other day to come upon such a passage. I had dragged along languidly after French words so bloodless, fleshless, and empty of matter and sense that they really were nothing but French words. At the end of a long and boring road I came to a bit that was sublime, rich, and lofty as the clouds. If I had found the slope gentle and the climb a bit slower, it would have been excusable; but it was a precipice so straight and steep that after the first six words I realized that I was flying off into another world. From there I saw the bog I had come out of, so low and deep that I never again had the stomach to go back down into it. If I stuffed one of my chapters with these rich spoils, it would show up too clearly the stupidity of the others.

To criticize my own faults in others seems to me no more unreasonable than to criticize, as I often do, others' faults in myself. We should denounce them everywhere and leave them no place of refuge. Still, I well know how audaciously I always attempt to pull myself up to the standard of my pilferings, to keep pace with them, not without a rash hope that I may deceive the eyes of the judges who try to discover them. But this is as much by virtue of my use of them as by virtue of my inventiveness or my power. And then, I do not wrestle with those old champions wholesale and body against body; I do so by snatches, by little light attacks. I don't go at them stubbornly; I only feel them out; and I don't go at all, as much as I think about going. If I could only hold my own with them I would be a good man, for I attack them only at their stiffest points.

As for doing what I have discovered others doing, covering themselves with borrowed armor until they don't even show their fingertips, and carrying out their plan, as is easy for the learned in common subjects, with ancient inventions pieced out here and there: for those who want to hide them and appropriate them, in the first place it is injustice and cowardice, that, having nothing of their own worth bringing out, they try to present themselves under false colors; and also a great piece of stupidity, that contenting themselves with gaining deceitfully the ignorant approbation of the common herd, they discredit themselves in the eyes of men of understanding, whose praise alone has any weight, and who turn up their noses at our borrowed incrustations. For my part, there is nothing I want less to do. I speak the minds of others only to speak my own mind better. This does not apply to the compilations that are published as compilations; and I have seen some very ingenious ones in my time; among others, one under the name of Capilupus, besides the ancients. These are minds that stand out both there and elsewhere, like Lipsius in the learned and laborious web of his *Politics*.

However that may be, I mean to say, and whatever these absurdities may be, I have no intention of concealing them, any more than I would a bald and graying portrait of myself, in which the painter had drawn not a perfect face, but mine. For likewise these are my humors and opinions; I offer them as what I believe, not what is to be believed. I aim here only at revealing myself, who will perhaps be different tomorrow, if I learn something new which changes me. I have no authority to be believed, nor do I want it, feeling myself too ill-instructed to instruct others.

Well, someone who had seen the preceding article [1] was telling me at my home the other day that I should have enlarged a bit on the subject of the education of children. Now, Madame, if I had some competence in this matter, I could not use it better than to make it a present to the little man who threatens soon to come out so bravely from within you (you are too noble-spirited to begin otherwise than with a male). For having had so great a part in bringing about your marriage, I have a certain rightful interest in the greatness and prosperity of whatever comes out of it; besides that the ancient claim that you have on my servitude is enough to oblige me to wish honor, good, and advantage to all that concerns you. But in truth I know nothing about it save this, that the greatest and most important difficulty in human knowledge seems to lie in this branch which deals with the training and education of children.

Just as in agriculture the operations that come before the

---

[1] The essay "Of Pedantry," which is not included in this selection.

planting, as well as the planting itself, are certain and easy;
but as soon as the plant comes to life, there are various methods and great difficulties in raising it; so with men: little
industry is needed to plant them, but from the time they are
born we assume the burden of the varied task, full of care
and fear, in training them and bringing them up.

The manifestation of their inclinations is so slight and so
obscure at that early age, the promises so uncertain and mis-
leading, that it is hard to base any solid judgment on them.
Look at Cimon, look at Themistocles and a thousand others,
how they belied themselves. The young of bears and dogs
show their natural inclination, but men, plunging headlong
into certain habits, opinions, and laws, easily change and disguise themselves. Still it is difficult to force natural propensities. Whence it happens that, because we have failed to
choose their road well, we often spend a lot of time and effort
for nothing, trying to train children for things in which they
cannot get a foothold. However, in this difficulty, my advice
is to guide them always to the best and most profitable things,
and to pay little heed to those trivial conjectures and prognostications which we make from the actions of their childhood. Even Plato, in his *Republic*, seems to me to give them
too much authority.

Madame, learning is a great ornament and a wonderfully
serviceable tool, notably for people raised to such a degree
of fortune as you are. In truth, it does not receive its proper
use in mean and lowborn hands. It is much prouder to lend
its resources to conducting a war, governing a people, or
gaining the friendship of a prince or a foreign nation, than
to constructing a dialectical argument, pleading an appeal,
or prescribing a mass of pills. Thus, Madame, because I think
you will not forget this element in the education of your

children, you who have tasted its sweetness and who are of a literary race (for we still have the writings of those ancient Counts of Foix from whom Milord the Count, your husband and yourself are descended; and François, Monsieur de Candale, your uncle, every day brings forth others, which will extend for many centuries the knowledge of this quality in your family), I want to tell you a single fancy of mine on this subject, which is contrary to common usage; it is all that I can contribute to your service in this matter.

The task of the tutor that you will give your son, upon whose choice depends the whole success of his education, has many other important parts, but I do not touch upon them, since I cannot offer anything worth while; and in this matter on which I venture to give him advice, he will take it as far as it seems good to him. For a child of noble family who seeks learning not for gain (for such an abject goal is unworthy of the graces and favors of the Muses, and besides it looks to others and depends on them), or so much for external advantages as for his own, and to enrich and furnish himself inwardly, since I would rather make of him an able man than a learned man, I would also urge that care be taken to choose for him a guide with a well-made rather than a well-filled head; that both these qualities should be required of him, but more particularly character and understanding than learning; and that he should go about his job in a novel way.

Most tutors never stop bawling into our ears, as though they were pouring water into a funnel; and our task is only to repeat what has been told us. I should like the tutor to correct this practice, and from the start, according to the capacity of the mind he has in hand, to begin putting it through its paces, making it taste things, choose them and discern them by itself; sometimes clearing the way for him, sometimes letting him clear his own way. I don't want him to think and talk alone, I want him to listen to his pupil speaking in his turn. Socrates, and later Arcesilaus, first had their disciples speak, and then they spoke to them. *The authority of those who teach is often an obstacle to those who want to learn.* [Cicero]

It is good that he should have him trot before him, to judge his pace and how much he must stoop to match his strength. For lack of this proportion we spoil everything; and to be able to hit it right and to go along in it evenly is one of the hardest tasks that I know; and it is the achievement of a lofty and very strong mind to know how to come down to a childish gait and guide it. I walk more firmly and surely up hill than down.

If, as is our custom, the teachers undertake to regulate many minds of such different capacities and forms with the same lesson and a similar amount of guidance, it is no wonder if in a whole race of children they find barely two or three who reap any proper fruit from their instruction.

Let him not be asked for an account merely of the words of his lesson, but of its sense and substance, and let him judge the profit he has made not by the testimony of his memory, but of his life. Let him be made to show what he has just learned in a hundred aspects, and apply it to as many different subjects, to see if he has yet thoroughly grasped it and made it his own, taking stock of his progress by the pedagogical method of Plato. It is a sign of crudeness and indigestion to disgorge food just as we swallowed it. The stomach has not done its work if it has not changed the condition and form of what has been given it to cook.

Our mind will move only on trust, being bound and constrained to the whim of others' fancies, a slave and a captive under the authority of their teaching. We have been so well accustomed to leading strings that we have no free motion left; our vigor and liberty are extinct. *They never become their own guardians.* [Seneca] I had a private talk with a man at Pisa, a good man, but such an Aristotelian that the most sweeping of his dogmas is that the touchstone and measure of all solid speculations and of all truth is conformity with the teaching of Aristotle; that outside of that there is nothing but chimeras and witlessness; that he saw everything and said everything. This proposition, having been interpreted a little too broadly and unfairly, put him once, and kept him long, in great danger of the Inquisition at Rome.

Let the tutor make him pass everything through a sieve and lodge nothing in his head on mere authority and trust: let not Aristotle's principles be principles to him any more than those of the Stoics or Epicureans. Let variety of ideas be set before him; he will choose if he can; if not, he will remain in doubt. Only the fools are certain and assured.

> *For doubting pleases me no less than knowing.*
> [Dante]

For if he embraces Xenophon's and Plato's opinions by his own reasoning, they will no longer be theirs, they will be his. He who follows another follows nothing. He finds nothing; indeed he seeks nothing. *We are not under a king; let each one claim his own freedom.* [Seneca] Let him know that he knows, at least. He must imbibe their ways of thinking, not learn their precepts. And let him boldly forget, if he wants, where he got them, but let him know how to apply them to himself. Truth and reason are common to everyone, and no more belong to the man who first said them than to the man who says them later. It is no more according to Plato than according to me, since he and I understand and see it in the same way. The bees plunder the flowers here and there, but afterwards they make honey of them, which is all theirs; it is no longer thyme or marjoram. Even so with the pieces borrowed from others; he will transform and blend them to make a work that is all his own, to wit, his judgment. His education, work, and study aims only at forming this.

Let him hide all the help he has had, and show only what he has made of it. The pillagers, the borrowers, parade their buildings, their purchases, not what they get from others. You do not see the fees of a member of a parliament, you see the alliances and honors he has gained for his children. No one makes public his receipts; everyone makes public his acquisitions.

The gain from our study is to have become better and wiser by it.

It is the understanding, Epicharmus used to say, that sees and hears, it is the understanding that makes profit of everything, that arranges everything, that acts, dominates, and reigns; all other things are blind, deaf, and soulless. Truly we make it servile and cowardly, by leaving it no freedom to do anything by itself. Who ever asked his pupil what he thinks of rhetoric or grammar, or of such and such a saying of Cicero? They slap them into our memory with all their feathers on, like oracles in which the letters and syllables are the substance of the matter. To know by heart is not to know; it is to retain what we have given our memory to keep. What we know rightly we dispose of, without looking at the model, without turning our eyes towards our book. Sad competence, a purely bookish competence! I intend it to serve as decoration, not as foundation, according to the opinion of Plato, who says that steadfastness, faith, and sincerity are the real philosophy, and the other sciences which aim at other things are only powder and rouge.

I wish Paluel or Pompey, those fine dancers of my time, could teach us capers just by our seeing them done without moving from our seats, as those people want to train our understanding without setting it in motion; or that we could be taught to handle a horse, or a pike, or a lute, or our voice, without practicing at it, as those people want to teach us to judge well and to speak well, without having us practice speaking or judging.

Now, for this apprenticeship, everything that comes to our eyes is book enough: a page's prank, a servant's blunder, a remark at table, are so many new materials.

For this reason, mixing with men is wonderfully useful, and visiting foreign countries, not merely to bring back, in the manner of our French noblemen, knowledge of the measurements of the Santa Rotonda, or of the richness of Signora Livia's [1] drawers, or, like some others, how much longer or wider Nero's face is in some old ruin there than on some similar medallion; but to bring back knowledge of the characters and ways of those nations, and to rub and polish our brains by contact with those of others. I should like the tutor to begin to take him around from a tender age, and first, to kill two birds with one stone, in those neighboring nations where the language is farthest from our own and where the tongue cannot be bent to it unless you train it early.

Likewise it is an opinion accepted by all, that it is not wise to bring up a child in the lap of his parents. This natural love makes them too tender and lax, even the wisest of them.

---

[1] A dancer, popular in Rome in Montaigne's time.

They are capable neither of chastising his faults nor of seeing him brought up roughly, as he should be, and hazardously. They could not endure his returning sweating and dusty from his exercise, drinking hot, drinking cold, or see him on a skittish horse, or up against a tough fencer, foil in hand, or with his first arquebus. For there is no help for it: if you want to make a man of him, unquestionably you must not spare him in his youth, and must often clash with the rules of medicine:

> *Let him live beneath the open sky*
> *And dangerously.*

[Horace]

It is not enough to toughen his soul; we must also toughen his muscles. The soul is too hard pressed unless it is seconded, and has too great a task doing two jobs alone. I know how much mine labors in company with a body so tender and so sensitive, which leans so hard upon it. And I often perceive in my reading that in their writings my masters give weight, as examples of great spirit and stoutheartedness, to acts that are likely to owe more to thickness of skin and toughness of bones. I have seen men, women, and children naturally so constituted that a beating is less to them than a flick of the finger to me; who move neither tongue nor eyebrow at the blows they receive. When athletes imitate philosophers in endurance, it is strength of sinews rather than of heart.

Now practice at enduring work is practice at enduring pain: *Work hardens one against pain.* [Cicero] The boy must be broken in to the pain and harshness of exercises, to build him up against the pain and harshness of dislocation, colic, cauterization, and the dungeon, and torture. For he may yet be a prey to the last two, which threaten the good as well as the bad in a time like this. We have proof of this right now. Whoever fights the laws threatens even the best of men with the scourge and the noose.

And besides, the authority of the tutor, which should be sovereign over the boy, is checked and hampered by the presence of the parents. Add the fact that the respect the whole household pays him, and the consciousness of the power and greatness of his house, are in my opinion no slight drawbacks at that age.

In this school of dealing with men I have often noticed this flaw, that instead of gaining knowledge of others we strive only to give knowledge of ourselves, and take more pains to peddle our wares than to get new ones. Silence and modesty are very good qualities for social intercourse. This boy will be trained to be sparing and thrifty with his ability when he has acquired it; not to take exception to the stupid things and wild tales that will be told in his presence, for it is uncivil and annoying to hit at everything that is not to our taste. Let him be content with correcting himself, and not seem to reproach others for what he refuses to do, or set himself up against common practices. *A man may be wise without ostentation, without arousing envy.* [Seneca] Let him shun these domineering and uncivil airs, and this childish ambition to try to seem more clever by being different and to gain reputation by finding fault and being original. As it is becoming only to great poets to indulge in poetic license, so it is tolerable only for great and illustrious minds to take unusual liberties. *If Socrates and Aristippus have done something contrary to the rules of behavior and custom, let him not think that he has a right to do the same; for they have gained that privilege by outstanding and divine merits.* [Cicero]

He will be taught not to enter into discussion or argument except when he sees a champion worth wrestling with, and even then not to use all the tricks that can help him, but only those that can help him most. Let him be made fastidious in choosing and sorting his arguments, and fond of pertinence, and consequently of brevity. Let him be taught above all to surrender and throw down his arms before truth as soon as he perceives it, whether it be found in the hands of his opponents, or in himself, through reconsideration. For he will not be set in a professor's chair to deliver a prepared lecture. He is pledged to no cause, except by the fact that he approves of it. Nor will he take up the trade in which men sell for ready cash the liberty to repent and acknowledge their mistakes. *Nor is he forced by any necessity to defend everything that has been prescribed and commanded.* [Cicero]

If his tutor is of my disposition, he will form his will to be a very loyal, very affectionate and very courageous servant of his prince; but he will cool in him any desire to attach himself to him otherwise than by sense of public duty. Besides several other disadvantages which impair our freedom by these private obligations, the judgment of a man who is hired and bought is either less whole and less free, or is taxed with imprudence and ingratitude. A courtier can have neither the right nor the will to speak and think otherwise than favorably of a master who among so many thousands of other subjects has chosen him to feed him and raise him up with his own hand. This favor and advantage corrupt his freedom, not without some reason, and dazzle him. Therefore we generally find the language of those people different from any other language in a state, and little to be trusted in such matters.

Let his conscience and his virtue shine forth in his speech, and be guided only by reason. Let him be made to understand that to confess the flaw he discovers in his own argument, though it is still unnoticed except by himself, is an act of judgment and sincerity, which are the principal qualities he seeks; that obstinacy and contention are vulgar qualities, most often seen in the meanest souls; that to change his mind and correct himself, to give up the bad side at the height of his ardor, are rare, strong and philosophical qualities.

He will be warned, when he is in company, to have his eyes everywhere; for I find that the chief places are commonly seized by the least capable men, and that greatness of fortune is rarely found in combination with ability. While people at the upper end of a table were talking about the beauty of a tapestry or the flavor of Malmsey wine, I have seen many fine sallies wasted at the other end. He will sound the depth of each man: a cowherd, a mason, a passer-by; he must put everything to use, and borrow from each man according to his wares, for everything is useful in a household; even the stupidity and weakness of others will be education to him. By taking stock of the graces and manners of others, he will create in himself desire of the good ones and contempt for the bad.

Put into his head an honest curiosity to inquire into all things; whatever is unusual around him he will see: a building, a fountain, a man, the field of an ancient battle, the place where Caesar or Charlemagne passed:

Which land is parched with heat, which numb with frost,
What wind drives sails to the Italian coast.

[Propertius]

He will inquire into the conduct, the resources and the alliances of this prince and that. These are things very pleasant to learn and very useful to know.

In this association with men I mean to include, and foremost, those who live only in the memory of books. He will associate, by means of histories, with those great souls of the best ages. It is a vain study, if you will; but also, if you will, it is a study of inestimable value, and the only study, as Plato tells us, that the Lacedaemonians had kept for their province. What profit will he not make in that province by reading the lives of our Plutarch? But let my guide remember the object of his task; let him not impress on his pupil so much the date of the destruction of Carthage as the characters of Hannibal and Scipio, nor so much where Marcellus died as why it was unworthy of his duty for him to die there. Let him be taught not so much the histories as how to judge them. That, in my opinion, is of all matters the one to which we apply our minds in the most varying degree. I have read in Livy a hundred things that another man has not read in him. Plutarch has read in him a hundred besides the ones I could read, and perhaps besides what the author had put in. For some it is a purely grammatical study; for others, the skeleton of philosophy, into which the most abstruse parts of our nature penetrate.

There are in Plutarch many extensive discussions, well worth knowing, for in my judgment he is the master workman in that field; but there are a thousand that he has only just touched on; he merely points out with his finger where we are to go, if we like, and sometimes is content to make only a stab at the heart of a subject. We must snatch these bits out of there and display them properly for sale. Just as that remark of his, that the inhabitants of Asia served one single man because they could not pronounce one single syllable, which is "No," may have given the matter and the

impulsion to La Boétie for his *Voluntary Servitude*. Just to
see him pick out a trivial action in a man's life, or a word
which seems unimportant: that is a treatise in itself. It is a
pity that men of understanding are so fond of brevity; doubtless their reputation gains by it, but we lose by it. Plutarch
would rather we praised him for his judgment than for his
knowledge; he would rather leave us wanting more of him
than over-full. He knows that even of good things one may
say too much, and that Alexandridas justly reproached the
man who was talking sensibly but too long to the Ephors:
*O stranger, you say what you should, but otherwise than you
should*. Those who have a thin body fill it out with padding,
those who have slim substance swell it out with words.

Wonderful brilliance may be gained for human judgment
by getting about in the world. We are all huddled and concentrated in ourselves, and our vision is reduced to the length
of our noses. Socrates was asked where he was from. He did
not answer "Athens," but "the world." He, whose imagination was fuller and more extensive, embraced the universe as
his city, and distributed his knowledge, his company, and his
affections to all mankind, unlike us who look only at what
is underfoot. When the vines freeze in my village, my priest
infers that the wrath of God is upon the human race, and
judges that the cannibals already have the pip. Seeing our
civil wars, who does not cry out that this mechanism is
already turned topsy-turvy and that the Judgment Day has
us by the throat, without reflecting that many worse things
have happened, and that ten thousand parts of the world,
to our one, are meanwhile having a gay time? Myself, considering their licentiousness and impunity, I am amazed
to see our wars so gentle and mild. When the hail comes
down on a man's head, it seems to him that the whole hemi-

sphere is in tempest and storm. And a Savoyard said that if that fool of a French king had known how to play his cards right, he was man enough to become chief steward to the Duke. His imagination conceived no higher dignity than that of his master. We are all unconsciously in this error, an error of great consequence and harm. But whoever considers as in a painting the great picture of our mother Nature in her full majesty; whoever reads such universal and constant variety in her face; whoever finds himself there, and not merely himself, but a whole kingdom, as a dot made with a very fine brush; that man alone estimates things according to their true proportions.

This great world, which some multiply further as being only a species under one genus, is the mirror in which we must look at ourselves to recognize ourselves from the proper angle. All in all, I want it to be the book of my student. So many humors, sects, judgments, opinions, laws, and customs teach us to judge sanely of our own, and teach our judgment to recognize its own imperfection and natural weakness, which is no small lesson. So many state disturbances and changes of public fortune teach us not to make a great miracle out of our own. So many names, so many victories and conquests, buried in oblivion, make it ridiculous to hope to perpetuate our name by the capture of ten mounted archers and some chicken-coop known only by its fall. The pride and arrogance of so many foreign pomps, the puffed-up majesty of so many courts and dignities, strengthens our sight and makes it steady enough to sustain the brilliance of our own without blinking. So many millions of men buried before us encourage us not to fear to go and find such good company in the other world. And likewise for other things.

Our life, Pythagoras used to say, is like the great and popuious assembly at the Olympic games. Some exercise their bodies, to win glory in the games, others bring merchandise to sell for gain. There are some, and not the worst, who come for no other profit than to see how and why everything is done, and to be spectators of the lives of other men, thereby to judge and regulate their own.

To the examples may properly be fitted all the most profitable lessons of philosophy, which human actions must measure up to as their rule. He will be told:

> *What you may justly wish; the use and ends*
> *Of hard-earned coin; our debt to country and to friends;*
> *What heaven has ordered us to be, and where our stand,*
> *Amid humanity, is fixed by high command;*
> *What we now are, what destiny for us is planned;*
>
>   [Propertius]

what it is to know and not to know, and what must be the aim of study; what are valor, temperance, and justice; what the difference is between ambition and avarice, servitude and submission, license and liberty; by what signs we may recognize true and solid contentment; how much we should fear death, pain, and shame;

> *What hardships to avoid, what to endure, and how;*
>
>   [Virgil]

what springs move us, and the cause of all our different gaits. For it seems to me that the first lessons in which we should soak his mind must be those that regulate his behavior and his common sense, that will teach him to know himself and to die well and live well. Among the liberal arts, let us begin with the art that liberates us. They are all somewhat useful for the edification and service of our life, just as everything else is somewhat useful. But let us choose the one that is directly and professedly useful for it.

If we knew how to confine the appurtenances of our life to their just and natural limits, we should find that the better part of the sciences that are now in use are no use to us; and that even in those which are, there are very useless stretches and depths that we would do better to leave alone, in accord with the teaching of Socrates, limiting the extent of our study in those regions where utility is lacking.

> *Dare to be wise! Begin!*
> *The man who would reform his life, but hesitates, is kin*
> *Unto the rustic boor who waits until the stream is gone;*
> *But ever rolling flows the stream, and ever will flow on.*
> [Horace]

It is very silly to teach our children,

> *What influence have Pisces and Leo, fierce and brave,*
> *Or Capricorn, that bathes in the Hesperian wave,*
> [Propertius]

the knowledge of the stars and the movement of the eighth sphere, before the knowledge of themselves and their movements:

> *What are the Pleiades to me,*
> *And what to me Boötes' stars?*
> [Anacreon]

Anaximines, writing to Pythagoras: "What sense have I if I can amuse myself with the secret of the stars, having death or slavery ever present before my eyes?" For at that time the kings of Persia were preparing to make war on his country. Everyone should speak thus: "When I am harassed by ambition, avarice, temerity, and superstition, and have other such

enemies to life within me, shall I go dreaming about the revo‹
lutions of the earth?"

After the tutor has told him what will help make him wiser
and better, he will explain to him the meaning of logic,
physics, geometry, rhetoric; and the science he chooses, now
that his judgment is already formed, he will soon master. His
lesson will be now in talk, now in a book; now his tutor will
give him some of the author himself who is suited to this
purpose of his education, now he will give him the marrow
and the substance pre-digested. And if by himself the tutor
is not familiar enough with books to find all the fine parts
that are in them, some man of letters may be associated with
him to effect his purpose, who at every turn will provide the
necessary supplies to be distributed and dispensed to his foster
child. And who can doubt that this kind of teaching is easier
and more natural than that of Gaza? [1] There we find thorny
and unpleasant precepts and empty and fleshless words that
you cannot get a hold on, nothing that rouses your mind.
Here the mind finds something to bite and feed on. The fruit
of it is incomparably greater, and also it will be sooner ripe.

It is a strange fact that things should be in such a pass in our
century that philosophy, even with people of understanding,
should be an empty and fantastic name, a thing of no use and
no value, both in common opinion and in fact. I think those
quibblings which have taken possession of all the approaches
to her are the cause of this. It is very wrong to portray her
as inaccessible to children, with a surly, frowning, and terri‹
fying face. Who has masked her with this false face, pale

----

[1] A fifteenth-century translator of Aristotle and author of a Greek
grammar.

and hideous? There is nothing more gay, more lusty, more
sprightly, and I might also say more frolicsome. She preaches
nothing but merrymaking and a good time. A sad and dejected
look shows that she does not dwell there. Demetrius, the
grammarian, finding a group of philosophers seated together
in the temple of Delphi, said to them: "Either I am mistaken,
or, judging by your serene and cheerful countenances, you
are not engaged in any deep discussion." To which one of
them, Heracleon, the Megarian, replied: "It is for those who
are inquiring whether the verb βάλλω has a double λ, or seeking the derivation of the comparatives χεῖρον and βέλτιον and
the superlatives χεῖριστον and βέλτιστον, to knit their brows
when discussing their science. But as for the teachings of
philosophy, they are wont to delight and rejoice those who
discuss them, not to make them sullen and sad."

> *You'll find the hidden torments of the mind*
> *Shown in the body, and the joys you'll find;*
> *The face puts on a cloak of either kind.*
>
> [Juvenal]

The soul in which philosophy dwells should by its health
make even the body healthy. It should make its tranquillity
and gladness shine out from within; should form in its own
mold the outward demeanor, and consequently arm it with
graceful pride, an active and joyous bearing, and a contented
and good-natured countenance. The surest sign of wisdom is
constant cheerfulness; her state is like that of things above
the moon, ever serene. It is *Baroco* and *Baralipton*[1] that make

---

[1] Artificial words in scholastic logic whose vowels represent forms
of syllogisms.

their disciples dirt-caked and grimy, and not she; they know her only by hearsay. Why, her business is to calm the tempests of the soul and to teach hungers and fevers to laugh, not by some imaginary epicycles, but by natural and palpable reasons. She has virtue as her goal, which is not, as the schoolmen say, set on the top of a steep, rugged, inaccessible mountain. Those who have approached virtue maintain, on the contrary, that she is established in a beautiful plain, fertile and flowering, from where, to be sure, she sees all things beneath her; but you can get there, if you know the way, by shady, grassy, sweetly flowering roads, pleasantly, by an easy smooth slope, like that of the celestial vaults. For lack of association with this virtue that is supreme, beautiful, triumphant, loving, as delightful as she is courageous, a professed and implacable enemy of sourness, displeasure, fear, and constraint, having Nature for her guide, Fortune and Pleasure for companions—they have gone, as befitted their weakness, and made up this stupid image, sad, quarrelsome, sullen, threatening, scowling, and set it on a rock, in a solitary place, among brambles: a phantom to frighten people.

My tutor, who knows he must fill his pupil's mind as much, or more, with affection as with reverence for virtue, will be able to tell him that the poets agree with the common view, and to set his finger on the fact that the gods have arranged for more sweat in the approaches to the chambers of Venus than of Pallas. And when he begins to feel his oats, and Bradamante or Angelica is offered him as a mistress to be enjoyed—a natural, active, spirited, manly but not mannish beauty, next to a soft, affected, delicate, artificial beauty; one disguised as a boy, wearing a shining helmet, the other dressed as a girl, wearing a headdress of pearls—the tutor will think that even the pupil's love is manly, if he chooses quite differently from that effeminate shepherd of Phrygia.[1]

He will teach him this new lesson, that the value and height of true virtue lies in the facility, utility, and pleasure of its practice, which is so far from being difficult that children can master it as well as men, the simple as well as the subtle. Her tool is moderation, not strength. Socrates, virtue's prime favorite, deliberately gives up his strength, to slip into the naturalness and ease of her gait. She is the nursing mother of human pleasures. By making them just she makes them sure and pure. By moderating them, she keeps them in breath and appetite. By withdrawing the ones she refuses, she makes us keener for the ones she allows us; and she allows us abundantly all those that Nature wills, even to satiety, in maternal fashion, if not to the point of lassitude (unless perchance we want to say that the regime that stops the drinker short of drunkenness, the glutton short of indigestion, the lecher short of baldness, is an enemy of our pleasures). If she lacks the fortune of ordinary men, she rises above it or does without it, and makes herself a different sort of fortune that is all her own, and no longer fluctuating and unsteady. She knows how to be rich and powerful and learned, and lie on perfumed mattresses. She loves life, she loves beauty and glory and health. But her own particular task is to know how to enjoy those blessings with temperance, and to lose them with fortitude: a task far more noble than harsh, without which the course of any life is denatured, turbulent, and deformed, and fit to be associated with those reefs, thickets, and monsters.

---

[1] Paris, whose award of the golden apple, the prize of beauty, to Aphrodite instead of Hera or Athene led to the Trojan War. Bradamante and Angelica are two heroines of Ariosto's *Orlando Furioso*.

If this pupil happens to be of such an odd disposition that he would rather listen to some idle story than to the account of a fine voyage or a wise conversation when he hears one; if, at the sound of the drum that calls the youthful ardor of his companions to arms, he turns aside to another that invites him to the tricks of the jugglers; if, by his own preference, he does not find it more pleasant and sweet to return dusty and victorious from a combat than from tennis or a ball with the prize for that exercise, I see no other remedy than for his tutor to strangle him early, if there are no witnesses, or apprentice him to a pastry cook in some good town, even though he were the son of a duke; in accordance with Plato's precept that children should be placed not according to the faculties of their father, but according to the faculties of their minds.

Since it is philosophy that teaches us to live, and since there is a lesson in it for childhood as well as for the other ages, why is it not imparted to children?

> *He still is moist and yielding clay; now, now, ere he*
> *congeal,*
> *We must make haste and tirelessly shape him on the sharp*
> *wheel.* [Persius]

They teach us to live, when life is past. A hundred students have caught the pox[1] before they came to Aristotle's lesson on temperance. Cicero used to say that even if he lived the lives of two men, he would not take the time to study the lyric poets. And I find these quibblers still more wretchedly useless. Our child is in much more of a hurry: he owes to education only the first fifteen or sixteen years of his life;

-----
[1] Syphilis

the rest he owes to action. Let us use so short a time for the necessary teachings. The others are abuses: away with all those thorny subtleties of dialectics, by which our lives cannot be amended. Take the simple teachings of philosophy, know how to choose them and treat them at the right time; they are easier to understand than a tale of Boccaccio. A child is capable of that when he leaves his nurse, much more than of learning to read and write. Philosophy has lessons for the birth of men as well as for their decrepitude.

I am of Plutarch's opinion, that Aristotle did not amuse his great pupil so much with the trick of constructing syllogisms or with the principles of geometry, as by instructing him in the good precepts concerning valor, prowess, magnanimity, and temperance, and the security of fearing nothing; and with this ammunition he sent him, still a child, to subjugate the empire of the whole world with only thirty thousand foot, four thousand horse, and forty-two thousand crowns. As for the other arts and sciences, says Plutarch, Alexander honored them no doubt, and praised their excellence and prettiness; but for the sake of the pleasure he found in them, he was not easily surprised into a desire to try to practice them.

> *Young men and old, seek here a purpose for the soul,*
> *And comfort for the woes that over gray hairs roll.*
>
> [Persius]

It is what Epicurus says in the beginning of his letter to Meniceus: *Neither let the youngest refuse to study philosophy, nor the oldest weary of it.* He who does otherwise seems to say either that it is not yet time to live happily, or that it is no longer time.

For all this education I do not want the boy to be made

a prisoner. I do not want him to be given up to the moody humors of a choleric schoolmaster. I do not want to spoil his mind by keeping him in torture and at work, as others do, fourteen or fifteen hours a day, like a porter. Nor would I think it good, if by virtue of some solitary and melancholy streak he were found to be addicted to the study of books with excessive application, for him to be encouraged in that; this makes them unfit for social intercourse and diverts them from better occupations. And how many men I have seen in my time besotted by rash avidity for learning! Carneades became so mad about it that he had no time left to take care of his hair and nails.

Nor do I want to spoil his noble manners by the uncivilized barbarism of others. French wisdom was proverbial of old as a wisdom that took hold early, and lost its hold soon. Indeed we still see that there is nothing as well-mannered as the little children in France; but ordinarily they disappoint the hopes that have been conceived for them, and as grown men they have no distinction. I have heard intelligent men maintain that these schools they are sent to, of which there are plenty, make them so besotted.

For our boy, a closet, a garden, the table and the bed, solitude, company, morning and evening, all hours will be the same, all places will be his study; for philosophy, which, as the molder of judgment and conduct, will be his principal concern, has this privilege of mixing in everything. When the orator Isocrates was entreated at a feast to speak of his art, everyone agrees that he was right to answer: *It is not the time now for what I can do; what it is time for now, I cannot do*. For to deliver harangues or rhetorical disputations to a company assembled to laugh and make merry would be too discordant a mixture. And as much could be said of all the other sciences. But as for philosophy, in the part where she treats of man and his duties and functions, it has been the common judgment of all the sages that because of the sweetness of her society she should not be excluded either from feasts or from games. And Plato having invited her to his Symposium, we see how she entertains the company in a mellow manner suited to the time and the place, though this is one of his loftiest and most salutary treatises:

> *Upon the rich and poor alike its blessings flow,*
> *And its neglect to young and old alike brings woe.*
>
> [Horace]

Thus he will doubtless be less idle than others. But, as the steps we take walking back and forth in a gallery, though there be three times as many, do not tire us like those we take on a set journey, so our lesson, occurring as if by chance, not bound to any time or place, and mingling with all our actions, will slip by without being felt. Even games and exercises will be a good part of his study: running, wrestling, music, dancing, hunting, handling horses and weapons. I want proper outward behavior, and social grace, and physical adaptability to be fashioned at the same time with his mind. It is not a mind, it is not a body that is being trained; it is a man; these parts must not be separated. And, as Plato says, they must not be trained one without the other, but driven abreast like a pair of horses harnessed to the same pole. And, to hear him, does he not seem to give more time and care to exercises of the body, and to think that the mind gets its exercise at the same time, and not the other way around?

For the rest, this education is to be carried on with severe gentleness, not as is customary. Instead of inviting children to letters, they offer them in truth nothing but horror and cruelty. Away with violence and compulsion! There is nothing to my mind which so depraves and stupefies a wellborn nature. If you would like him to fear shame and chastisement, don't harden him to them. Harden him to sweat and cold, wind and sun, and the dangers that he must scorn; wean him from all softness and delicacy in dressing and sleeping, eating and drinking; accustom him to everything. Let him not be a pretty boy and a little lady, but a lusty and vigorous youth.

As a boy, a man, and a graybeard, I have always thought and judged in the same way. But, among other things, I have always disliked the discipline of most of our schools. They might have erred less harmfully by leaning towards indulgence. They are a regular jail of imprisoned youth. They make them slack, by punishing them for slackness before they show it. Go in at lesson time: you hear nothing but cries, both from tortured boys and from masters drunk with rage. What a way to arouse zest for their lesson in these tender and timid souls, to guide them to it with a horrible scowl and hands armed with rods! Wicked and pernicious system! Besides, as Quintilian very rightly remarked, this imperious authority leads to dangerous consequences, and especially in our manner of punishment. How much more fittingly would their classes be strewn with flowers and leaves than with bloody stumps of birch rods! I would have portraits there of Joy and Gladness, and Flora and the Graces, as the philosopher Speusippus did in his school. Where their profit is, let their frolic be also. Healthy foods should be sweetened for the child, and harmful ones dipped in gall.

It is wonderful how solicitous Plato shows himself in his Laws about the gaiety and pastimes of the youth of his city, and how he dwells upon their races, games, songs, jumping, and dancing, whose conduct and patronage he says antiquity gave to the gods themselves: Apollo, the Muses, and Minerva. He extends this to a thousand precepts for his gymnasia; as for the literary studies, he wastes little time on them, and seems to recommend poetry in particular only for the sake of the music.

Any strangeness and peculiarity in our conduct and ways is to be avoided as inimical to social intercourse, and unnatural. Who would not be astonished at the constitution of Demophon, Alexander's steward, who sweated in the shade and shivered in the sun? I have seen men flee from the smell of apples more than from musket fire, others take fright at a mouse, others throw up at the sight of cream, and others at the plumping of a feather bed; as Germanicus could not endure either the sight or the crowing of cocks. There may perhaps be some occult quality in this; but a man could exterminate it, in my opinion, if he set about it early. Education has won this much from me—it is true that it was not without some trouble—that except for beer, my appetite adapts itself indiscriminately to everything people eat.

While the body is still supple, it should for that reason be bent to all fashions and customs. And provided his appetite and will can be kept in check, let a young man boldly be made fit for all nations and companies, even for dissoluteness and excess, if need be. Let his training follow usage. Let him be able to do all things, and love to do only the good. The philosophers themselves do not think it praiseworthy in Callisthenes to have lost the good graces of his master Alexander the Great by refusing to keep pace with him in drinking. He will laugh, he will carouse, he will dissipate with his prince. Even in dissipation I want him to outdo his comrades in vigor and endurance; and I want him to refrain from doing evil, not for lack of power or knowledge, but for lack of will. *There is a great difference between not wishing to do evil and not knowing how.* [Seneca]

I thought I was doing honor to a lord who was as far removed from such excesses as any lord in France, by asking him, in gay company, how many times in his life he had got drunk in the interest of his king's affairs in Germany. He took it as it was intended, and answered that he had done so three times, which he related. I know some who for lack of this faculty have made themselves a lot of trouble when they had to deal with that nation. I have often noticed with great admiration the wonderful nature of Alcibiades, who could change so easily to suit such different fashions, without damage to his health; now outdoing the Persians in luxury and pomp, now the Lacedaemonians in austerity and frugality; as pure in Sparta as he was voluptuous in Ionia.

> *Any costume, rank or fortune, Aristippus carried well.*
> [Horace]

So I would make my pupil.

> *Him I admire whom patience clothes in shabby dress,*
> *If he can grace a different way of life no less,*
> *And if he plays both parts with equal comeliness.*
> [Horace]

These are my lessons. He who shows them has profited by them better than he who knows them. If you see him, you hear him; if you hear him, you see him.

God forbid, says someone in Plato, that philosophizing should mean learning a number of things and discussing the arts! *This richest of all arts, the art of living well, they followed rather in their lives than in their studies.* [Cicero] Leon, prince of the Phliasians, asking Heraclides Ponticus what science or art he professed, he said: "I know neither art nor science; but I am a philosopher." Someone reproached Diogenes for meddling, though ignorant, with philosophy. "I meddle with it," he said, "all the more appropriately." Hegesias begged him to read him some book. "You are jesting," he replied; "you choose real and natural figs, not painted ones; why don't you also choose real and natural exercises, not written ones?"

He will not so much say his lesson as do it. He will repeat it in his actions. We shall see if there is prudence in his enterprises, if he shows goodness and justice in his conduct, if he shows judgment and grace in his speaking, fortitude in his illnesses, modesty in his games, temperance in his pleasures, unconcern in his tastes, whether flesh or fish, wine or water, order in his economy: *Who makes his learning not a display of knowledge, but the law of his life; who obeys himself and submits to his own injunctions.* [Cicero] The true mirror of our discourse is the course of our lives.

Zeuxidamus replied to a man who asked him why the Lacedaemonians did not draw up in writing the rules of prowess and give them to their young men to read, that it was because they wanted to accustom them to deeds, not words. Compare with our pupil, after fifteen or sixteen years, one of your school Latinizers, who has spent that much time merely learning to speak. The world is nothing but babble, and I never saw a man who did not say rather more than less than he should. And yet half of our life is wasted on that. They keep us for four or five years learning to understand words and stitch them into sentences; as many more, to mold them into a great body, extending into four or five parts; and another five, at least, learning how to mix and interweave them briefly in some subtle way. Let us leave that to those who make a special profession of it.

Going to Orleans one day, I met, in that plain this side of Cléry, two teachers coming to Bordeaux, about fifty yards apart. Further off, behind them, I perceived a company and a lord at the head, who was the late Monsieur le Comte de la Rochefoucault. One of my men inquired of the first of these teachers who was the gentleman that came behind him. He, not having seen the retinue that was following him, and thinking that my man was talking about his companion, replied comically: "He is not a gentleman; he is a grammarian, and I am a logician."

Now, we who are trying on the contrary to make not a grammarian or a logician, but a gentleman, let us allow them to misuse their free time; we have business elsewhere. Provided our pupil is well equipped with substance, words will follow only too readily; if they won't follow willingly, he will drag them. I hear some making excuses for not being able to express themselves, and pretending to have their heads full of many fine things, but to be unable to express them for lack of eloquence. That is all bluff. Do you know what I think those things are? They are shadows that come to them of some shapeless conceptions, which they cannot untangle and clear up within, nor consequently set forth without: they do not understand themselves yet. And just watch them stammer on the point of giving birth; you will conclude that they are not laboring for delivery, but for conception, and that they are only trying to lick into shape this unfinished matter. For my part I hold, and Socrates makes it a rule, that whoever has a vivid and clear idea in his mind will express it, if necessary in Bergamask dialect, or, if he is dumb, by signs:

> *Master the stuff, and words will freely follow.*
> [Horace]

And as another said just as poetically in his prose, *When things have taken possession of the mind, words come thick and fast.* [Seneca] And another: *The things themselves carry the words along.* [Cicero]

He knows no ablatives, conjunctives, substantives, or grammar; nor does his lackey, or a fishwife of the Petit Pont, and yet they will talk your ear off, if you like, and will perhaps be as little bothered by the rules of their language as the best master of arts in France. He does not know rhetoric, nor how in a preface to capture the favor of the gentle reader; nor does he care to know it. In truth, all this fine painting is easily eclipsed by the luster of a simple natural truth. These niceties serve only to amuse the common herd, who are incapable of taking their meat tougher or in bigger morsels, as Aper very clearly shows in Tacitus. The ambassadors of Samos had come to Cleomenes, King of Sparta, ready with a fine long oration, to incite him to war against the tyrant Polycrates. After letting them have their say, he replied to them: *As for your beginning and exordium, I no longer remember it, nor consequently the middle; and as for your conclusion, I will do nothing of the sort.* That was a fine answer, it seems to me, and speechifiers well snubbed.

And what about this other? The Athenians were to choose between two architects to build a big structure. The first, more affected, came forward with a fine prepared speech on the subject of this job, and was winning the judgment of the people in his favor. But the other, in three words: *Athenian lords, what this man has said, I will do.*

When Cicero's eloquence was at its height, many were struck with admiration; but Cato only laughed and said: *We have an amusing consul.* Early or late, a useful maxim or a shrewd remark is always in season. If it does not suit what precedes or what follows, it is good in itself. I am not one of those who think that good rhythm makes a good poem. Let him make a short syllable long if he wants, that doesn't matter; if the inventions are pleasant, if wit and judgment have done their work well, I shall say: There is a good poet, but a bad versifier.

> *His taste is keen, but harsh his verse.*
>
> [Horace]

Let his work, says Horace, lose all its seams and measures—

> *The rhythm and the measure; and what goes*
> *Foremost, make last, and last to first transpose;*
> *Yet still the poet's scattered limbs it shows;*
>
> [Horace]

—he will not belie himself for all that; the very fragments will be beautiful. That is what Menander answered, when, as the day drew near for which he had promised a comedy, he was chided for not having set his hand to it yet: *It is composed and ready; there remains only to add the verses.* Having the substance and the materials arranged in his mind, he took little account of the rest. Since Ronsard and Du Bellay have brought honor to our French poetry, I never see a little apprentice who doesn't swell his words and arrange his rhythms almost as they do. *It makes more sound than sense.* [Seneca] In the eyes of the common people, there never were so many poets. But just as it was very easy for them to reproduce their rhythms, just so they fall far short of imitating the rich descriptions of the one and the delicate inventions of the other.

True, but what will he do if someone presses him with the sophistic subtlety of some syllogism? "Ham makes us drink; drinking quenches thirst; therefore ham quenches thirst." Let him laugh at it; it is subtler to laugh at it than to answer it.

Let him borrow from Aristippus this amusing counter-thrust: *Why shall I untie it, since it gives me so much trouble tied?* Someone was using dialectical tricks against Cleanthes, when Chrysippus said to him: *Play those tricks with children, and don't divert the thoughts of a grown man to that stuff.* If those silly quibbles, *tortuous and thorny sophisms* [Cicero], are intended to convince him of a lie, they are dangerous; but if they remain without effect and only make him laugh, I do not see why he need be on his guard against them.

There are some men so stupid that they go a mile out of their way to chase after a fine word, *or who do not fit words to things, but seek irrelevant things which their words may fit.* [Quintilian] And as another says, *There are some who are led by the charm of some attractive word to write something they had not intended.* [Seneca] I much more readily twist a good saying to sew it on me than I twist the thread of my thought to go and fetch it. On the contrary, it is for words to serve and follow; and let Gascon get there if French cannot. I want the substance to stand out, and so to fill the imagination of the listener, that he will have no memory of the words. The speech I love is a simple, natural speech, the same on paper as in the mouth; a speech succulent and sinewy, brief and compressed, not so much dainty and well-combed as vehement and brisk:

The speech that strikes the mind will have most taste;
[Epitaph of Lucan]

rather difficult than boring, remote from affectation, irregular, disconnected and bold; each bit making a body in itself; not pedantic, not monkish, not lawyer-like, but rather soldierly, as Suetonius calls Julius Caesar's speech; and yet I do not quite see why he calls it so.

I have been prone to imitate that disorder in dress which we see in our young men—a cloak worn like a scarf, the hood over one shoulder, a neglected stocking—which shows a pride disdainful of these foreign adornments and careless of art. But I think it is even better employed in our form of speech. Any affectation, especially in the gaiety and freedom of French, is unbecoming to a courtier. And in a monarchy every gentleman should be trained in the manner of a courtier. Wherefore we do well to lean a little in the direction of naturalness and negligence.

I do not like a fabric in which the seams and stitches show, just as in a handsome body we must not be able to count the bones and veins: *Let the language devoted to truth be plain and simple. Who speaks carefully unless he wants to speak affectedly?* [Seneca] The eloquence that diverts us to itself is unfair to the content.

As in dress it is pettiness to seek attention by some peculiar and unusual fashion, so in language the search for novel phrases and little-known words comes from a childish and pedantic ambition. Would that I might use only those that are used in the markets of Paris! Aristophanes, the grammarian, did not know what he was talking about when he criticized Epicurus for the simplicity of his words and the aim of his oratorical art, which was simply perspicuity of speech. The imitation of speech, because of its facility, may be quickly picked up by a whole people; the imitation of judgment and invention does not come so fast. Most readers, because they have found a similar robe, think very wrongly that they have a similar body. Strength and sinews are not to be borrowed; the attire and the cloak may be borrowed. Most of the people who often visit me speak like these Essays; but I don't know whether they think like them.

The Athenians, says Plato, give their attention to fullness and elegance in speech, the Lacedaemonians to brevity, and the Cretans to fertility of thought rather than of language; the last are the best. Zeno used to say that he had two kinds of disciples: some that he called φιλολόγους, curious to learn things, who were his favorites; the others, λογοφίλους, who cared only for the language. This is not to say that it is not a fine and excellent thing to speak well, but it is not as fine as they make it out; and I am vexed that we keep busy all our life at that. I would want first to know my own language well, and that of my neighbors, with whom I have the commonest dealings. There is no doubt that Greek and Latin are great and handsome ornaments, but we buy them too dear. I shall tell you here a way to get them cheaper than usual, which was tried out on myself. Anyone who wants to can use it.

My late father, having made all the inquiries a man can make, among men of learning and understanding, about a superlative system of education, was advised of the drawbacks that were prevalent; and he was told that the long time we put into learning languages which cost the ancient Greeks and Romans nothing was the only reason why we could not attain their greatness in soul and in knowledge. I do not think

that that is the only reason for this. At all events, the expe-
dient my father hit upon was this, that while I was nursing
and before the first loosening of my tongue, he put me in
the care of a German, who has since died a famous doctor
in France, wholly ignorant of our language and very well
versed in Latin.[1] This man, whom he had sent for expressly,
and who was very highly paid, had me constantly in his
hands. There were also two others with him, less learned, to
attend me and relieve him. These spoke to me in no other
language than Latin. As for the rest of my father's household, it was an inviolable rule that neither himself, nor my
mother, nor any valet or housemaid, should speak anything
in my presence but such Latin words as each had learned in
order to jabber with me.

It is wonderful how everyone profited from this. My
father and mother learned enough Latin this way to understand it, and acquired sufficient skill to use it when necessary,
as did also the servants who were most attached to my service. Altogether, we Latinized so much that it overflowed all
the way to our villages on every side, where there still remain
several Latin names of artisans and tools that have taken root
by usage. As for me, I was over six before I understood any
more French or Perigordin than Arabic. And without artificial means, without a book, without grammar or precept,
without rod and without tears, I had learned some Latin, quite
as pure as what my schoolmaster knew, for I could not have
contaminated or spoiled it. If as a test they wanted to give
me a theme in the college fashion, where they give it to others
in French, they had to give it to me in bad Latin, to turn it

---

[1] Doctor Horstanus, later a professor at the Collège de Guienne at
Bordeaux.

into good. And Nicholas Grouchy, who wrote *De Comitiis Romanorum*, Guillaume Guerente, who wrote a commentary on Aristotle, George Buchanan, that great Scottish poet, Marc Antoine Muret, whom France and Italy recognize as the best orator of his time, my private tutors, have often told me that in my childhood I had that language so ready and handy that they were afraid to accost me. Buchanan, whom I afterwards saw in the employ of the late Monsieur le Maréchal de Brissac, told me that he was writing on the education of children and that he was taking my education as a model; for he was then in charge of that Count de Brissac who has since shown himself so valorous and brave.

As for Greek, of which I have practically no knowledge at all, my father planned to have me taught it artificially, but in a new way, in the form of amusement and exercise. We volleyed our conjugations back and forth, like those who learn arithmetic and geometry by such games as checkers and chess. For among other things he had been advised to teach me to enjoy knowledge and duty by my own free will and desire, and to educate my mind in all gentleness and freedom, without rigor and constraint. He did this so religiously that because some hold that it troubles the tender brains of children to wake them in the morning with a start, and to snatch them suddenly and violently from their sleep, in which they are plunged much more deeply than we are, he had me awakened by the sound of some instrument; and I was never without a man for that purpose.

This example will be enough to let you judge the rest, and also to commend both the prudence and the affection of so good a father, who is not at all to be blamed if he reaped no fruit corresponding to such an excellent cultivation. Two things were the cause of this: firstly, the sterile and unfit soil;

for though my health was sound and complete and my nature gentle and tractable, I was withal so sluggish, lax, and drowsy that they could not tear me from my sloth, not even to make me play. What I saw, I saw well, and beneath this inert appearance nourished bold ideas and opinions beyond my years. I had a slow mind, which would go only as far as it was led; a tardy understanding, a weak imagination, and on top of all this an incredible lack of memory. It is no wonder if he could get nothing worth while from all this.

Secondly, just as people frantically eager to be cured will try any sort of advice, that good man, being very much afraid to fail in a thing so close to his heart, at last let himself be carried away by the common opinion, which always follows the leader like a flock of cranes, and fell in line with custom, having no longer about him the men who had given him those first instructions, which he had brought from Italy. And he sent me, when I was about six, to the Collège de Guienne, which was then very flourishing, and the best in France. And there, nothing could be added to the care he took, both to choose me competent tutors and in all the other aspects of my education, in which he held out for certain particular practices contrary to school usage. But for all that, it was still school. My Latin promptly degenerated, and since then, for lack of practice, I have lost all use of it. And all this novel education of mine did for me was to make me skip immediately to the upper classes; for when I left the school at thirteen, I had finished my course (as they call it), and in truth without any benefit that I can make out now.

The first taste I had for books came to me from my pleasure in the fables of the *Metamorphoses* of Ovid. For at about seven or eight years of age I would steal away from any other pleasure to read them, since this language was my mother tongue, and it was the easiest book I knew and the best suited by its content to my tender age. For as regards the Lancelots of the Lake, the Amadises, the Huons of Bordeaux, and such books of rubbish on which children waste their time, I did not know even their names, and I still do not know their substance, so strict was my discipline. Thereby I grew more careless in the study of my other prescribed lessons. At that point, I happened by remarkable good fortune to come in contact with a tutor who was an understanding man, who knew enough to connive cleverly at this frivolity of mine and others like it. For by this means I went right through Virgil's *Aeneid*, and then Terence, and then Plautus, and some Italian comedies, always lured on by the pleasantness of the subject. If he had been foolish enough to break this habit, I think I should have gotten nothing out of school but a hatred of books, as do nearly all our noblemen. He went about it cleverly. Pretending to see nothing, he whetted my appetite, letting me gorge myself with these books only in secret, and gently keeping me at my work on the regular studies. For the chief qualities my father sought in those he put in charge of me were good nature and an easygoing disposition. Correspondingly, my own character had no other vice than inertia and laziness. The danger was not that I should do ill, but that I should do nothing. No one predicted that I should become wicked, but only useless. They foresaw loafing, not knavery.

I realize that it has turned out that way. The complaints that ring in my ears are of this sort: "Idle. Cool in the duties of friendship and kinship, and in public functions. Too self-centered." The most insulting do not say, "Why did he take? Why didn't he pay?" but "Why doesn't he cancel? Why doesn't he give?"

I should take it as a favor that men should find me wanting only in such acts of supererogation. But they are unjust to demand what I do not owe, much more rigorously than they demand of themselves what they do owe. By condemning me to an action they wipe out all the pleasure of it and the gratitude that would be due me for it; whereas the good that I do should have greater weight coming from me, considering that I have none at all done me. I may dispose of my fortune the more freely the more it is my own. However, if I were a great blazoner of my own actions, perhaps I might well throw back these reproaches. And I might inform some people that they are not so much offended that I do not do enough, as that I could do a lot more than I do.

Meanwhile, for all that, my mind was not lacking in strong stirrings of its own, and certain and open-minded judgments about the things it understood; and it digested them by itself, alone. And, among other things, I really do believe that it would have been wholly incapable of submitting to force and violence.

Shall I include in my account this faculty of my boyhood assurance in expression and flexibility in voice and gesture, in adapting myself to the parts I undertook to act? For before the usual age,

Scarce had my twelfth year snatched me from the year before,

[Virgil]

I played the leading parts in the Latin tragedies of Buchanan, Guerente and Muret, which were performed with dignity in our Collège de Guienne. In this matter, as in all other parts of his task, Andreas Goveanus, our principal, was incomparably the greatest principal of France; and I was considered a master craftsman. It is an exercise that I do not at all disapprove of for young children of good family; and since then I have seen our princes take part in it in person, honorably and commendably, after the example of some of the ancients.

It was even permissible for people of quality to make a profession of it in Greece. *He revealed the matter to the tragic actor Ariston. This man was distinguished both in birth and fortune; nor did his art spoil his position, since nothing of that sort is considered a disgrace by the Greeks.* [Livy]

For I have always blamed as undiscerning those who condemn these recreations, and as unjust those who refuse entry into our good towns to the comedians who deserve it, and begrudge the people these public amusements. Good governments take care to assemble the citizens and bring them together for sports and amusements as well as for the serious functions of piety; sociability and friendliness are thereby increased. And besides, they could not be granted more orderly pastimes than those that take place in the presence of everyone and right in the sight of the magistrate. And I should think it reasonable that the magistrate and the prince, at their own expense, should sometimes give the people this treat, out of a sort of paternal kindness and affection; and that in populous cities there should be places intended and arranged for these spectacles—a diversion from worse and hidden doings.

To return to my subject, there is nothing like arousing appetite and affection; otherwise you make nothing but asses loaded with books. By whipping them we give them their pocketful of learning to keep; which, if it is to do any good, we must not merely lodge in us: we must espouse it.

It Is Folly to Measure the True and False by Our Own Capacity[1]

PERHAPS it is not without reason that we attribute facility in belief and conviction to simplicity and ignorance; for it seems to me I once learned that belief was a sort of impression made on our mind, and that the softer and less resistant the mind, the easier it was to imprint something on it. *As the scale of the balance must necessarily sink under the weight placed upon it, so must the mind yield to evident things.* [Cicero] The more a mind is empty and without counterpoise, the more easily it gives beneath the weight of the first persuasive argument. That is why children, common people, women, and sick people are most subject to being led by the ears. But then, on the other hand, it is foolish presumption to go around disdaining and condemning as false whatever does not seem likely to us; which is a common vice in those who think they have more than normal ability. I used to do so once; and if I heard of returning spirits, prognostications

---

[1] Chapter 27.

of future events, enchantments, sorcerv or some other story
that I could not swallow,

> *Dreams, witches, miracles, magic alarms,*
> *Nocturnal specters, and Thessalian charms,*
>
> [Horace]

I felt compassion for the poor people who were taken in by
these follies. And now I think that I was at least as much to
be pitied myself. Not that experience has since shown me
anything surpassing my first beliefs, and that through no
fault of my curiosity; but reason has taught me that to condemn a thing thus, dogmatically, as false and impossible, is
to assume the distinction of knowing the bounds and limits
of God's will and of the power of our mother Nature; and
that there is no more notable folly in the world than to measure these things by our capacity and competence. If we call
prodigies or miracles whatever our reason cannot reach, how
many of these appear continually before our eyes! Let us
consider through what clouds and how gropingly we are
led to the knowledge of most of the things that are right in
our hands; assuredly we shall find that it is rather familiarity
than knowledge that takes away their strangeness,

> *But no one now, so tired of seeing are our eyes,*
> *Deigns to look up at the bright temples of the skies,*
>
> [Lucretius]

and that if those things were presented to us for the first
time, we should find them as incredible, or more so, than
any others.

> *If they were here for the first time for men to see,*
> *If they were set before us unexpectedly,*

Nothing more marvelous than these things could be told,
Nothing more unbelievable for men of old.

[Lucretius]

He who had never seen a river thought that the first one
he came across was the ocean. And the things that are the
greatest within our knowledge we judge to be the utmost
that nature can do in that category.

> *A fair-sized stream seems vast to one who until then*
> *Has never seen a greater; so with trees, with men.*
> *In every field each man regards as vast in size*
> *The greatest objects that have come before his eyes.*
> [Lucretius]

The mind becomes accustomed to things by the habitual
sight of them, nor wonders nor inquires about the reasons for
the things it sees all the time. [Cicero]

The novelty of things incites us more than their greatness
to seek their causes.

We must judge with more reverence the infinite power
of nature, and with more consciousness of our ignorance
and weakness. How many things of slight probability there
are, testified by trustworthy people, which, if we cannot be
convinced of them, we should at least leave in suspense! For
to condemn them as impossible is to pretend, with rash presumption, to know the limits of possibility. If people rightly
understood the difference between the impossible and the
unusual, and between what is contrary to the orderly course
of nature and what is contrary to the common opinion of
men, not believing rashly nor disbelieving easily, they would
observe the rule of "nothing too much," enjoined by Chilo.

When we find in Froissart that the Count de Foix, in Béarn,

learned of the defeat of King John of Castile at Juberoth the day after it happened, we can laugh at it; and also at the story our annals tell, that Pope Honorius performed public funeral rites for King Philip Augustus and commanded them to be performed throughout Italy on the very day he died at Mantes. For the authority of these witnesses is perhaps not high enough to keep us in hand. But then, if Plutarch, after several examples that he cites from antiquity, says that he knows with certain knowledge that in the time of Domitian, the news of the battle lost by Antonius in Germany was published in Rome, several days' journey from there, and dispersed throughout the whole world, on the same day it was lost; and if Caesar maintains that it has often happened that the report has preceded the event—shall we say that these simple men let themselves be hoaxed like the common herd, because they were not clear-sighted like ourselves? Is there anything more delicate, clearer and more alert than Pliny's judgment, when he sees fit to bring it into play, or anything farther from inanity? Leaving aside the excellence of his knowledge, which I count for less, in which of these qualities do we surpass him? However, there is no school boy so young but he will convict him of falsehood, and want to give him a lesson on the progress of Nature's works.

When we read in Bouchet about the miracles done by the relics of Saint Hilary, let it go: his credit is not great enough to take away our right to contradict him. But to condemn wholesale all similar stories seems to me a singular impudence. The great Saint Augustine testifies that he saw a blind child restored to sight upon the relics of Saint Gervaise and Saint Protasius at Milan; a woman at Carthage cured of a cancer by the sign of the cross that a newly baptized woman made over her; Hesperius, a close friend of his, cast out the

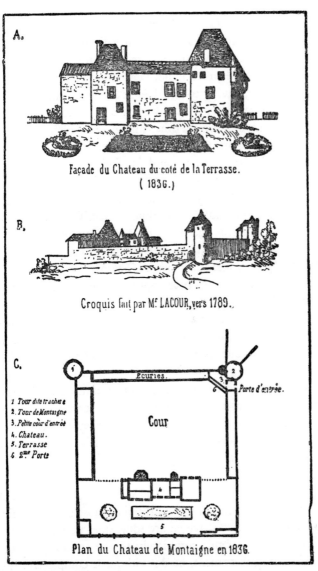

A.

Façade du Chateau du coté de la Terrasse.
(1836.)

B.

Croquis fait par Mr LACOUR, vers 1789.

C.

1 Tour dite trachat e
2. Tour de Montaigne
3. Petite cour d'entrée
4. Chateau.
5. Terrasse
6 2me Porte

Ecuries.

Porte d'entrée.

Cour

Plan du Chateau de Montaigne en 1836.

Façade and ground plan of Montaigne's château

spirits that infested his house, with a little earth from the sepulcher of our Lord, and a paralytic promptly cured by this earth, later, when it had been carried to church; a woman in a procession, having touched Saint Stephen's shrine with a bouquet, and rubbed her eyes with this bouquet, recover her long-lost sight; and several other miracles at which he says he himself was present. Of what shall we accuse both him and two holy bishops, Aurelius and Maximinus, whom he calls upon as his witnesses? Shall it be of ignorance, simplicity, and credulity, or of knavery and imposture? Is there any man in our time so impudent that he thinks himself comparable to them, either in virtue and piety, or in learning, judgment, and ability? *Who, though they brought forth no proof, might crush me by their mere authority.* [Cicero]

It is dangerous and presumptuous, besides the absurd temerity that it implies, to disdain what we do not comprehend. For after you have established, according to your fine understanding, the limits of truth and falsehood, and it turns out that you must necessarily believe things even stranger than those you deny, you are obliged from then on to abandon them. Now, what seems to me to bring as much disorder into our consciences as anything, is this partial surrender of their beliefs by Catholics. It seems to them that they are being very moderate and understanding when they yield to their opponents some of the articles in dispute. But, besides the fact that they do not see what an advantage it is to a man charging you for you to begin to give ground and withdraw, and how much that encourages him to pursue his point, those articles which they select as the most trivial are sometimes very important. Either we must submit completely to the authority of our ecclesiastical government, or do without it completely. It is not for us to decide what portion of obedience we owe it.

Moreover, I can say this for having tried it, having in other days exercised this freedom of personal choice and selection, regarding with negligence certain points in the observances of our Church which seemed more pointless or strange than others; coming to tell learned men about them, I found that these things have a massive and very solid foundation, and that it is only stupidity and ignorance that makes us receive them with less reverence than the rest. Why do we not remember how much contradiction we sense even in our own judgment, how many things were articles of faith to us yesterday, which are fables to us today? Vainglory and curiosity are the two scourges of our soul. The latter leads us to thrust our noses into everything, and the former forbids us to leave anything unresolved and undecided.

Of Friendship[1]

As I was considering the way a painter I employ went about his work, I had a mind to imitate him. He chooses the best spot, the middle of each wall, for a picture labored over with all his skill, and the empty space all around it he fills with grotesques, which are fantastic paintings whose only charm lies in their variety and strangeness. And what are these essays, in truth, but grotesques and monstrous bodies, pieced together of divers members, without definite shape, having no order, sequence, or proportion other than accidental?

A lovely woman's body tapers off into a fish.
[Horace]

I readily keep up with my painter to this second point, but I fall short in the first and better part; for my ability does not go far enough for me to dare to undertake a rich, polished picture, formed according to art. It has occurred to me to borrow one from Étienne de la Boétie, which will do honor to all the rest of this work. It is a discourse to which he gave the name *La Servitude Volontaire*; but those who did not know this have since very fitly rebaptized it *Le Contre Un*.[2] He wrote it

---

[1] Chapter 28.
[2] *La Servitude Volontaire,* Voluntary Servitude. *Le Contre Un,* Against One Man.

by way of essay in his early youth, in honor of liberty against tyrants. It has long been circulating in the hands of men of understanding, not without great and well-merited commendation; for it is noble, and as full as can be. Still, it is far from being the best he could do; and if at the more mature age when I knew him, he had adopted a plan such as mine, of putting his ideas in writing, we should see many rare things which would bring us very close to the glory of antiquity; for particularly in the matter of natural gifts, I know no one who can be compared with him. But nothing of his remains except this treatise—and that by chance, and I think he never saw it after it left his hands—and a few observations on that Edict of January, made famous by our civil wars, which will perhaps yet find their place elsewhere. That was all I could recover of what he left—I, to whom in his will, with such loving recommendation, with death at his throat, he bequeathed his library and his papers—except for the little volume of his works which I had published.

And yet I am particularly obliged to this work, since it was the medium of our first acquaintance. For it was shown to me long before I had seen him, and gave me my first knowledge of his name, thus starting on its way this friendship which together we fostered, as long as God willed, so entire and so perfect that certainly you will hardly read of the like, and among men of today you will see no trace of it in practice. So many coincidences are needed to build it up that it is a lot if Fortune can do it once in three centuries.

There is nothing to which nature seems to have inclined us more than to society. And Aristotle says that good legislators have had more care for friendship than for justice. Now the ultimate point in the perfection of society is this. For in general, all associations that are forged and nourished by pleasure or profit, by public or private needs, are less beautiful, noble, and so much the less friendships, in so far as they mix into friendship another cause and object and reward than friendship itself. Nor do the four ancient types—natural, social, hospitable, venerian—come up to real friendship, either separately or together.

From children toward fathers, it is rather respect. Friendship feeds on communication, which cannot exist between them because of their too great inequality, and might perhaps interfere with the duties of nature. For neither can all the secret thoughts of fathers be communicated to children, lest this beget an unbecoming intimacy, nor could the admonitions and corrections, which are one of the chief duties of friendship, be administered by children to fathers. There have been nations where by custom the children killed their fathers, and others where the fathers killed their children, to avoid the mutual interference that can sometimes arise; and by nature the one depends on the destruction of the other. There have been philosophers who disdained this natural tie, witness Aristippus: when pressed about the affection he owed his children for having come out of him, he began to spit, saying that that had come out of him just as much, and that we also bred lice and worms. And that other, whom Plutarch wanted to reconcile with his brother, said: *I don't think any more of him for having come out of the same hole.*

Truly the name of brother is a beautiful name and full of affection, and for that reason we made our alliance a brotherhood. But that confusion of ownership, the dividing, and the fact that the richness of one is the poverty of the other, wonderfully softens and loosens the solder of brotherhood. Brothers having to guide the progress of their advancement along the same path and at the same rate, it is inevitable that they often jostle and clash with each other. Furthermore, why should the harmony and kinship which begets these true and perfect friendships be found in them? Father and son may be of entirely different dispositions, and brothers also. He is my son, he is my kinsman, but he is an unsociable man, a knave, or a fool. And then, the more they are friendships which law and natural obligation impose on us, the less of our choice and free will there is in them. And our free will has no product more properly its own than affection and friendship. Not that I have not experienced all the friendship that can exist in that situation, having had the best father that ever was, and the most indulgent, even in his extreme old age, and being of a family famous and exemplary, from father to son, in this matter of brotherly concord:

> *Known to others*
> *For fatherly affection toward my brothers.*
>
> [Horace]

As for comparing with it affection for women, though this is born of our choice, we cannot do it, nor can we put it in this class. Its fire, I confess,

> *Of us that goddess is not unaware*
> *Who blends a bitter sweetness with her care,*
>
> [Catullus]

is more active, more scorching and more intense. But it is an impetuous and fickle flame, wavering and variable, a fever flame, subject to fits and lulls, that holds us only by one corner. In friendship it is a general and universal warmth, moderate and even, besides, a constant and settled warmth, all gentleness and smoothness, with nothing bitter and stinging about it. What is more, in love there is nothing but a frantic desire for what flees from us:

> *Just as a huntsman will pursue a hare*
> *O'er hill and dale, in weather cold or fair;*
> *The captured hare is worthless in his sight;*
> *He only hastens after things in flight.*

[Ariosto]

As soon as it enters the boundaries of friendship, that is to say harmony of wills, it grows faint and languid. Enjoyment destroys it, as having a fleshly end, subject to satiety. Friendship, on the contrary, is enjoyed according as it is desired; it is bred, nourished, and increased only in enjoyment, since it is spiritual, and the soul grows refined by practice. During the reign of this perfect friendship those fleeting affections once found a place in me, not to speak of my friend, who confesses only too many of them in these verses. Thus these two passions within me have come to be known to each other, but to be compared, never; the first keeping its course in proud and lofty flight, and disdainfully watching the other making its way far, far beneath it.

As for marriage, besides its being a bargain to which only the entrance is free, its continuance being constrained and forced, depending otherwise than on our will, and a bargain ordinarily made for other ends, there supervene a thousand foreign tangles to unravel, enough to break the thread and trouble the course of a lively affection; whereas in friendship there are no dealings or business except with itself. Besides, to tell the truth, the ordinary capacity of women is inadequate for that communion and fellowship which is the nurse of this sacred bond; nor does their soul seem firm enough to endure the strain of so tight and durable a knot. And indeed,

but for that, if such a familiarity, free and voluntary, could
be built up, in which not only would the souls have this complete enjoyment, but the bodies would also share in the alliance; in which the entire man would be engaged, it is certain that the friendship would be fuller and more complete.
But this sex in no instance has yet succeeded in attaining it,
and by the common agreement of the ancient schools is excluded from it.

And that other Greek license is justly abhorred by our
morality. Since this involved, moreover, according to their
practice, such a necessary disparity in age and such a difference in the lovers' obligations, it did not correspond closely
enough with the perfect union and harmony that we require
here: *For what is this love of friendship? Why does no one
love either an ugly youth, or a handsome old man?* [Cicero]
For even the picture the Academy paints of it will not contradict me, I think, if I say this about it: that this first frenzy
which the son of Venus inspired in the lover's heart at the
sight of the flower of tender youth, in which they allow all
the insolent and passionate acts that unrestrained ardor can
produce, was simply founded on external beauty, the false
image of corporeal generation. For it could not be founded
on the spirit, the signs of which were still hidden, which was
only at its birth and before the age of budding. If this frenzy
seized a base heart, the means of his courtship were riches,
presents, favor in advancement to dignities, and other such
base merchandise, which they condemn. If it fell on a nobler
heart, the medium was also noble: philosophical instruction,
precepts to revere religion, obey the laws, die for the good
of the country; examples of valor, prudence, justice; the
lover studying to make himself acceptable by the grace and
beauty of his soul, that of his body being long since faded,

and hoping by this mental fellowship to establish a firmer and more lasting pact.

When this courtship attained its effect in due season (for whereas they do not require of the lover that he use leisure and discretion in his enterprise, they strictly require it of the loved one, because he had to judge an inner beauty, difficult to know and hidden from discovery), there was born in the loved one the desire of spiritual conception through the medium of spiritual beauty. This was the main thing here, and corporeal beauty accidental and secondary; quite the opposite of the lover. For this reason they prefer the loved one, and prove that the gods also prefer him, and strongly rebuke the poet Aeschylus for having, in the love of Achilles and Patroclus, given the lover's part to Achilles, who was in the first beardless bloom of his youth, and the handsomest of all the Greeks.

After this general communion is established, the stronger and worthier partner in it exercising his functions and predominating, they say that there resulted from it fruits very useful personally and to the public; that it constituted the strength of the countries which accepted the practice, and the principal defense of equity and liberty: witness the salutary loves of Harmodius and Aristogeiton. Therefore they call it sacred and divine. And, by their reckoning, only the violence of tyrants and the cowardice of the common people are hostile to it. In short, all that can be said in favor of the Academy is that it was a love ending in friendship; which corresponds pretty well to the Stoic definition of love: *Love is the attempt to form a friendship inspired by beauty.* [Cicero]

I return to my description of a more equitable and more equable kind of friendship. *Only those are to be judged friendships in which the characters have been strengthened and matured by age.* [Cicero]

For the rest, what we ordinarily call friends and friendships are nothing but acquaintanceships and familiarities formed by some chance or convenience, by means of which our souls are bound to each other. In the friendship I speak of, our souls mingle and blend with each other so completely that they efface the seam that joined them, and cannot find it again. If you press me to tell why I loved him, I feel that this cannot be expressed, except by answering: Because it was he, because it was I.

Beyond all my understanding, beyond what I can say about this in particular, there was I know not what inexplicable and fateful force that was the mediator of this union. We sought each other before we met because of the reports we heard of each other, which had more effect on our affection than such reports would reasonably have; I think it was by some ordinance from heaven. We embraced each other's names. And at our first meeting, which by chance came at a great feast and gathering in the city, we found ourselves so taken with each other, so well acquainted, so bound together, that from that time on nothing was so close to us as each other. He wrote an excellent Latin satire, which is published, in which he condones and explains the precipitancy of our mutual understanding, so promptly grown to its perfection. Having so little time to last, and having begun so late, for we were both grown men, and he some years older than I, it could not lose time and conform to the pattern of mild and regular friendships, which need so many precautions in the form of long preliminary association. Our friendship has no other model than itself, and can be compared only with itself. It is not one special consideration, nor two, nor three, nor four, nor a thousand: it is I know not what quintessence of all this mixture, which, having seized my whole will, led it to plunge and lose itself in his; which, having seized his whole will, led it to plunge and lose itself in mine, with equal hunger, equal rivalry. I say lose, in truth, for neither of us reserved anything for himself, nor was anything either his or mine.

When Laelius, in the presence of the Roman consuls, who, after condemning Tiberius Gracchus, prosecuted all those who had been in his confidence, came to ask Caius Blossius, who was his best friend, how much he would have been willing to do for him, he answered: "Everything." "What, everything?" pursued Laelius. "And what if he had commanded you to set fire to our temples?" "He would never have commanded me to do that," replied Blossius. "But what if he had?" Laelius insisted. "I would have obeyed," he replied. If he was such a perfect friend to Gracchus as the histories say, he did not need to offend the consuls by this last bold confession, and he should not have abandoned the assurance he had of Gracchus' disposition. But nevertheless, those who charge that this answer is seditious do not fully understand this mystery, and fail to assume first what is true, that he had Gracchus' will up his sleeve, both by power over him and by knowledge of him. They were friends more than citizens, friends more than friends or enemies of their country or friends of ambition and disturbance. Having committed themselves absolutely to each other, they held absolutely the reins of each other's inclination; and if you assume that this team was guided by the strength and leadership of reason, as indeed it is quite impossible to harness it without that, Blossius' answer is as it should have been. If their actions went astray, they were by my measure neither friends to each other, nor friends to themselves.

For that matter, this answer has no better ring than would mine if someone questioned me in this fashion: "If your will commanded you to kill your daughter, would you kill her?" and I said yes. For that does not bear witness to any consent to do so, because I have no doubt at all about my will, and just as little about that of such a friend. It is not in the power of all the arguments in the world to dislodge me from the certainty I have of the intentions and judgments of my friend. Not one of his actions could be presented to me, whatever appearance it might have, that I could not immediately find the motive for it. Our souls pulled together in such unison, they regarded each other with such ardent affection, and with a like affection revealed themselves to each other to the very depths of our hearts, that not only did I know his soul as well as mine, but I should certainly have trusted myself to him more readily than to myself.

Let not these other, common friendships be placed in this rank. I have as much knowledge of them as another, and of the most perfect of their type, but I advise you not to confuse the rules of the two; you would make a mistake. You must walk in those other friendships bridle in hand, with prudence and precaution; the knot is not so well tied that there is no cause to mistrust it. *Love him,* Chilo used to say, *as if you have to hate him some day; hate him as if you have to love him.* This precept, which is so abominable in this sovereign and masterful friendship, is healthy in the practice of common and customary friendships, in regard to which we must use the remark that Aristotle so often repeated: *O my friends, there is no friend.*

In this noble relationship, services and benefits, on which

other friendships feed, do not even deserve to be taken into account; the reason for this is the complete blending of our wills. For as the friendship I feel for myself receives no increase from the help I give myself in time of need, whatever the Stoics say, and as I feel no gratitude to myself for the service I do myself; so the union of such friends, being truly perfect, makes them lose the sense of such duties, and hate and banish from between them these words implying separation and distinction: benefit, obligation, gratitude, request, thanks, and the like. Everything actually being in common between them—wills, thoughts, judgments, goods, wives, children, honor, and life—and their relationship being that of one soul in two bodies, according to Aristotle's very apt definition, they can neither lend nor give anything to each other. That is why the lawmakers, to honor marriage with some imaginary resemblance to this divine union, forbid gifts between husband and wife, wishing thus to imply that everything should belong to each of them and that they have nothing to divide and split up between them.

If, in the friendship I speak of, one could give to the other, it would be the one who received the benefit who would oblige his friend. For, each of them seeking above all things to benefit the other, the one who provides the matter and the occasion is the liberal one, giving his friend the satisfaction of doing for him what he most wants to do. When the philosopher Diogenes was short of money, he used to say that he asked it back of his friends, not that he asked for it. And to show how this works in practice, I will tell you an ancient example that is singular.

Eudamidas of Corinth had two friends, Charixenus, a Sicyonian, and Aretheus, a Corinthian. When he came to die, being poor, and his two friends rich, he made his will thus: *I leave this to Aretheus, to feed my mother and support her in her old age; this to Charixenus, to see my daughter married and give her the biggest dowry he can; and in case one of them should chance to die, I substitute the survivor in his place.* Those who first saw this will laughed at it; but his heirs, having been informed of it, accepted it with singular satisfaction. And one of them, Charixenus, dying five days later, and the place of substitute being open to Aretheus, he supported the mother with great care, and of five talents he had in his possession, he gave two and a half to his only daughter for her marriage, and two and a half for the marriage of the daughter of Eudamidas, holding their weddings on the same day.

This example is quite complete except for one circumstance, which is the plurality of friends. For this perfect friendship I speak of is indivisible: each one gives himself so wholly to his friend that he has nothing left to distribute elsewhere; on the contrary, he is sorry that he is not double, triple, or quadruple, and that he has not several souls and several wills, to confer them all on this one object. Common friendships can be divided up: one may love in one man his beauty, in another his easygoing ways, in another liberality, in one paternal love, in another brotherly love, and so forth; but this friendship that possesses the soul and rules it with absolute sovereignty cannot possibly be double. If two called for help at the same time, which one would you run to? If they demanded conflicting services of you, how would you arrange it? If one confided to your silence a thing that would be useful for the other to know, how would you extricate yourself? A single dominant friendship dissolves all other obligations. The secret I have sworn to reveal to no other man, I can impart without perjury to the one who is not another man, he is myself. It is a great enough miracle to be doubled, and those who talk of tripling themselves do not know the height of it: nothing is superlative if it has an equal. And he who supposes that of two men I love one just as much as the other, and that they love each other and me just as much as I love them, multiplies into a brotherhood the most single and unified of all things, of which even a single one is the rarest thing in the world to find.

The rest of this story fits in very well with what I was saying, for Eudamidas grants his friends, as a kindness and a favor, to use them for his need. He leaves them heirs to this liberality of his, which consists of putting into their hands a chance to do him good. And without doubt the strength of friendship is shown much more richly in his action than in that of Aretheus.

In short, these are actions inconceivable to anyone who has not tasted friendship, and which make me honor wonderfully the answer of that young soldier to Cyrus, who asked him for how much he would sell a horse with which he had just won the prize in a race, and whether he would exchange him for a kingdom: "No indeed, Sire, but I would most willingly let him go to gain a friend, if I found a man worthy of such an alliance." That was not badly spoken, "if I found one"; for it is easy to find men fit for a superficial acquaintance. But for this kind, in which we act from the very bottom of our hearts, which holds nothing back, truly it is necessary that all the springs of action be perfectly clean and true.

In the relationships which bind us only by one small part, we need look out only for the imperfections that particularly concern that part. The religion of my doctor or my lawyer does not matter. That consideration has nothing in

common with the functions of the friendship they owe me.
And in the domestic relationship between me and those who
serve me, the same is true. And I scarcely inquire of a lackey
whether he is chaste; I try to find out whether he is diligent.
And I am not as much afraid of a gambling mule driver as of
a stupid one, or a profane cook as an ignorant one. I do not
take it upon myself to tell the world what it should do—
enough others do that—but what I do in it.

> *That is my practice: do as you see fit.*
> [Terence]

For the familiarity of the table I look for wit, not prudence;
for the bed, beauty before goodness; in the association of
conversation, competence, even without uprightness. Likewise in other matters.

Just as the man who was found astride a stick, playing with
his children, asked the man who surprised him thus to say
nothing about it until he was a father himself, in the belief
that the passion which would then be born in his soul would
make him an equitable judge of such an act, so I should like
to talk to people who have experienced what I tell. But knowing how far from common usage and how rare such a friendship is, I do not expect to find any good judge of it. For the
very discourses that antiquity has left us on this subject seem
to me weak compared with the feeling I have. And in this
particular the facts surpass even the precepts of philosophy:

> *Nothing shall I, while sane, compare with a dear friend.*
> [Horace]

The ancient Menander declared that man happy who had
been able to meet even the shadow of a friend. He was certainly right to say so, especially if he spoke from experience.

For in truth, if I compare all the rest of my life—though by the grace of God I have spent it pleasantly, comfortably, and, except for the loss of such a friend, free from any grievous affliction, and full of tranquillity of mind, having accepted my natural and original advantages without seeking other ones—if I compare it all, I say, with the four years which were granted me to enjoy the sweet company and society of that man, it is nothing but smoke, nothing but dark and dreary night. Since the day I lost him,

> *Which evermore I shall recall with pain,*
> *With reverence—thus, Gods, did you ordain—*
>
> [Virgil]

I only drag on a weary life; and the very pleasures that come my way, instead of consoling me, redouble my grief for his loss. We went halves in everything; it seems to me that I am robbing him of his share,

> *Nor is it right for me to taste of pleasures here alone,*
> *—So I resolved—as long as he who shared my life is gone.*
>
> [Terence]

I was already so formed and accustomed to being double everywhere that only half of me seems to be alive now.

> *Since an untimely blow has snatched away*
> *Part of my soul, why then do I delay,*
> *I the remaining part, less dear than he,*
> *And not entire surviving? The same day*
> *Brought ruin equally to him and me.*
>
> [Horace]

There is no action or thought in which I do not miss him, as indeed he would have missed me. For just as he surpassed me

infinitely in every other ability and virtue, so he did in the
duty of friendship.

> *Why should I be ashamed or exercise control*
> *When I mourn so dear a soul?*
>
> [Horace]

> *Brother, your death has left me sad and lone;*
> *Since you departed all our joys have gone,*
> *Which while you lived your sweet affection fed;*
> *My pleasures all lie shattered, with you dead.*
> *Our soul lies in the tomb, with yours entwined;*
> *And since then I have banished from my mind*
> *My studies, and my spirit's dearest joys.*
> *Shall I ne'er speak to you, or hear your voice?*
> *Or see your face, more dear than life to me?*
> *At least I'll love you to eternity.*
>
> [Catullus]

But let us listen a while to this boy of sixteen.

Because I have found that this work has since been brought
to light, and with evil intent, by those who seek to disturb
and change the state of our government without worrying
whether they will improve it, and because they have mixed
his work up with some of their own concoctions, I have
changed my mind about putting it in here. And so that the
memory of the author may not be damaged in the eyes of
those who could not know his opinions and actions at close
hand, I beg to advise them that this subject was treated by
him in his boyhood, only by way of an exercise, as a common theme hashed over in a thousand places in books. I have
no doubt that he believed what he wrote, for he was so conscientious as not to lie even in jest. And I know further that
if he had had the choice, he would rather have been born in

Venice than in Sarlac, and with reason. But he had another maxim sovereignly imprinted in his soul, to obey and submit most religiously to the laws under which he was born. There never was a better citizen, or one more devoted to the tranquillity of his country, or more hostile to the commotions and innovations of his time. He would much rather have used his ability to suppress them than to give them material that would excite them further. His mind was molded in the pattern of other ages than this.

Now, in exchange for this serious work, I shall substitute another, produced in that same season of his life, gayer and more jovial.[1]

---

[1] In the next chapter (29), Montaigne had originally inserted twenty-nine sonnets of La Boétie.

Of Cannibals[1]

WHEN King Pyrrhus passed over into Italy, after studying the formation of the army that the Romans sent to meet him, he said: "I do not know what barbarians these are" (for so the Greeks called all foreign nations), "but the formation of this army that I see is not at all barbarous." The Greeks said as much of the army that Flaminius brought into their country, and so did Philip, seeing from a knoll the order and distribution of the Roman camp, in his kingdom, under Publius Sulpicius Galba. That is how we should beware of clinging to common opinions, and judge things by reason's way, not by popular say.

I had with me for a long time a man who had lived for ten or twelve years in that other world which was discovered in our century, in the place where Villegaignon landed, and which he called Antarctic France.[2] This discovery of a boundless country seems worthy of consideration. I don't know if I can guarantee that some other such discovery will not be made in the future, so many personages greater than ourselves having been mistaken about this one. I am afraid we have eyes bigger than our stomachs, and more curiosity

---

1 Chapter 31.
2 In Brazil, in 1557.

than capacity. We embrace everything, but we clasp only wind.

Plato brings in Solon, telling how he had learned from the priests of the city of Saïs in Egypt that in days of old, before the Flood, there was a great island named Atlantis, right at the mouth of the Straits of Gibraltar, which contained more countries than Africa and Asia put together, and that the kings of that country, who not only possessed that island but had stretched out so far on the mainland that they held the breadth of Africa as far as Egypt, and the length of Europe as far as Tuscany, attempted to step over into Asia and sub-jugate all the nations that border on the Mediterranean, as far as the gulf of the Black Sea; and to accomplish this, crossed the Spains, Gaul, Italy, as far as Greece, where the Athenians checked them; but that some time after, both the Athenians and themselves and their island were swallowed up by the Flood.

It is quite likely that that phenomenal havoc of waters made amazing changes in the habitations of the earth, as people maintain that the sea cut off Sicily from Italy—

> *'Tis said an earthquake once asunder tore*
> *These lands with dreadful havoc, which before*
> *Formed but one land, one shore,*
>
>   [Virgil]

—Cyprus from Syria, the island of Euboea from the main-land of Boeotia; and elsewhere joined lands that were divided, filling the channels between them with sand and mud:

> *A sterile marsh, long fit for rowing, now*
> *Feeds neighbor towns, and feels the heavy plow.*
>
>   [Horace]

But there appears little likelihood that that island was the new world which we have just discovered; for it almost touched Spain, and it would be an incredible result of a flood to have forced it away as far as it is, more than twelve hundred leagues; besides, the travels of the moderns have already almost revealed that it is not an island, but a mainland connected with the East Indies on one side, and elsewhere with the lands under the two poles; or, if it is separated from them, it is by so narrow a strait and interval that it does not deserve to be called an island on that account.

It seems that there are movements, some natural, others feverish, in these great bodies, just as in our own. When I consider the inroads that my river, the Dordogne, is making in my lifetime into the right bank in its descent, and that in twenty years it has gained so much ground and stolen away the foundations of several buildings, I clearly see that this is an extraordinary disturbance; for if it had always gone at this rate, or was to do so in the future, the face of the world would be turned topsy-turvy. But rivers are subject to changes: now they overflow in one direction, now in another, now they keep to their course. I do not speak of the sudden inundations whose causes are manifest. In Médoc, along the seashore, my brother, the Sieur d'Arsac, can see an estate of his buried under the sands that the sea vomits in front of it; the tops of some buildings are still visible; his rents and domains have changed into very thin pasturage. The inhabitants say that for some time the sea has been pushing toward them so hard that they have lost four leagues of land. These sands are its harbingers; and we see great dunes of moving sand that march half a league ahead of it and gain territory.

The other testimony of antiquity with which some would connect this discovery is in Aristotle, at least if that little book *Of Unheard-of Wonders* is by him. He there relates that certain Carthaginians, having set out upon the Atlantic Ocean from the Straits of Gibraltar, and sailed a long time, had at last discovered a great fertile island, all clothed in woods and watered by great deep rivers, far remote from any mainland; and that they, and others since, attracted by the goodness and fertility of the soil, went there with their wives and children, and began to settle there. The lords of Carthage, seeing that their country was gradually becoming depopulated, expressly forbade anyone to go there any more, on pain of death, and drove out these new inhabitants, fearing, it is said, that in course of time they might come to multiply so greatly as to supplant themselves and ruin their state. This story of Aristotle does not fit our new lands any better than the other.

This man I had was a simple crude fellow [1]—a character fit to bear true witness; for clever people observe more things and more curiously, but they interpret them; and to lend weight and conviction to their interpretation, they cannot help altering history a little. They never show you the things as they are, but bend and disguise them according to the way they have seen them; and to give credence to their judgment and attract you to it, they are prone to add something to their matter to stretch it out and amplify it. We need a man either very honest, or so simple that he has not the stuff to build up false inventions and give them plausibility; and wedded to no theory. Such was my man; and besides this, he has at various times brought sailors and merchants, whom he had known

[1] The traveler Montaigne spoke of at the beginning of the chapter.

on that trip, to see me. So I content myself with his information, without inquiring what the cosmographers say about it.

We ought to have topographers who would give us an
exact account of the places where they have been. But because they have this advantage over us that they have seen
Palestine, they want to enjoy the privilege of telling us news
about all the rest of the world. I would like everyone to write
what he knows, and as much as he knows, not only in this,
but in all other subjects; for a man may have some special
knowledge and experience of the nature of a river or a fountain, who in other matters knows only what everybody
knows. However, to circulate this little scrap of knowledge,
he will undertake to write down the whole of physics. From
this vice spring many great abuses.

Now, to return to my subject, I think there is nothing
barbarous and savage in this nation, from what I have been
told, except that each man calls barbarism whatever is not
his own practice; for indeed it seems we have no other test of
truth and reason than the example and pattern of the opinions and customs of the country we live in. *There* is always
the perfect religion, the perfect government, the perfect and
accomplished usage in all things. Those people are wild, just
as we call wild the fruits that Nature has produced by herself and in her normal course; whereas really it is those that
we have changed artificially and led astray from the common
order, that we should rather call wild. In the former the
genuine, most useful and natural virtues and properties are
alive and vigorous, which we have debased in the latter, and
have only adapted to the pleasure of our corrupted taste.
And yet for all that, the savor and delicacy of some uncul-
tivated fruits of those countries is quite as excellent, even to
our taste, as that of our own. It is not reasonable that art

should win the place of honor over our great and powerful mother Nature. We have so overloaded the beauty and richness of her works by our inventions that we have quite smothered her. Yet wherever she shines forth in her purity, she wonderfully puts to shame our vain and frivolous attempts:

> *Ivy comes readier without our care;*
> *In lonely caves the arbutus grows more fair;*
> *No art with artless bird-song can compare.*
>
> [Propertius]

All our efforts cannot even succeed in reproducing the nest of the tiniest little bird, its contexture, its beauty and convenience; nor even the web of the puny spider. All things, says Plato, are produced by nature, by chance, or by art; the greatest and most beautiful by one or the other of the first two, the least and most imperfect by the last.

These nations, then, seem to me barbarous in this sense, that they have been fashioned very little by the human mind, and are still very close to their original naturalness. The laws of nature still rule them, very little corrupted by ours; but they are in such a state of purity that I am sometimes vexed that knowledge of them did not come earlier, in the days when there were men able to judge them better than we. I am sorry that Lycurgus and Plato did not have this knowledge; for it seems to me that what we actually see in these nations surpasses not only all the pictures in which poets have embellished the golden age, and all their ingenuity in imagining a happy state of man, but also the conceptions and the very desire of philosophy. They could not imagine a naturalness so pure and simple as that which we see by experience; nor could they believe that our society can be maintained with so little artifice and human solder. This is a nation, I should say to Plato, in which there is no sort of traffic, no knowledge of letters, no science of numbers, no name for a magistrate or for political superiority, no custom of servitude, no riches or poverty, no contracts, no successions, no partitions, no occupations but leisure ones, no care for any but common kinship, no clothes, no agriculture, no metal, no use of wine or corn. The very words that signify lying, treachery, dissimulation, avarice, envy, belittling, pardon, unheard of. How far from this perfection would he find the republic that he imagined: *Men fresh sprung from the gods.* [Seneca]

> *These manners nature first ordained.*
> [Virgil]

For the rest, they live in a country with a very pleasant and temperate climate, so that according to my witnesses you rarely see a sick man there; and they have assured me that they never saw one palsied, bleary-eyed, toothless, or bent with age. They are settled along the sea and shut in on the land side by great high mountains, with a stretch about a hundred leagues wide in between. They have a great abundance of fish and flesh which bear no resemblance to ours, and they eat them with no other artifice than cooking. The first man who rode a horse there, though he had had dealings with them on several other trips, so horrified them in this posture that they shot him dead with arrows before they could recognize him.

Their buildings are very long, with a capacity of two or three hundred souls, covered with the bark of great trees, the strips fastened to the ground at one end and supporting and leaning on one another at the top, in the manner of some

Sire

c'est estre au dessus du pois et de la foule de nos
grans & importuns affaires que de nous sçauoir
prester & desmettre aus petits a leur tour
suiuant. le denoir de uostre authorité royalle
qui nous expose a toute heure a toute sorte et
degré d'homes & d'occupations touteffois ce que
uostre maiesté a deigné considerer mes lettres et y
comander responce i'estime mieus le denoir a la
benignité qu'à la uigur de son ame. J'ay de tout
temps regardé en uous cette mesme forture ou uous
estes et uous peut sonuenir que lors mesme qu'il
uien faloit confesser a mon cure ie ne laissois. de
uoir anciennemant de bon euil uos succez a pre sant
aues plus de raison et de liberté ie les embrasse
de pleine affection Ils uous seruent la par effait
mais ils ne uous seruent pas moins icy plor réputation
le retentissemant porte autant que le coup Nous ne
sourions tirer de la iustice de uostre cause des
argumans si fers a meintenir ou reduire uos subietz
come nous fesons des nouuelles de la prosperité de
uos entreprises et puis assurer uostre maiesté que
les changemans nouueaus qu'elle uoit par deça a
son aduantage son heureuse issue de Diepe y a bien
a point secondé le franc zelle & meruilleuse
prudance de monsieur le mareschal de Matignon.

47

Two pages of a letter from Montaigne to Henry IV. Montaigne offers
congratulations and advice to the new king of France and hopes that he
may soon come to Paris, then still rebellious, in response to Henry's invitation. He assures the king that he is his, even more by affection than by
duty, and commends Henry's bearing in these words: "Your Majesty has
very laudably adapted your outward manner to the height of your new

et chastiemant il doit estre remis apres la possession
de la maistrise Vn grand conquerur du temp passé
se vante d'auoir donc autant d'occasion a ses enemis
subiuguer de l'eimer qu'a ses amis Et icy nous
sentons desia quelqu'effaict de bon prognostique
de l'impression que reçoivent nos villes disvnices
par la comparaison de leur rude tretement a
celluy des villes qui sont sous nostre obeissance.
Desirant a vostre maiesté vne felicité plus presante
& moins hazardeuse & qu'elle soit plustost cherie
que crainte de ses peuples et tenant son bien
necessairement attaché au leur ie ne voudrois que
ce mesme aduancemant qu'elle faict vers la victoire
l'auance aussi vers des conditions de paix plus faciles
Sire vostre lettre du dernier de nouambre m'est
venue a moi qu'asture et au dela du terme qu'il vous
plaisoit me prescrire de vostre seiour a Tours. Ie reçois
a grace singuliere qu'elle ait daigné me faire sentir
qu'elle gronderoit a gré de me voir/ personne si inutille
mais sienne plus par affection encore que par devoir.
Elle a raisonnablemant rangé ses formes externes a la
hautur de sa nouvelle fortune mais la debonaireté
& facilité de ses humeurs internes elle faict autant
raisonnablemont de ne les changer. Il luy a pleu aussi
respect non sulemant a mon cage mais a mon desir aussi
de m'apeler en lieu ou elle fut vn peu en repos de ses
laborieuses agitations Sera ce pas bien tost a
Paris Sire et ij m'a il moiens ny sante que ie
n'estande pour m'y randre

48

de mr d'auigne le 18 de Janu.

Vostre treshumble
tresobeissant seruitur et
subiect montaigne

fortune, but as for the affability and ease of your inward character,
you act as laudably in not changing them." The date is January 18, 1590.

of our barns, whose covering hangs down to the ground and acts as a side. They have wood so hard that they cut with it and make of it their swords and grills to cook their food. Their beds are of a cotton weave, hung from the roof like those in our ships, each man having his own; for the wives sleep apart from their husbands.

They get up with the sun, and eat right after they get up, for the whole day, having no other meal than that one. They do not drink then, as Suidas tells us of some other Eastern peoples, who drank apart from meals; but they drink several times a day, and to capacity. Their drink is made of some root, and is of the color of our claret wines. They only drink it lukewarm. This beverage keeps only two or three days; it has a slightly sharp taste, is not at all heady, good for the stomach, and laxative for those who are not used to it; it is a very pleasant drink for anyone who is accustomed to it. In place of bread they use a certain white substance like preserved coriander. I have tried it; it tastes sweet and a little flat.

The whole day is spent in dancing. The younger men go to hunt animals with bows. Some of the women busy themselves meanwhile in warming their drink, which is their chief duty. Some one of the old men, in the morning before they begin to eat, preaches to the whole barnful in common, walking from one end to the other, and repeating one single sentence several times until he has completed the circuit (for the buildings are fully a hundred paces long). He recommends to them only two things: valor against the enemy and love for their wives. And they never fail to point out this obligation, as their refrain, that it is their wives who keep their drink warm and seasoned.

There may be seen in several places, including my own

house, the shape of their beds, of their ropes, of their wooden swords and the bracelets with which they cover their wrists in combats, and of the big canes, open at one end, by whose sound they keep time in their dances. They are close shaven all over, and shave themselves much more cleanly than we, with nothing but a wooden or stone razor. They believe that souls are immortal, and that those who have deserved well of the gods are lodged in that part of heaven where the sun rises, and the damned in the west.

They have some sort of priests and prophets, who very rarely appear before the people, having their home in the mountains. On their arrival there is a great feast and solemn assembly of several villages—each barn, as I have described it, makes up a village, and they are about one French league from each other. This prophet speaks to them in public, exhorting them to virtue and their duty; but their whole ethical science contains only these two articles: resoluteness in war and affection for their wives. This man prophesies to them things to come and the results they are to expect from their undertakings, and urges them to war or holds them back from it; but this is on the condition that when he fails to prophesy correctly, and if things turn out otherwise than he has predicted, he is cut into a thousand pieces if they catch him, and condemned as a false prophet. For this reason, the prophet who has once been mistaken is never seen again.

Divination is a gift of God; that is why it should be a punishable imposture to abuse it. Among the Scythians, when the soothsayers failed to hit the mark, they were laid, chained hand and foot, on carts full of heather and drawn by oxen, on which they were burned. Those who handle matters subject to the conduct of human capacity are excusable if they do the best they can. But these others, who come and trick us with assurances of an extraordinary faculty that is beyond our ken, should they not be punished for not making good their promise, and for the temerity of their imposture?

They have their wars with the nations beyond the mountains, further inland, to which they go quite naked, with no other arms than bows or wooden swords pointed at one end, in the manner of the tongues of our boar spears. It is marvelous what firmness they show in their combats, which never end but in slaughter and bloodshed; for as for routs and terror, they do not know what that means.

Each man brings back as his trophy the head of the enemy he has killed, and sets it up at the entrance to his dwelling. After treating their prisoners well for a long time with all the hospitality they can think of, the captor of each one calls a great assembly of his acquaintances. He ties a rope to one of the prisoner's arms, by the end of which he holds him, a few steps away, for fear of being hurt, and gives his dearest friend the other arm to hold in the same way; and these two, in the presence of the whole assembly, dispatch him with their swords. This done, they roast him and eat him in common and send some pieces to their absent friends. This is not, as people think, for nourishment, as of old the Scythians used to do; it is to betoken an extreme revenge. And the proof of this is that having perceived that the Portuguese, who had joined forces with their adversaries, inflicted a different kind of death on them when they took them prisoner, which was to bury them up to the waist, shoot the rest of their bodies full of arrows, and afterwards hang them; they thought that these people from the other world, being men who had sown the knowledge of many vices among their neighbors and were much greater masters than themselves in every sort of wickedness, did not adopt this sort of vengeance without some reason, and that it must be more painful than their own; so they began to give up their old method and follow this one.

I am not sorry that we notice the barbarous horror of such acts, but I am heartily sorry that, judging their faults rightly, we should be so blind to our own. I think there is more barbarity in eating a man alive than in eating him dead, in tearing by tortures and the rack a body still full of feeling, in roasting him bit by bit, having him bitten and mangled by dogs and swine (as we have not only read but seen within fresh memory, not among ancient enemies, but among neighbors and fellow citizens, and what is worse, on the pretext of piety and religion) than in roasting and eating him after he is dead.

Indeed, Chrysippus and Zeno, heads of the Stoic sect, thought that there was nothing wrong in using our carcasses for any purpose in case of need, and getting nourishment from them; just as our ancestors, being besieged by Caesar in the city of Alésia, resolved to relieve the famine of this siege with the bodies of the old men, women, and other people useless for fighting.

> *The Gascons once, 'tis said, their life renewed*
> *By eating of such food.*
>
> [Juvenal]

And physicians do not fear to use human flesh in all sorts of ways for our health, applying it either inwardly or outwardly. But there never was any opinion so diseased as to excuse treachery, disloyalty, tyranny, and cruelty, which are our common vices.

Then we may well call these people barbarians, in respect

to the rules of reason, but not in respect to ourselves, who surpass them in every kind of barbarity.

Their warfare is wholly noble and generous, and as excusable and beautiful as this human disease can be; its only basis among them is the jealousy of valor. They are not fighting for the conquest of new lands, for they still enjoy that natural abundance that provides them without toil and trouble with all necessary things in such profusion that they have no wish to enlarge their boundaries. They are still in that happy state of desiring only as much as their natural needs demand; anything beyond that is superfluous to them.

They generally call each other thus: those of the same age, brothers; those who are younger, children; and the old men are fathers to all the others. These leave to their heirs in common the full possession of their property, without division or any other title at all than just the one that Nature gives to her creatures in bringing them into the world.

If their neighbors cross the mountains to come and attack them, and win victory over them, the gain of the victor is glory, and the advantage of having proven the master in valor and virtue; for otherwise they have no use for the goods of the vanquished, and they return to their own country, where they have no lack of anything necessary, nor yet lack of that great thing, the knowledge of how to enjoy their condition happily and be content with it. These do the same in their turn. They demand of their prisoners no other ransom than their confession and acknowledgment of being vanquished. But there is not one in a whole century who does not choose to die rather than to relax a single bit, by word or look, from the grandeur of an invincible courage; you do not see one who does not choose to be killed and eaten rather than so much as ask not to be. They treat them very freely, so that life may be all the dearer to them, and usually talk to them of the threats of their coming death, the torments they will have to suffer, the preparations that are being made for that purpose, the cutting up of their limbs, and the feast that will be made at their expense. All this is done for the sole purpose of extorting from their lips some weak or base word, or making them want to flee, so as to gain the advantage of having terrified them and broken down their firmness. For indeed, if you take it the right way, it is in this point alone that true victory lies:

> *It is no victory*
> *Unless the vanquished foe admits your mastery.*
>
> [Claudian]

The Hungarians, very bellicose fighters, did not in olden times pursue their advantage beyond putting the enemy at their mercy. For having wrung this confession from him, they let him go unharmed, unransomed, except, at most, for making him give his word never again to take arms against them.

We win quite enough advantages over our enemies that are borrowed advantages, not really our own. It is the quality of a porter, not of valor, to have sturdier arms and legs; agility is a dead and corporal quality; it is a stroke of luck to make our enemy stumble, or dazzle his eyes by the light of the sun; it is a trick of art and science, which may be found in a worthless coward, to be an able fencer. The worth and value of a man is in his heart and his will; there lies his real honor. Valor is the strength, not of legs and arms, but of heart and soul; it does not consist in the worth of our horse, or our weapons, but in our own. He who falls obstinate in his courage, *if he has fallen, he fights on his knees.* [Seneca] He who relaxes none of his assurance for any danger of imminent death; who, giving up his soul, still looks firmly and scornfully at his enemy, he is beaten not by us, but by fortune; he is killed, not conquered.

The most valiant are sometimes the most unfortunate. Thus there are triumphant defeats that rival victories. Nor did those four sister victories, the fairest that the sun ever beheld with his eyes—Salamis, Plataea, Mycale, and Sicily—ever dare match all their combined glory against the glory of the annihilation of King Leonidas and his men at the pass of Thermopylae.

Who ever hastened with more glorious and ambitious desire to win a battle than Captain Ischolas to lose one? Who ever secured his safety more ingeniously and painstakingly than he did his destruction? He was charged to defend a certain pass in the Peloponnesus against the Arcadians. In order to do so, finding himself quite powerless in view of the nature of the place and the inequality of the forces, and making up his mind that all who confronted the enemy would necessarily have to remain on the field; on the other hand, deeming it unworthy both of his own virtue and magnanimity and of the name of a Lacedaemonian to fail in his charge, he took a middle course between these two extremes, in this way. The youngest and fittest of his band he preserved for the defense and service of their country, and sent them home; and with those whose loss was less vital, he determined to hold this pass, and by their death to make the enemy buy their entry as dearly as he could. And so it turned out. For being presently surrounded on all sides by the Arcadians, after slaughtering a large number of them, he and his men were all put to the sword. Is there a trophy dedicated to victors that would not be more due to these vanquished? The role of true victory is in fighting, not in coming off safely; and the honor of valor consists in combating, not in beating.

To return to our story. These prisoners are so far from giving in, in spite of all that is done to them, that on the contrary, during the two or three months that they are kept, they wear a gay expression; they urge their captors to hurry and put them to the test; they defy them, insult them, reproach them with their cowardice and the number of battles lost to their men.

I have a song composed by a prisoner which contains this challenge, that they should all come boldly and gather to dine off him, for they will be eating at the same time their own fathers and grandfathers, who have served to feed and nourish his body. "These muscles," he says, "this flesh and these veins are your own, poor fools that you are. You do not recognize that the substance of your ancestors' limbs is still contained in them? Savor them well; you will find in them the taste of your own flesh." An idea that certainly does not smack of barbarity. Those that paint these people dying, and who show the execution, portray the prisoner spitting in the face of his slayers and making faces at them. Indeed, to the last gasp they never stop braving and defying them by word and look. Truly here are real savages by our standards; for either they must be thoroughly so, or we must be; there is an amazing distance between their character and ours.

The men there have several wives, and the higher their reputation for valor, the more wives they have. It is a remarkably beautiful thing about their marriages that the same jealousy our wives have to keep us from the affection and favors of other women, theirs have to win this for them. Being more concerned for their husbands' honor than for anything else, they strive and worry to have as many companions as they can, since that is a sign of their husband's valor.

Our wives will cry "Miracle!"; but it is not. It is a properly matrimonial virtue, but one of the highest order. And in the Bible, Leah, Rachel, Sarah, and Jacob's wives gave their beautiful handmaids to their husbands; and Livia seconded the appetites of Augustus, to her own disadvantage; and Stratonice, the wife of King Deiotarus, not only lent her husband for his use a very beautiful young chambermaid in her service, but carefully brought up her children, and backed them up to succeed to their father's estates.

And lest it be thought that all this is done through a simple and servile bondage to usage and through the pressure of the authority of their ancient customs, without reasoning or judgment, and because their minds are so stupid that they cannot take any other course, I must cite some examples of their capacity. Besides the warlike song I have just quoted, I have another, a love song, which begins in this vein: "Adder, stay; stay, adder, that from the pattern of your coloring my sister may draw the model and the workmanship of a rich girdle that I may give to my love; so may your beauty and your disposition be forever preferred to all other serpents." This first couplet is the refrain of the song. Now I am familiar enough with poetry to be a judge of this: that not only is there nothing barbarous in this fancy, but that it is altogether Anacreontic. Their language, moreover, is a soft language, with an agreeable sound, somewhat like Greek in its endings.

Three of these men, not knowing how much their repose and happiness will pay some day for the knowledge of the corruptions of this side of the ocean, and that of this intercourse will come their ruin, which I suppose is already well advanced—poor wretches, to have let themselves be tricked by the desire for new things, and to have left the serenity of their own sky to come and see ours—were at Rouen, at the time when the late King Charles the Ninth [1] was there. The King talked to them for a long time; they were shown our ways, our pomp, the form of a fine city. After that someone asked their opinion, and wanted to know what they had found most amazing. They replied that there were three things, of which I have forgotten the third, and I am very sorry for it; but I still remember two of them. They said that in the first place they thought it very strange that so many grown men, bearded, strong, and armed, who were around the King (it is likely that they were talking about the Swiss of his guard) should submit to obey a child, and that one of them was not chosen to command instead; secondly (they have a way in their language of speaking of men as halves of one another), that they had noticed that there were among us men full and gorged with all sorts of good things, and that their other halves were beggars at their doors, emaciated with hunger and poverty; and they thought it strange that these needy halves could suffer such an injustice, and did not take the others by the throat, or set fire to their houses.

I had a long talk with one of them; but I had an interpreter who followed my meaning so badly, and who was so hindered by his stupidity in taking in my ideas, that I could get hardly any satisfaction from the man. When I asked him what profit he gained from his superior position among his people (for he was a captain, and our sailors called him king), he told me that it was to march foremost in war. How many men followed him? He pointed to a piece of ground,

1 In 1562.

to signify as many as such a space could hold; it might have been four or five thousand men. Did all this authority expire with the war? He said that this much remained, that when he visited the villages dependent on him, they made paths for him through the underbrush by which he might pass quite comfortably.

All this is not too bad. But wait! They don't wear trousers.

Of Solitude[1]

LET us leave aside the tedious comparison between the solitary and the active life; and as for that fine statement under which ambition and avarice take cover, "That we are not born for our private selves, but for the public," let us boldly appeal to those who are in the midst of the dance; and let them cudgel their conscience and say whether, on the contrary, the titles, the offices, and the hustle and bustle of the world are not sought out to gain private profit from the public. The evil means men use in our day to push themselves show clearly that the end is not worth much. Let us reply to ambition that it is she herself that gives us a taste for solitude. For what does she shun so much as society? What does she seek so much as elbow-room? There is opportunity everywhere for doing good or evil. However, if Bias' statement is true, that the wicked are in the majority, or what Ecclesiastes says, that not one in a thousand is good—

The good are rare: if all their numbers you compile,
They'll scarcely match the gates of Thebes, the mouths
of Nile,   [Juvenal]

—contagion is very dangerous in the crowd. One must either

---

imitate the vicious, or hate them. Both these things are dangerous: to resemble them, because they are many; and to hate many of them, because they are unlike.

And merchants who go to sea are right to be careful that those who embark on the same ship are not dissolute, blasphemous, or wicked, regarding such company as unlucky. Wherefore Bias said humorously to those who were undergoing with him the danger of a great tempest and calling on the gods for help: "Be quiet, so they may not realize that you are here with me." And in a more pressing emergency, Albuquerque, Viceroy in the Indies for King Emanuel of Portugal, in great peril of shipwreck at sea, took a young boy upon his shoulders for this purpose alone, that in their common danger the boy's innocence might serve him as a guarantee and a recommendation to divine favor, and bring him to safety.

It is not that the wise man cannot live anywhere content, yes, and alone in a palace crowd; but if he has the choice, says he, he will flee even the sight of it. He will endure it, if need be, but if it is up to him, he will choose the other. He does not feel sufficiently rid of vices, if he must still contend with those of other men. Charondas chastised as evil those who were convicted of keeping evil company.

There is nothing so unsociable and so sociable as man; one by his vice, the other by his nature. And Antisthenes does not seem to me to have given a satisfactory answer to the man who reproached him for associating with wicked men, when he said that doctors lived well enough among the sick; for if they improve the health of the sick, they impair their own by the contagion, the constant sight, and the treatment of diseases.

Now the aim of all solitude, I take it, is the same: to live more at leisure and at one's ease. But people do not always find the right way. Often they think they have left business, and they have only changed it. There is scarcely less trouble in governing a family than an entire state: whatever the mind is wrapped up in, it is all wrapped up in it, and domestic occupations are no less importunate for being less important. Furthermore, by getting rid of the court and the market place we have not gotten rid of the chief worries of our life:

> *Reason and sense remove anxiety,*
> *Not houses that look out upon the sea.*
> [Horace]

Ambition, avarice, irresolution, fear, and lusts do not leave us when we change our country.

> *Behind the horseman sits black care.*
> [Horace]

They often follow us even into the cloisters and the schools of philosophy. Neither deserts, nor rocky caves, nor hair shirts, nor fastings will free us of them:

> *The fatal shaft sticks in her side.*
> [Virgil]

Someone said to Socrates that a certain man had grown no better by his travels. "I should think not," he said; "he took himself along with him."

> *Why should we move to find*
> *Countries and climates of another kind?*
> *What exile leaves himself behind?*
> [Horace]

If a man does not first unburden himself and his soul of the load that weighs upon it, movement will crush it still more,

as in a ship the cargo is less cumbersome when it is settled.
You do a sick man more harm than good by moving him.
You imbed the malady by disturbing it, as stakes penetrate
deeper and grow firmer when you budge them and shake
them. Wherefore it is not enough to have gotten away from
the crowd, it is not enough to move; we must get away from
the love of crowds that is within us, we must sequester ourselves and regain possession of ourselves.

> *"At last," you'll say, "I've snapped my chains."*
> *No; when a dog runs off, rope broken at great pains,*
> *Yet dangling from his neck the greater part remains.*
> [Persius]

We take our chains away with us; it is not complete freedom; we still turn our eyes to what we have left behind, our
fancy is full of it.

> *Unless the heart is purged, what must we undergo!*
> *What battles and what perils, to our fruitless woe!*
> *How great the bitter cares of lust that rend apart,*
> *With terrors in their train, an agitated heart!*
> *What great disasters pride and filth and wantonness*
> *Bring after them! And luxury and idleness!*
> [Lucretius]

Our illness grips us by the soul, and the soul cannot escape
from itself:

> *The soul's at fault, which ne'er escapes itself.*
> [Horace]

Therefore we must bring it back and withdraw it into itself:
that is the real solitude, which may be enjoyed in the midst
of cities and the courts of kings; but it is enjoyed more
handily alone.

Now since we are undertaking to live alone and do without company, let us make our contentment depend on ourselves; let us cut loose from all the ties that bind us to others; let us win from ourselves the power to live really alone and to live that way contentedly.

Stilpo having escaped the burning of his city, in which he had lost wife, children, and property, Demetrius Poliorcetes, seeing him unperturbed in expression amid the great ruin of his country, asked him if he had not suffered loss. He replied No, that thanks to God he had lost nothing of his own. That is what the philosopher Antisthenes expressed humorously: that man should furnish himself with provisions that would float on water and could swim ashore with him from a shipwreck.

Certainly a man of understanding has lost nothing, if he has himself. When the city of Nola was ruined by the barbarians, Paulinus, who was bishop of the city, having lost everything and being their prisoner, prayed God thus: "Lord, keep me from feeling this loss; for Thou knowest that they have yet touched nothing of what is mine." The riches that made him rich and the goods that made him good were still entire. That is what it is to choose wisely the treasures that can be secured from harm, and to hide them in a place where no one may go and which can be betrayed only by ourselves.

We should have wife, children, goods, and above all health, if we can; but we must not bind ourselves to them so strongly that our happiness depends on them. We must reserve a back shop all our own, entirely free, in which to establish our real liberty and our principal retreat and solitude. Here our ordinary conversation must be between us and ourselves, and so private that no outside association or communication can find a place; here to talk and laugh as if without wife, with-out children and without possessions, without retinue and without servants, so that, when the time comes to lose them, it may be nothing new to us to do without them. We have a soul that can be turned upon itself; it can keep itself com-pany; it has the means to attack and the means to defend, the means to receive and the means to give: let us not fear that in this solitude we shall stagnate in tedious idleness:

> *In solitude be to thyself a throng.*
>
> [Tibullus]

Virtue, says Antisthenes, is content with itself, without rules, without words, without deeds.

Among our customary actions there is not one in a thou-sand that concerns ourselves. The man you see climbing atop the ruins of that wall, frenzied and beside himself, a mark for so many musket shots; and that other, all scarred, pale and faint with hunger, determined to die rather than open the gates to him, do you think that they are there for their own sake? For the sake of a man whom perhaps they never saw, and who is not in the least concerned about their doings, being meanwhile plunged in idleness and pleasures.

This other fellow, dirty, with running nose and eyes, whom you see coming out of his study after midnight, do you think he is seeking among his books how to make him-self a better, happier, and wiser man? Nothing doing. He will die in the attempt, or teach posterity the meter of Plautus' verses and the proper spelling of a Latin word. Who does not willingly exchange health, rest, and life for reputation and glory, the most useless, worthless, and false coin that is cur-rent among us? Our own death did not frighten us enough; let us burden ourselves also with that of our wives, our children, and our servants. Our own affairs did not give us enough trouble; let us also torment ourselves and get headaches over those of our neighbors and friends.

> *What! Shall a man establish in his soul, or prize*
> *Anything dearer than himself in his own eyes?*
> [Terence]

Solitude seems to me more appropriate and reasonable for those who have given to the world their most active and vigorous years, following the example of Thales.

We have lived enough for others; let us live at least this remaining bit of life for ourselves. Let us bring back our thoughts and plans to ourselves and our comfort. It is no small matter to arrange our retirement securely; it keeps us busy enough without mixing other undertakings with it. Since God gives us leisure to make arrangements for moving out, let us prepare for it; let us pack our bags; let us take an early leave of the company; let us break free from these violent clutches that engage us elsewhere and draw us away from ourselves. We must untie these bonds that are so powerful, and henceforth love this and that, but be wedded only to ourselves. That is to say, let the other things be ours, but not joined and glued to us so strongly that they cannot be detached without tearing off our skin and some part of our body as well. The greatest thing in the world is to know how to belong to ourselves.

It is time to untie ourselves from society, since we can contribute nothing to it. And he who cannot lend, let him keep from borrowing. Our powers are failing us; let us withdraw them and concentrate them on ourselves. He who can turn the offices of friendship and fellowship around and fuse them into himself, let him do so. In this decline, which makes him useless, burdensome, and troublesome to others, let him keep from being troublesome to himself, and burdensome, and useless. Let him indulge and care for himself, and especially govern himself, respecting and fearing his reason and his conscience, so that he cannot make a false step in their presence without shame. *For it is rare for anyone to respect himself enough.* [Quintilian]

Socrates says that the young should get instruction, grown men should practice doing good, old men should withdraw from all civil and military occupations, living at their own discretion, without being tied down to any fixed office.

There are some temperaments more suited to these precepts for retirement than others. Those whose grasp of things is weak and slow, and whose affection and will are fastidious and slow to enter service or employment, of whom I am one, both by natural disposition and by reflection, will comply with this advice better than the active and busy souls who embrace everything and engage themselves everywhere, who grow passionate about all things, who offer, present, and give themselves on all occasions. We should use these accidental and external conveniences, so far as they are agreeable to us, but without making them our mainstay; they are not; neither reason nor nature will have it so. Why should we, contrary to their laws, make our contentment a slave to the power of others? Moreover, to anticipate the accidents of fortune, to deprive ourselves of the commodities that are in our hands, as many have done through piety and some philosophers through reason, to wait on ourselves, to sleep on the hard ground, to put out our eyes, to throw our riches into the river, to seek pain, some in order to win bliss in another life by torment in this, others to make themselves safe from a new fall by settling on the lowest step—these are the acts of an excessive virtue. Let the sturdier and stronger natures make even their hiding place glorious and exemplary:

> *When riches fail, I praise*
> *The safe and simple life, content with humble ways;*
> *But then, when better, richer fortune smiles on me,*
> *I say that only they live well and sensibly*
> *Whose wealth in country manors glistens brilliantly.*
> [Horace]

I have enough on my hands without going that far. It is enough for me while under fortune's favor, to prepare for its disfavor, and while I am well off, to picture the evil that is to come, as far as my imagination can reach; just as we accustom ourselves to jousts and tournaments, and imitate war in the midst of peace.

I do not consider Arcesilaus, the philosopher, less virtuous because I know that he used gold and silver vessels as much as the condition of his fortune allowed him to; and I esteem him more highly for having used them moderately and liberally than if he had given them up.

I see to what limits natural necessity goes; and, seeing the poor beggar at my door, often merrier and healthier than myself, I put myself in his place, I try to fit my mind to his bias. And running over the other examples in the same way, though I may think that death, poverty, contempt, and disease are at my heels, I easily resolve not to take fright at what a humbler man than I accepts with such patience. And I cannot believe that weakness of understanding can do more than vigor, or that the results of reason cannot match the results of habit. And knowing how precarious these incidental comforts are, I do not fail, while in full enjoyment of them, to make it my sovereign request of God that he make me content with myself and the good things I bring forth. I see healthy young men who never fail to carry in their trunks a mass of pills to take when afflicted with a cold, which they fear the less because they think they have the remedy at hand. Thus we must do; and further, if we feel ourselves subject to some graver malady, we must provide ourselves with the drugs that benumb and put to sleep the affected part.

The occupation we must choose for such a life must be neither laborious nor tedious, otherwise there would be no point in having come to it in search of rest. This depends on each man's particular taste: mine is not at all adaptable to management. Those who like it should apply themselves to it with moderation:

They try to make things yield to them, not them to things.
[Horace]

Besides, the care of an estate is a job for slaves, as Sallust calls it. Some parts of it are more excusable, like the care of gardens, which Xenophon attributes to Cyrus; and a mean may be found between that base and sordid concern, tense and full of anxiety, which is seen in men who plunge themselves deep into it, and that profound and extreme negligence, letting everything go to seed, which we see in others:

Democritus's herds devour his crops, his season's yield,
While on swift wings his soul without his body roams
*   afield.*

[Horace]

But let us hear the counsel that the younger Pliny gives his friend Cornelius Rufus on this matter of solitude: *I advise you, in this full and prosperous retreat in which you are, to leave to your servants the sordid and abject care of the household, and to devote yourself to the study of letters, in order to derive from them something that is all your own.* He means reputation, being of a like mind with Cicero, who says he wants to use his solitude and rest from public affairs to gain by his writings immortal life:

> *Is knowledge naught to you*
> *Unless another knows that you know all you do?*
> [Persius]

It seems reasonable, when a man talks of retiring from the world, that he should set his gaze outside of it. These men do so only half way. They indeed arrange their affairs for the time when they will no longer be there; but by a ridiculous contradiction they still aspire to reap the fruit of their plan from the world when they have left it.

The idea of those who seek solitude for religious reasons, filling their hearts with the certainty of divine promises for the other life, is much more sane and consistent. They set before their eyes God, an object infinite both in goodness and in power; in him the soul has the wherewithal to satisfy its desires abundantly in complete freedom. Afflictions, sufferings come to them as profit, being used for the acquisition of eternal health and rejoicing; death, as desirable, being the passage to so perfect a state. The harshness of their rules is promptly smoothed by habit; and the carnal appetites are frustrated and then put to sleep by denial, for nothing keeps them up but use and exercise. Only this one goal of another life, happily immortal, rightly deserves that we abandon the comforts and pleasures of this life of ours. And he who can really and constantly kindle his soul with the flame of that living faith and hope builds himself in solitude a life that is voluptuous and delightful beyond any other kind of life.

Therefore I am satisfied neither with the purpose nor the means of Pliny's advice; we are only falling out of an ague into a burning fever. This occupation with books is as laborious as any other, and as much an enemy to health, which should be our chief consideration. And we must not let ourselves be lulled to sleep by the pleasure we take in it; it is the same pleasure that ruins the frugal man, the miser, the voluptuous man, and the ambitious man. The sages teach us often enough to beware of the treachery of our appetites, and to distinguish the real and complete pleasures from the pleasures that are mixed and streaked with still more pain. For most pleasures, they say, caress and embrace us only to strangle us, as did those thieves that the Egyptians called Philistas. And if we got our headache before getting drunk, we should take care not to drink too much. But pleasure, to deceive us, walks ahead and hides her retinue from us. Books are pleasant; but if by associating with them we end by losing gaiety and health, the best parts of us, let us leave them. I am one of those who think that their benefits cannot counterbalance this loss.

As men who have long felt weakened by some indisposition at last put themselves at the mercy of medicine and have certain rules of living prescribed for them by art, which are nevermore to be transgressed; so he who retires, wearied and disgusted with the common way of life, must model this one on the rules of reason, order it and arrange it by premeditation and reflection. He must have taken leave of every kind of labor, whatever aspect it may bear, and flee in general the passions that prevent tranquillity of body and soul, and choose the way that suits his humor best:

> *Let each one know the way that he should go.*
> [Propertius]

In management, in study, in hunting, and in all other pursuits, we should take part up to the utmost limits of pleasure, but beware of engaging ourselves further, where pain begins to mingle with it. We must keep only so much business and occupation as is necessary to keep us in trim and protect us from the inconveniences that the other extreme, slack and sluggish idleness, brings in its train.

There are sterile and thorny sciences, for the most part created for the busy life; we must leave them to those who are in the service of the world. For myself, I like only books that are either pleasant and easy, which entertain me, or those that console me and counsel me to regulate my life and my death:

> *To saunter silent through the wholesome wood,*
> *Bent on thoughts worthy of the wise and good.*
> [Horace]

Wiser men, having a strong and vigorous soul, can make for themselves a wholly spiritual repose. But I, who have a commonplace soul, must help support myself by bodily comforts; and age having lately robbed me of those that were more to my fancy, I train and sharpen my appetite for those that remain and are more suitable to this present season. We must hold on, tooth and nail, to our enjoyment of the pleasures of life, which our years tear, one after the other, from our hands:

> *Let us seize pleasures; life is ours to claim;*
> *Too soon we shall be ashes, ghosts, a name.*
>
> [Persius]

Now, as for glory, the goal that Pliny and Cicero set up for us, it is very far from my reckoning. The humor most directly opposite to retirement is ambition. Glory and repose are things that cannot lodge in the same dwelling. As far as I can see, these men have only their arms and legs outside the crowd; their souls, their intentions are more than ever in the thick of it:

> *Old man, do you collect titbits for others' ears?*
>
> [Persius]

They have only stepped back to make a better jump, and with a stronger impetus to plunge deeper into the crowd. Do you want to see how they shoot a grain's length too short? Let us put into the scales the advice of two philosophers,[1] and of two very different sects, one writing to Idomeneus, the other to Lucilius, their friends, to draw them out of handling affairs and high positions into solitude.

"You have," they say, "lived until now swimming and floating; come away and die in port. You have given the rest of your life to light, give this part to the shade. It is impossible to abandon occupations if you do not abandon the fruits of them; therefore rid yourself of all care for renown and glory. There is danger that the gleam of your past actions may give you only too much light and follow you right into your lair.

---

[1] Epicurus and Seneca.

Abandon with the other pleasures that which comes from the approbation of others; and as for your knowledge and ability, don't worry, it will not lose its effect if it makes you yourself a better man. Remember the man who, when he was asked why he took so much pains in an art which could come to the knowledge of scarcely anyone, replied: 'Few are enough for me, one is enough for me, none at all is enough for me.' He spoke truly: you and one companion are an adequate theater for each other, or you for yourself. Let the people be one to you, and let one be a whole people to you. It is a base ambition to want to gain glory from our idleness and our concealment. We must do like the animals that rub out their tracks at the entrance to their lairs.

"What you must seek is no longer that the world should speak of you, but how you should speak to yourself. Retire into yourself, but first prepare to receive yourself there; it would be madness to trust in yourself if you do not know how to govern yourself. There are ways to fail in solitude as well as in company. Until you have made yourself such that you dare not trip up in your own presence, and until you are self-respecting and ashamed, *let true ideals be kept before your mind* [Cicero], keep ever in your mind Cato, Phocion, and Aristides, in whose presence even fools would hide their faults; make them controllers of all your intentions; if these intentions get off the track, your reverence for those men will set them on their way again. They will keep you on the way of being content with yourself, of borrowing nothing except from yourself, of holding your mind in check and fixing it on definite and limited thoughts in which it may take pleasure; and, having recognized the true blessings, which we enjoy in so far as we recognize them, of resting content with them, without any desire to prolong life and reputation."

That is the counsel of true and natural philosophy, not of an ostentatious and loquacious philosophy like that of the first two.

Of Democritus and Heraclitus[1]

JUDGMENT is a tool to use on all subjects, and comes in everywhere. Therefore in the tests[2] that I make of it here, I use every sort of occasion. If it is a subject I do not understand at all, even on that I essay my judgment, sounding the ford from a good distance; and then, finding it too deep for my height, I stick to the bank. And this acknowledgment that I cannot cross over is a token of its effect, indeed one it is most proud of. Sometimes in a vain and non-existent subject I try to see if it will find material to give it body, prop it up, and support it. Sometimes I lead it to a noble and well-worn subject in which it has nothing original to discover, the road being so beaten that it can only walk in others' footsteps. There it plays its part by choosing the way that seems best to it, and of a thousand paths it says that this one or that was the most wisely chosen.

I take the first subject that chance offers. They are all equally good to me. And I never plan to develop them completely. For I do not see the whole of anything; nor do those who promise to show it to us. Of a hundred members and faces that each thing has, I take one, sometimes only to lick

---

1 Chapter 50.
2 In the French, *essais;* hence, *tests* or *essays.*

it, sometimes to brush the surface, sometimes to pinch it to the bone. I give it a stab, not as wide but as deep as I know how. And most often I like to take them from some unaccustomed point of view. I would venture to treat some matter thoroughly, if I knew myself less well. Scattering a word here, there another, samples separated from their context, dispersed, without a plan and without a promise, I am not bound to make something of them or to adhere to them myself without varying when I please and giving myself up to doubt and uncertainty and my ruling quality, which is ignorance.

Every movement reveals us. That same mind of Caesar's, which comes to light in ordering and directing the battle of Pharsalia, is also shown in arranging idle and amorous affairs. We judge a horse, not only by seeing him handled on a race course, but also by seeing him walk, and even by seeing him resting in the stable.

Among the functions of the soul there are some lowly ones; he who does not see that side of her does not fully know her. And perhaps she is best observed when she goes at her simple pace. The winds of passion seize her more strongly on her lofty flights. Moreover, she applies her entire self to each matter, and works on it with all of her, and never treats more than one at a time. And she treats a matter not according to itself, but according to herself.

Things in themselves may have their own weights and measures and qualities; but once inside, within us, she allots them their qualities as she sees fit. Death is frightful to Cicero, desirable to Cato, a matter of indifference to Socrates. Health, conscience, authority, knowledge, riches, beauty, and their opposites, are stripped on entry and receive from the soul new clothing, and the coloring that she chooses

—brown, green, bright, dark, bitter, sweet, deep, superficial —and which each individual soul chooses; for they have not agreed together on their styles, rules and forms; each one is queen in her realm. Wherefore let us no longer make the external qualities of things our excuse; it is up to us to reckon them as we will. Our good and our ill depend on ourselves alone. Let us offer our offerings and vows to ourselves, not to Fortune; she has no power over our character; on the contrary, it drags her in its train and molds her in its own form.

Why shall I not judge Alexander at table, talking and drinking his fill? Or if he is playing chess, what sinew of his soul is not touched and employed in this silly and puerile game? I hate it and avoid it, because it is not enough of a game, and is too serious an amusement, being ashamed to devote to it the attention that would suffice for something good. He was no more absorbed when he prepared his glorious expedition to India; nor is this other in unraveling a passage on which depends the salvation of the human race. See how our mind swells and magnifies this ridiculous amusement; how all its muscles grow tense; what ample opportunity it here gives everyone to know himself, and to judge himself rightly. In no other situation do I see and check up on myself more thoroughly. What passion does not excite us in this game: anger, vexation, hatred, impatience, and a vehement ambition to win in a thing in which ambition to be beaten would be more excusable. For rare and extraordinary excellence in frivolous things is unbecoming a man of honor. What I say of this example may be said of all others: each particle, each occupation of a man betrays him and reveals him just as well as any other.

Democritus and Heraclitus were two philosophers, of

whom the first, finding the condition of man vain and ridiculous, never went out in public but with a mocking and laugh-
ing face; Heraclitus, having pity and compassion on this same
condition of ours, wore a face perpetually sad, and eyes filled
with tears:

> *One always, when he o'er his threshold stept,*
> *Laughed at the world; the other always wept.*
> [Juvenal]

I prefer the first humor; not because it is pleasanter to
laugh than to weep, but because it is more disdainful, and
condemns us more than the other; and it seems to me that we
can never be despised as much as we deserve. Pity and com-
miseration are mingled with some esteem for the thing we
pity; the things we laugh at we consider worthless. I do not
think there is as much unhappiness in us as frivolity, nor as
much wickedness as stupidity. We are not so full of evil as
of inanity; we are not as wretched as we are worthless.

Thus Diogenes, who pottered about by himself, rolling his
tub and turning up his nose at the great Alexander, considering us as flies or bags of wind, was really a sharper and
more stinging judge, and consequently juster, to my taste,
than Timon, who was surnamed the hater of men. For what
we hate we take seriously. This man wished us ill, passionately desired our ruin, shunned association with us as dangerous, as with wicked men depraved by nature. The other
esteemed us so little that our contact could neither disturb
him nor infect him, and avoided our company, not through
fear of association with us, but through disdain of it; he
considered us incapable of doing either good or evil.

Of the same stamp was the reply of Statilius, whom Brutus
asked to join the conspiracy against Caesar. He considered

the enterprise just, but he did not believe that men were worth taking any trouble about; in conformity with the teachings of Hegesias, who said that the wise man should do nothing except for himself, since he alone is worth having anything done for him; and that of Theodorus, that it is unjust for a wise man to risk his life for the good of his country, and endanger wisdom for the sake of fools.

Our own peculiar condition is that we are as fit to be laughed at as able to laugh.

BOOK II

BOOK II

Of the Inconsistency of Our Actions[1]

THOSE who make a practice of comparing human actions are never so much at a loss as to put them together and in the same light; for they commonly contradict each other so strangely that it seems impossible that they have come from the same shop. One moment Marius the Younger is a son of Mars, another moment a son of Venus. Pope Boniface the Eighth, they say, entered office like a fox, behaved in it like a lion, and died like a dog. And who would believe that it was Nero, that living image of cruelty, who said, when they brought him in customary fashion the sentence of a condemned criminal to sign: "Would to God I had never learned to write!" So much his heart was wrung at condemning a man to death!

All the world is so full of such examples, each man, in fact, can supply himself with so many, that sometimes I find it strange to see intelligent men going to great pains to match these pieces; seeing that irresolution seems to me the most

<hr>

[1] Chapter 1.

common and apparent defect of our nature, as witness that famous line of Publius, the farce writer:

> *Bad is the plan that never can be changed.*
> [Publius Syrus]

There is some justification for basing a judgment of a man on the most ordinary acts of his life; but in view of the natural instability of our conduct and opinions, it has often seemed to me that even good authors are wrong to insist on weaving a consistent and solid fabric out of us. They choose one general characteristic, and go and arrange and interpret all a man's actions to fit their picture; and if they cannot twist them enough, they go and set them down to dissimulation. Augustus has escaped them; for there is in this man throughout the course of his life such an obvious, abrupt, and continual variety of actions, that even the boldest judges have had to let him go, untouched and unsolved. It is harder for me to believe in men's consistency than in anything, and easier to believe in their inconsistency. He who would judge them in detail and distinctly, bit by bit, would more often hit upon the truth.

In all antiquity it is hard to pick out a dozen men who set their lives to a certain and constant course, which is the principal goal of wisdom. For, to comprise it all in a word, says an ancient, and to embrace all the rules of our life in one, it is "always to wish and not to wish the same thing." I would not deign, he says, to add "provided the wish is just"; for if it is not just, it is impossible for it always to be whole.

In truth, I once learned that vice is only unruliness and lack of moderation, and consequently it is impossible to attribute consistency to it. It is a maxim of Demosthenes, they say, that the beginning of all virtue is consultation and delib-

eration; and the end and perfection, consistency. If we undertook a definite course through reason, we should take the
fairest one; but no one has thought of that:

> *He spurns the thing he sought and seeks anew*
> *What he just spurned; he seethes, his life's askew.*
>> [Horace]

Our ordinary practice is to follow the inclinations of our
appetite, to the right, to the left, up hill and down, as the
wind of chance carries us. We think of what we want only
at the moment we want it, and we change like that animal
which takes the color of the place you set it on. What we
have just now planned, we presently change, and presently
again we retrace our steps: nothing but oscillation and inconstancy:

> *Like puppets we are moved by outside strings.*
>> [Horace]

We do not go; we are carried away, like floating objects, now
gently, now violently, according as the water is angry or
calm:

> *Do we not see all humans unaware*
> *Of what they want, and always searching everywhere,*
> *And changing place, as if to drop the load they bear?*
>> [Lucretius]

Every day a new fancy, and our humors shift with the shifts
in the weather:

> *Such are the minds of men, as is the fertile light*
> *That Father Jove himself sends down to make earth bright*
>> [Homer]

We float between different minds; we wish nothing freely,

nothing absolutely, nothing constantly. If any man had prescribed and established definite laws and a definite regime in his head, we should see shining throughout his life an evenness of habits, an order and infallible relation between his principles and his practice.

Empedocles noticed this inconsistency in the Agrigentines, that they abandoned themselves to pleasures as if they were to die on the morrow, and built as if they were never to die.

This man [1] would be easy to understand, as is the younger Cato: he who has touched one chord of him has touched all; he is a harmony of perfectly concordant sounds, which cannot conflict. With us, on the contrary, for so many actions, we need so many individual judgments. The surest thing, in my opinion, would be to trace them to the neighboring circumstances, without getting into any further research and without drawing from them any other conclusions.

During the disorders of our poor state, I was told that a girl, living near where I then was, had thrown herself out of a high window to avoid the violence of a knavish soldier quartered in her house; she had not been killed by the fall, and, doubling her efforts, she had tried to cut her throat with a knife, but had been prevented, after wounding herself gravely, however. She herself confessed that the soldier had as yet pressed her only with requests, solicitations, and gifts, but that she had been afraid that he would finally resort to force. And, on top of all that, words, expression, and this blood that testified to her virtue, all in the true manner of

---

[1] The disciplined man two paragraphs back. The paragraph about the Agrigentines, added to Montaigne's original text, breaks the continuity.

another Lucrece. Now, I learned that as a matter of fact, both before and since, she had been a wench not so hard to come to terms with. As the story says: Handsome and gentlemanly as you may be, when you have had no luck, do not promptly infer that your mistress is inviolably chaste; it does not prove that the muleteer won't have his chance.

Antigonus, having taken a liking to one of his soldiers for his virtue and valor, ordered his physicians to treat him for a persistent internal malady that had long tormented him; and perceiving after his cure that he was going to work much more coldly, asked him what had changed him and made him such a coward. "You yourself, Sire," he answered him, "by delivering me from the ills because of which I took no account of my life." A soldier of Lucullus, having been robbed of everything by the enemy, made a bold attack on them for revenge. When he had retrieved his loss, Lucullus, having formed a good opinion of him, urged him to some dangerous exploit with all the fine expostulations he could think of,

With words that might have stirred a coward's heart.
[Horace]

"Urge some poor soldier who has been robbed to do it," he replied;

Though but a rustic lout,
"He'll go where'er you wish who's lost his money," he
called out;

[Horace]

and resolutely refused to go.

When we read that Mohammed having outrageously berated Chasan, leader of his Janissaries, because he saw his troops driven back by the Hungarians and himself behaving like a coward in the fight, Chasan's only reply was to go and hurl himself madly, alone, just as he was, arms in hand, into the first body of enemies that he met, by whom he was promptly swallowed up; this was perhaps not so much self-justification as a change of mood, nor so much his natural prowess as fresh spite.

That man whom you saw so adventurous yesterday, do not think it strange to find him such a coward the day after: either anger, or necessity, or company, or wine, or the sound of a trumpet, had put his heart in his belly. This was not a courage shaped by reason; these circumstances have made it firm; it is no wonder if he has now been made different by other, contrary circumstances.

These supple variations and contradictions that are seen in us have made some imagine that we have two souls, and others, two powers which accompany us and drive us, each one in its own way, one toward good, the other toward evil; for such sudden diversity cannot well be reconciled with one simple subject.

Not only does the wind of accident move me at will, but, besides, I move and disturb myself by the instability of my position; and anyone who observes carefully can hardly find himself twice in the same state. I give my soul now one face, now another, according to the direction in which I turn it. If I speak of myself in different ways, that is because I look at myself in different ways. All contradictions may be found in me by some twist and in some fashion. Bashful, insolent; chaste, lascivious; talkative, taciturn; tough, delicate; clever, stupid; surly, affable; lying, truthful; learned, ignorant; and liberal and miserly and prodigal: all this I see in myself to some extent according to how I turn; and whoever studies himself really attentively finds in himself, yes, even in his judgment, this gyration and discord. I have nothing to say about myself absolutely, simply, and solidly, without confusion and without mixture, or in one word. *Distinguo* is the most universal member of my logic.

Although I am always minded to say good of what is good, and rather to interpret favorably anything that can be so interpreted, still it is true that the strangeness of our nature makes it happen that we are often driven to do good by vice itself—were it not that doing good is judged by intention alone.

Therefore one courageous deed must not be taken to prove a man valiant; a man who was really valiant would be so always and on all occasions. If it were a habit of virtue, and not a sally, it would make a man equally resolute in any accident, the same alone as in company, the same in single combat as in battle; for, whatever they say, there is not one valor for the pavement and another for the camp. As bravely would he bear an illness in his bed as a wound in camp, nor would he fear death more in his home than in an assault. We would not see the same man charging into the breach with brave assurance, and later tormenting himself, like a woman, over the loss of a lawsuit or a son. When, though a coward against infamy, he is brave against poverty; when, though weak against the surgeons' knives, he is steadfast against the enemy's swords, the action is praiseworthy, not the man.

Many Greeks, says Cicero, cannot look at the enemy, and are brave in sickness; the Cimbrians and Celtiberians, just the opposite: *for nothing can be uniform that does not spring from a firm principle.* [Cicero]

There is no more extreme valor of its kind than Alexander's; but it is only of one kind, and not complete and universal enough. Incomparable though it is, it still has its blemishes; which is why we see him worry so frantically when he conceives the slightest suspicion that his men are plotting against his life, and behave in these investigations with such violent and indiscriminate injustice and a fear that upsets his natural judgment. Also superstition, with which he was so badly tainted, bears some stamp of pusillanimity. And the excessiveness of the penance he did for the murder of Clytus is also evidence of the unevenness of his temper.

Our actions are nothing but a patchwork—*they despise pleasure, but are too cowardly in pain; they are indifferent to glory, but infamy breaks their spirit*—and we want to gain honor under false colors. Virtue will not be followed except for her own sake; and if we sometimes borrow her mask for some other purpose, she promptly snatches it from our face. It is a strong and vivid dye, once the soul is steeped in it, and will not go without taking the flesh with it. That is why, to judge a man, we must follow his traces long and carefully. If he does not maintain consistency for her own sake, *whose way of life has been well considered and preconcerted* [Cicero]; if changing circumstances make him change his pace (I should say his path, for his pace may be hastened or slowed), let him go: that man goes before the wind, as the motto of our Talbot says.

It is no wonder, says an ancient,[1] that chance has so much power over us, since we live by chance. A man who has not directed his life as a whole toward a definite goal cannot possibly set his particular actions in order. A man who does not have a picture of the whole in his head cannot possibly arrange the pieces. What good is a provision of colors for a

---

[1] Seneca.

man who does not know what he has to paint? No one makes a definite plan of his life, and we think about it only piece-meal. The archer must first know what he is aiming at, and then set his hand, his bow, his string, his arrow, and his movements for that goal. Our plans go astray because they have no direction and no aim. No wind serves the man who has no port of destination.

I do not agree with the judgment given in favor of Sopho-cles, on the strength of seeing one of his tragedies, that it proved him able to manage his domestic affairs, against the accusation of his son. Nor do I think that the conjecture of the Parians sent to reform the Milesians was sufficient ground for the conclusion they drew. Visiting the island, they no-ticed the best-cultivated lands and the best-run country houses; and having noted down the names of their owners, when they had assembled the citizens in the town, they ap-pointed these owners the new governors and magistrates, judging that they, careful of their private affairs, would be careful of those of the public.

We are all creatures of patches, and so shapeless and strange in composition that each bit at every moment plays its own game. And there is as much difference between us and ourselves as between us and others. *Consider it a great thing to play the part of one single man.* [Seneca] Since am-bition can teach men valor, and temperance, and liberality, and even justice; since greed can implant in the heart of a shop apprentice, brought up in obscurity and idleness, the confidence to cast himself so far from home and hearth, in a frail boat at the mercy of the waves and angry Neptune; since it also teaches discernment and wisdom; and since Venus herself supplies resolution and boldness to boys still subject to discipline and the rod, and arms the tender hearts of virgins who are still in their mothers' laps:

> *Furtively passing sleeping guards, with Love as guide,*
> *Alone by night the girl comes to the young man's side;*
> [Tibullus]

it is not a matter for a calm mind to judge us simply by our outward actions; we must sound the inside and see what springs set us in motion. But since this is a high and hazardous undertaking, I wish fewer people would meddle with it.

Of Presumption[1]

THERE is another kind of vainglory, which is an over-good opinion we form of our own worth. It is an unreasoning affection, by which we cherish ourselves, which pictures us to ourselves as other than we are; as the passion of love lends beauties and graces to the object it embraces, and makes its victims, with muddled and unsettled judgment, think that what they love is other and more perfect than it is.

However, I do not want a man to misjudge himself, for fear of erring in that direction, or to think himself less than he is. Judgment must maintain its rights in all matters; it is right that it should see, in this matter as elsewhere, what truth sets before it. If he is Caesar, let him boldly judge himself the greatest captain in the world.

We are nothing but ceremony; ceremony carries us away, and we leave the substance of things; we hang on to the branches and abandon the trunk and body. We have taught the ladies to blush at the mere mention of what they are not at all afraid to do; we dare not call our members by their right names, and we are not afraid to employ them in every kind of debauchery. Ceremony forbids our expressing in words things that are permissible and natural, and we obey

---

[1] Chapter 17.

it; reason forbids our doing things that are illicit and wicked, and no one obeys it. I find myself here entangled in the laws of ceremony, for she does not allow a man either to speak well of himself, or to speak ill. We shall let her alone for the moment.

Those whom Fortune (whether we should call it good or bad) has caused to spend their lives in some eminent station, can show what they are by their public actions. But those whom she has employed only in a mass, and of whom no one will speak unless they do so themselves, may be excused if they have the temerity to speak of themselves to those who are interested in knowing them, after the example of Lucilius:

> *As unto loyal friends and tried*
> *He to his notebook would confide*
> *His secrets; thither turning still,*
> *Though Fortune brought him good or ill;*
> *Hence all the old man's life is known*
> *As on a votive tablet shown.*

[Horace]

That man committed to his paper his actions and thoughts, and portrayed himself there as he felt he was. *Nor did anyone doubt the honesty or disparage the motives of Rutilius or Scaurus for doing so.* [Tacitus]

So I remember that from my tenderest childhood people noticed in me some indefinable way of carrying my body and certain gestures testifying to some empty and stupid pride. I want to say this about it first, that it is not unbecoming to have characteristics and propensities so much our own and so incorporated into us that we have no way of sensing and recognizing them. And of such natural inclinations

the body is likely to retain a certain bent, without our knowledge or consent. It was a certain affectation harmonious with
his beauty that made Alexander lean his head a little to one
side, and Alcibiades speak softly and with a lisp. Julius Caesar
used to scratch his head with one finger, which is the behavior of a man full of troublesome thoughts; and Cicero, it
seems to me, was in the habit of wrinkling his nose, which is
a sign of a mocking nature. Such gestures can grow on us
unperceived.

There are others that are artificial, of which I do not
speak, like bows and salutations, by which men gain credit,
most often wrongfully, for being very humble and courteous; a man may be humble through vainglory. I am rather
prodigal in taking off my hat, especially in summer, and I
never receive this salute without returning it, from whatever
class of man it may come, unless he is in my pay. I could
wish that certain princes I know would be more sparing and
just in dispensing these salutes; for when they are thus strewn
about indiscriminately, they have no more power; if they
are given without consideration, they are given without
effect.

Among the extraordinary mannerisms, let us not forget
the arrogance of the Emperor Constantius, who in public
always held his head straight, without turning or bending it
this way or that, not even to look at those who saluted him
from the side; keeping his body fixed and motionless, without letting himself move with the swaying of his coach, without daring either to spit, or blow his nose, or wipe his face
in front of the people.

I do not know whether those gestures that people noticed
in me were of the first kind, and whether I really had some
occult propensity to this fault, as may well be; and I cannot

answer for the movements of my body. But as for the movements of my soul, I want to confess here what I think about them.

There are two parts in this vainglory, namely, to esteem ourselves too highly, and not to esteem others highly enough.

As for the first, it seems to me that first of all, these considerations should be taken into account: that I feel myself oppressed by an error of my soul which I dislike, both as unjust and, even more, as troublesome. I try to correct it, but uproot it I cannot. It is that I lower the value of the things I possess, because I possess them, and raise the value of things when they are foreign, absent, and not mine. This humor goes very far. As the prerogative of authority makes husbands regard their own wives, and many fathers their children, with wicked disdain; so it is with me, and between two similar works I should always decide against my own. Not so much that jealousy for my progress and improvement disturbs my judgment and keeps me from being satisfied with myself, as that ownership, of itself, breeds contempt of what we hold and control. Far-off governments, customs, and languages delight me; and I realize that Latin, by its dignity, beguiles me more than it should, as it does children and common people. My neighbor's housekeeping, his house, his horse, if equal in value, seem better than my own, because they are not mine—the more so because I am very ignorant of my affairs. I admire the assurance and optimism each man has about himself, when there is virtually nothing that I know I know, or that I dare give my word that I can do. I do not have my means catalogued and arranged; and I know about them only after doing something: as doubtful of myself as of anything else. Whence it comes about that if I happen to do well in a task, I attribute it more to my luck than to my ability; for I plan them all at random and in fear.

Likewise this is generally true of me, that of all the opinions antiquity has held of man as a whole, the ones I embrace most willingly and adhere to most firmly are those that despise, humiliate, and nullify us most. Philosophy seems to me never to have such an easy game as when she combats our presumption and vanity, when she candidly admits her uncertainty, weakness, and ignorance. It seems to me that the nursing mother of the falsest opinions, public and private, is the over-good opinion man has of himself.

These people who perch astride the epicycle of Mercury, and who see so far into the sky, yank out my teeth. For in the study I am making, the subject of which is man, when I find such an extreme variety of judgments, so deep a labyrinth of difficulties one on top of the other, so much diversity and uncertainty in the very school of wisdom, you may well wonder—since these people have not been able to come to an agreement in the knowledge of themselves and their own state, which is ever present before their eyes, which is in them; since they do not know the motion of what they move themselves, or how to depict and decipher to us the springs that they hold and manage themselves—how I should take their word about the cause of the ebb and flow of the river Nile. Curiosity for the knowledge of things was given to men as a scourge, says the Holy Scripture.

But to come to my own particular case, it would be very difficult, it seems to me, for anyone else to esteem himself less, or indeed for anyone else to esteem me less, than I esteem myself. I consider myself one of the common sort, except in that I consider myself so; guilty of the commoner and humbler faults, but not of faults disavowed or ~~excused~~; and I value myself only for knowing my value.

If there is vainglory in me, it is infused in me superficially by the treachery of my nature, and has no body of its own to appear before my judgment. I am sprinkled with it, but not dyed.

For in truth, as regards any kind of products of the mind, I have never brought forth anything that satisfied me; and the approbation of others does not repay me. My taste is delicate and hard to please, and especially regarding myself; I am incessantly disowning myself; and I feel myself, in every part, wavering and bending with weakness. I have nothing of my own good enough to satisfy my judgment. My sight is clear and controlled enough; but when I put it to work, it grows blurred, as I find most evidently in poetry. I have an infinite love for it; I am a pretty good judge of other men's works; but in truth, I play the child when I try to set my hand to it; I cannot endure myself. A man may play the fool anywhere else, but not in poetry:

> *For Gods and men and booksellers refuse*
> *To countenance a mediocre Muse.*
>
> [Horace]

Would God that maxim were written on the front of all our printers' shops, to deny entrance to so many versifiers:

> *No man has more assurance than a bad poet.*
> [Martial]

Why have we no such nations as these? Dionysius the father esteemed nothing of his own so highly as his poetry. At the time of the Olympic games, with chariots surpassing all others in magnificence, he also sent poets and musicians to present his verses, with royally gilded and tapestried tents and pavilions. When they came to deliver his verses, the grace and excellence of the pronunciation at first drew the attention of the people; but when later they pondered the ineptitude of the work, they first grew scornful, and, becoming more and more bitter in their judgment, they presently flew into a rage, and ran to all his pavilions and knocked them down and tore them to bits in resentment. And when his chariots no longer made any kind of a showing in races, and the ship bringing his men back missed Sicily and was driven and shattered by the tempest against the coast of Tarentum, the people felt certain that it was the wrath of the gods, irritated, like themselves, against this bad poem. And even the sailors who escaped from the shipwreck backed up the opinion of the people.

The oracle that predicted his death also seemed to support this somewhat. It said that Dionysius would be near his end when he had vanquished men better than himself; which he took to mean the Carthaginians, who surpassed him in power. And in fighting them he often side-stepped victory and tempered it so as not to incur the fate predicted. But he misunderstood it; for the god was referring to the time he gained the award at Athens over better tragic poets than he, by favor and injustice, presenting in the competition his play entitled *The Leneians*; after which victory he suddenly died, partly because of the excessive joy that he got from it.

What I find excusable in my own work I find so, not in itself and in reality, but in comparison with other and worse things to which I see people give credit. I am envious of the happiness of those who can rejoice and find gratification in their work, for it is an easy way to give oneself pleasure, since the source of the pleasure is oneself. Especially so if there is a little firmness in their self-conceit. I know a poet to whom the strong and the weak, in the crowd and in the chamber, and heaven and earth, cry out that he does not know his business. For all that, he will not reduce one bit of the measure for which he has cut himself out; he is always beginning again, always getting fresh advice, and always persisting, all the stronger and more set in his opinion because it depends on him alone to maintain it. My works are so far from delighting me that as many times as I sample them again, so many times I am vexed with them:

> *When I re-read I blush, for even I perceive enough*
> *That ought to be erased, though it was I who wrote the*
> *stuff.*

[Ovid]

I have always an idea in my mind, and some blurred picture, which offers me as if in a dream a better form than the one I have framed, but I cannot grasp it and exploit it. And that idea itself is on only a mediocre plane. From that I conclude that the productions of those great rich minds of the past are very far beyond the utmost stretch of my imagination and desire. Their writings not only satisfy me and leave me full, but they astonish me and transfix me with admiration. I judge their beauty; I see it, if not in full, at least enough so that I cannot aspire to it myself.

Whatever I undertake, I owe a sacrifice to the Graces, as Plutarch says of someone, to win their favor:

> *If anything gives pleasure that I write,*
> *If it affects men's senses with delight,*
> *Unto the charming graces it is due.*

[Author unknown]

They abandon me at every turn. Everything I write is crude;

it lacks elegance and beauty. I do not know how to make things appear more precious than they really are; my fashioning is no help to the matter. That is why I need my matter strong, gripping, and shining by its own light. When I take hold of popular and gayer matters, it is so as to go my own way, for I do not love a solemn and gloomy wisdom, as does the world, and to cheer up myself, not my style, which rather takes to grave and austere matters (at least if I should give the name of style to a shapeless and undisciplined way of talking, a popular jargon, and a way of proceeding without definitions, without divisions, without conclusions, and vague, like that of Amafanius and Rabirius).

I do not know how to please, or delight, or tickle: the best story in the world dries up in my hands and becomes dull. I do not know how to talk except in good earnest, and am wholly devoid of that facility, which I see in several of my friends, of entertaining the first comer and holding the attention of a whole group, or tirelessly amusing the ear of a prince with all kinds of small talk, matter never failing them, because of the gift they have of knowing how to use the first subject that comes to mind, and suiting it to the humor and capacity of the people they are dealing with. Princes are not very fond of serious talk, nor I of telling stories. The first and readiest arguments, which are usually the best received, I do not know how to use: a bad popular preacher. On all matters I like to say the deepest things I know. Cicero thinks that in philosophical treatises the hardest part is the exordium. If that is so, I shall stick to the conclusion.

Yet we must tune the string to all sorts of notes; and the sharpest is the one that least often comes into play. There is at least as great perfection in lifting an empty subject to its feet as in holding up a heavy one. Sometimes we must handle things superficially, sometimes go into them deeply. I well know that most people keep on that low plane, since they can grasp things only by that outer bark; but I also know that the greatest masters, both Xenophon and Plato, are often seen relaxing into that humble and popular way of speaking and treating matters, enhancing it with the charm that never fails them.

Furthermore, my language has no ease or polish; it is harsh and disdainful, with a free and unruly disposition. And I like it that way, by inclination if not by judgment. But I am quite conscious that sometimes I let myself go too far, and that in the effort to avoid art and affectation, I fall back into them in another direction:

> *I try to be concise, and grow obscure.*
>
> [Horace]

Plato says that length and brevity are properties which neither decrease nor increase the worth of style.

If I should attempt to follow that other style that is even, smooth, and orderly, I could not attain it. And even though the concision and rhythm of Sallust are more to my humor, yet I consider Caesar both greater and less easy to imitate. And if my inclination leads me more to imitate Seneca's style, I nonetheless admire Plutarch's more. As in action, so in speech I simply follow my natural bent; which is perhaps the reason why I can do better in speech than in writing. Movement and action animate words, notably in men who move briskly, as I do, and become heated. Bearing, countenance, voice, robe, and posture can lend weight to things which in themselves are nothing but babble. Messala complains, in Tacitus, of certain tight garments of his time, and of the form of the benches where the orators had to speak, which weakened their eloquence.

My French is spoiled, both in pronunciation and in other respects, by the barbarism of my home soil; I never saw a man from the South of France whose accent was not clearly marked and offending to pure French ears. Yet this is not because I am very expert in my Périgordian, for I have scarcely more command of it than of German; and that does not worry me much. It is a language like others around me, in one strip of land or another, those of Poitou, Saintonge, Angoumois, Limoges, and Auvergne: soft, drawling, long-winded. To be sure, there is above us, toward the mountains, a Gascon dialect that I consider singularly good, dry, brief, expressive, and indeed a more virile and military language than any that I understand; as sinewy, powerful, and pertinent as French is graceful, delicate, and flowing.

As for Latin, which was given me for my mother tongue, I have lost through lack of practice the ability to use it quickly in speaking; yes, and in writing, in which they used to call me Master John. That is how poor I am in that field.

Beauty is a great recommendation in dealings with men; it is the prime means of conciliation between one another, and there is no man so barbarous and surly as not to be somewhat struck by its charm. The body has a great part in our being, it holds a high rank in it; so its structure and composition are well worth consideration. Those who want to split up our two principal parts and sequester them from each other are wrong. On the contrary, we must couple and join them together again. We must order the soul not to draw aside and entertain itself alone, scorning and abandoning the body (nor can it do so except by some hypocritical monkey trick), but to rally to the body, embrace it, cherish it, assist it, control it, advise it, set it right and bring it back when it goes astray; in short, to marry it and be a husband to it, so that together they may produce results not different and contrary, but harmonious and uniform.

Christians are particularly instructed about this bond; for they know that divine justice embraces this association and union of body and soul, to the point of making the body capable of eternal rewards, and that God watches the whole man in action and wills that he receive, in his entirety, punishment or reward, according to his merits.

The Peripatetic sect, of all sects the most sociable, attributes to wisdom one single care, to provide and procure the common good of these two associated parts. And they show that the other sects, for not having devoted themselves enough to the consideration of this mixture, have taken sides, one for the body, another for the soul, with equal error, and have abandoned their subject, which is man, and their guide, which they generally avow is Nature.

The first distinction that existed between men, and the first consideration that gave some men pre-eminence over others, was probably the advantage of beauty:

> *They portioned out the fields, and gave the most to the elect,*
> *To each according to his beauty, strength, and intellect;*
> *For in those days beauty was prized, and strength enjoyed respect.*

> [Lucretius]

Well, I am a little below medium height. This is not only an ugly defect, but also a disadvantage, especially for men in command or office; for they lack the authority given by a fine presence and bodily majesty. C. Marius was reluctant to accept soldiers under six feet in height. The Courtier[1] is quite right to prefer an average height to any other for the gentleman he is training, and to reject any peculiarity that will make people point him out. But as for choosing to have him shorter rather than taller if he fails to be of this medium height, that would not be my choice for a military man.

Little men, says Aristotle, may well be pretty, but not handsome; and in greatness is a great soul known, as is beauty in a great tall body. The Ethiopians and Indians, he says, in electing their kings and magistrates, considered the beauty and lofty stature of their persons. They were right; for it breeds respect in his followers and terror in the enemy to see marching at the head of a troop a leader of handsome and majestic stature:

> *Turnus himself moves with the foremost, arms in hand,*
> *Splendid in build, a full head taller than his band.*
>
> [Virgil]

Our great, divine, and heavenly King, whose every particular should be carefully, religiously, and reverently noted, did not reject the recommendation of a handsome body: *fairer than the children of men.* [Psalms] And Plato desires beauty, as well as temperance and courage, in the guardians of his Republic.

It is a great annoyance to be addressed in the midst of your servants with the question: "Where is the master?" and to get only the tail end of the salute made to your barber or your secretary. As happened to poor Philopoemen. Being the first of his company to arrive at a house where he was expected, his hostess, who did not know him and saw his

---

[1] *Il Libro del Cortegiano* (1528), by Baldesar Castiglione.

rather unimpressive appearance, set him to work helping her maids draw water and stir up the fire in honor of Philo-poemen. The gentlemen of his suite, having arrived and sur-prised him busy at this fine occupation (for he had not failed to obey the command given him), asked him what he was doing there. "I am paying," he answered them, "the penalty of my ugliness."

The other kinds of beauty are for women; the beauty of stature is the only beauty of men. Where smallness dwells, neither breadth and roundness of forehead, nor clarity and softness of eyes, nor the moderate form of the nose, nor small size of ears and mouth, nor regularity and whiteness of teeth, nor the smooth thickness of a chestnut beard, nor curly hair, nor proper roundness of head, nor freshness of color, nor a pleasant facial expression, nor an odorless body, nor fit proportion of limbs, can make a handsome man.

For the rest, I have a strong, thick-set body, a face not fat, but full, a temperament between the jovial and the melan-choly, moderately sanguine and warm—

My legs are stiff with bristles, my chest with shaggy hair,
[Martial]

—sound and lusty health, rarely troubled by illnesses, until I was well along in years. Such I was, for I am not considering myself at this moment, when I am well on the road to old age, having long since passed forty:

Old age breaks bit by bit their powers and ripened strength,
And melts into complete decrepitude at length.

[Lucretius]

What I shall be from now on will be nothing but half a man,

it will no longer be myself. I escape and steal away from myself every day:

> *The passing years steal from us all things, one by one.*
> [Horace]

I have never had any adroitness or agility; and yet I am the son of a very nimble father whose sprightliness lasted him until his extreme old age. He scarcely ever found a man of his condition who was his equal in any bodily exercise; just as I have scarcely found any who did not surpass me, except in running, in which I was just fair. Of music, either vocal, for which my voice is very poor, or instrumental, they never succeeded in teaching me anything. At dancing, tennis, wrestling, I have never been able to acquire any but very slight and ordinary ability; at swimming, fencing, vaulting, and jumping, none at all. My hands are so clumsy that I cannot even write so I can read it; so that I would rather do over what I have scribbled than give myself the trouble of unscrambling it. And I read hardly any better. I feel that I weigh upon my listeners. Otherwise, a good scholar.[1] I cannot close a letter the right way, nor could I ever cut a pen, nor carve at table worth a rap, nor saddle a horse, nor properly carry a bird and release it, nor talk to dogs, birds, or horses.

My bodily qualities, in short, are very well matched with those of my soul. There is no liveliness; there is only solid and persistent vigor. I stand up well under hard work; but I do so

---

[1] A possible reminiscence of Clément Marot's well-known line, "Au demeurant, ie meilleur fils du monde" ("For the rest, the best son in the world"), which follows an impressive enumeration of the vices of his valet.

only if I go to **it** of my own will, and as much as my desire leads me to it,

> *When gently zest beguiles the rigors of the toil.*
>
> [Horace]

Otherwise, if I am not lured to it by some pleasure, and if I have a different guide than my own sheer free will, I am good for nothing. For I have come to the point where except for health and life, there is nothing for which I am willing to gnaw at my nails and that I am willing to buy at the price of mental torment and constraint:

> *I would not buy at such a fee*
> *All shady Tagus' sands, and all the gold it rolls to sea.*
>
> [Juvenal]

Extremely idle, extremely independent, both by nature and by art. I would as soon lend my blood as my care.

I have a soul that is all its own, accustomed to conducting itself in its own way. Having had neither governor nor master forced on me to this day, I have gone just so far as I pleased, and at my own pace. This has made me soft and useless for serving others, and no good to anyone but myself. And for my own sake there was no need to force that inert, lazy, and do-nothing nature. For having found myself from birth in such a degree of fortune that I had reason to be content with it, and as much sense as I felt I had occasion for, I have sought for nothing, and have acquired nothing either:

> *I am not wafted by fair winds with swelling sails;*
> *Yet neither do I steer my life through adverse gales.*
> *In strength, wit, beauty, virtue, rank, and wealth, I'm cast*
> *The last among the first, the first among the last.*
>
> [Horace]

The only means I have needed is the means of contenting myself, which, however, if you take it rightly, is a well-ordered state of mind, equally difficult in every kind of fortune, and which we see by experience is more readily found in want than in plenty; perhaps because, as is the case with our other passions, hunger for riches is sharpened more by the use of them than by the lack of them, and because the virtue of moderation is rarer than that of patience. And all I needed was to enjoy pleasantly the good things that God in his liberality had placed in my hands. I have never tasted of any sort of tedious work. I have had hardly anything to manage but my own affairs; or, if I have, it has been on condition of managing them at my own times and in my own way, commissioned by people who trusted me and knew me, and did not hustle me. For experts get some service out of even a restive and broken-winded horse.

Even my childhood was guided in a mild, free fashion, exempt from rigorous subjection. All this has built up in me a delicate disposition, unable to endure worry—to such a point that I like to have the losses and disorders that concern me hidden from me; I put under the heading of expenses what my nonchalance costs me for its food and upkeep:

> *Superfluous things, delighting thieves,*
> *But which the master ne'er perceives.*
>
> [Horace]

I like to be ignorant of the count of what I have, so as to feel my loss less exactly. I ask those who live with me, if they lack affection for me and honest dealings, to cheat me and pay me with decent appearances. Not having enough fortitude to endure the annoyance of the adverse accidents to which we are subject, and being unable to keep up the tension of regulating and ordering affairs, I foster as best I can this idea of abandoning myself completely to fortune, expecting the worst in everything, and resolving to bear that worst meekly and patiently. It is for that alone that I labor; that is the goal toward which I direct all my reflections.

In danger, I do not think so much how I shall escape it, as how little it matters that I escape it. Even if I should fall, what would it matter? Not being able to control events, I control myself, and adapt myself to them if they do not adapt themselves to me. I have hardly the skill to dodge Fortune and escape her or force her, and to direct and lead things foresightedly to serve my purpose. I have even less patience to stand the harsh and painful care that is needed for that. And the most painful situation for me is to be in suspense about urgent matters, and tossed between fear and hope. Deliberation, even about the slightest things, annoys me; and I feel my mind harder put to it to endure the various shocks and ups and downs of doubt and deliberation, than to settle down and accept any course whatever, after the die is cast. Few passions have troubled my sleep; but as for deliberations, the slightest one troubles it. Even as in roads I like to avoid the sloping and slippery sides, and cast myself into the beaten part, even the muddiest and boggiest, from which I cannot sink lower, and seek security there; just so I like pure misfortunes, which do not try me and worry me any more, once the uncertainty about mending them is over, and which drive me at a single bound directly into suffering:

> *Uncertain ills torment us most.*
> [Seneca]

When things happen, I bear myself like a man; in conducting them, like a child. The dread of falling gives me a greater fever than the fall. The game is not worth the candle. The miser is worse off for his passion than the poor man, and the jealous man than the cuckold. And often it is not as bad to lose your vineyard as to go to court for it. The lowest step is the firmest. It is the seat of constancy. There you need nothing but yourself. Constancy is founded there and leans only upon itself.

Is there not a certain philosophical air about the case of a gentleman known to many? He married when well along in years, having spent his youth in gay company, a great story-teller, a merry lad. Remembering how the subject of cuck-oldry had given him material for talking and jesting about others, to take cover, he married a woman whom he picked up in the place where each man can find one for his money, and adopted these formulas to be used with her: "Good morning, whore."—"Good morning, cuckold." And there was nothing about which he talked more often and openly to visitors at his home than this arrangement of his; by which he checked the secret gossip of mockers, and blunted the point of their reproach.

As for ambition, which is neighbor to presumption, or rather daughter, it would have been necessary, to advance me, for Fortune to come and take me by the hand. For as for taking pains for the sake of some uncertain hope, and sub-mitting to all the difficulties that attend those who try to push themselves into favor at the beginning of their career, I could never have done it:

I do not purchase hope with ready cash.
[Terence]

I cling to what I see and hold, and do not go far from port:

> *Let one oar row in water, the other on the shore.*
>
> [Propertius]

And then, a man seldom gains these advancements except by first risking what he has. And it is my opinion that if what a man has is enough to maintain the way of life to which he is born and brought up, it is folly to let go of it on the chance of increasing it. The man whom Fortune denies a foothold and the means of arranging a calm and restful life is excusable if he tosses what he has to chance, since in any case necessity sends him questing:

> *In evil we must take a risky path.*
>
> [Seneca]

And I sooner excuse a younger son for casting his portion to the winds than a man who has the honor of his house in his charge, and cannot become needy without being at fault.

I have certainly found the road shorter and easier, with the advice of my good friends of past days, by getting rid of this desire and keeping quiet;

> *Who would enjoy the prize without the dust;*
>
> [Horace]

also judging very sanely that my powers were not capable of great things, and remembering this saying of the late Chancellor Olivier, that the French are like monkeys who climb to the top of a tree, from branch to branch, and never stop moving until they have reached the highest branch, and show their rear ends when they get there.

> *'Tis shameful to take on a load that is too great,*
> *Then leave it when our knees buckle beneath its weight.*
>
> [Propertius]

Even the qualities that were not reproachable in me, I considered useless in this age. My easygoing ways would have been called cowardice and weakness; fidelity and conscience would have been thought scrupulous and squeamish; frankness and independence, troublesome, thoughtless, and rash.

Misfortune has its uses. It is good to be born in a very depraved time; for by comparison with others, you are considered virtuous for a cheap price. Anyone who is only sacrilegious and a parricide in our days is a good and honorable man:

> *If now a friend denies not what was given him in trust,*
> *If he restores an ancient purse with all its coins and rust,*
> *This prodigy of honesty deserves to be enrolled*
> *In Tuscan books, and with a sacrificial lamb extolled.*
> [Juvenal]

And there was never time and place where a surer and greater reward was offered to princes for goodness and justice. I am much mistaken if the first man who thinks to push himself into favor and credit by that path will not outstrip his fellows without much effort. Force and violence can do something, but not always everything.

We see merchants, village justices, and artisans keeping up with the nobility in valor and military knowledge. They do honorably in both private and public combats; they fight, they defend cities in our wars. A prince's eminence is smothered amid this crowd. Let him shine by his humanity, his truthfulness, his loyalty, his moderation, and especially his justice, marks that are rare, unknown, and banished. It is only by the will of the people that he can do his job, and no other qualities can flatter their will as much as those, they being more useful to them than the others. *Nothing is so popular as goodness.* [Cicero]

By such a comparison I would have thought myself great and unusual, just as I think myself dwarfish and ordinary in comparison with certain past ages, in which it was a commonplace, if other stronger qualities were absent, to see a man moderate in his revenge, slow to resent offenses, religious in keeping his word, neither double-dealing nor supple, nor accommodating his faith to the wishes of others or to the occasion. I would rather let affairs break their necks than twist my faith for the sake of them. For as for this new-fangled virtue of hypocrisy and dissimulation, which is so highly honored at present, I mortally hate it; and of all vices, I know none that testifies to so much cowardice and baseness of heart. It is a craven and servile idea to disguise ourselves and hide behind a mask, and not to dare to show ourselves as we are. In that way our men train for perfidy; being accustomed to speak false words, they have no scruples about breaking their word. A noble heart should not belie its thoughts; it wants to reveal itself even to its inmost depths. There everything is good, at least everything is human.

Aristotle considers it the function of magnanimity to hate and love openly, to judge, to speak with complete frankness, and to have no regard for the approbation or reprobation of others at the price of truth. Apollonius said that it was for slaves to lie, and for free men to speak truth.

Truth is the first and fundamental part of virtue. It must be loved for itself. He who tells the truth because he has some external obligation to do so and because it serves him, and who does not fear to tell a lie when it is not important to anybody, is not truthful enough.

My soul by nature shuns lying and hates even to think a

lie. I feel an inward shame and a stinging remorse if one escapes me, as sometimes it does, for occasions surprise me and move me contrary to my premeditation.

We must not always say everything, for that would be folly; but what we say must be what we think; otherwise it is wickedness. I do not know what people expect to gain by incessant feigning and dissimulating, unless it is not to be believed even when they speak truth. That may deceive people once or twice; but to make a profession of covering up, and to boast, as some of our princes have done, that they would throw their shirt in the fire if it were aware of their real intentions (which is a saying of the ancient Metellus of Macedon), and that a man who does not know how to dissemble does not know how to rule—this is warning those who have to deal with them that they speak nothing but deceit and lies. *The more artful and cunning a man is the more he is hated and suspected, when he loses his reputation for honesty.* [Cicero] It would be very naïve for a man to let himself be taken in by either the face or the words of one who takes pride in being always different outside and inside, as Tiberius did; and I do not know what part such people can play in human dealings, since they never offer anything that is accepted as good money. He who is disloyal to truth is also disloyal to falsehood.

Those who, in our time, in establishing the duties of a prince,[1] have considered only his advantage, and have preferred that to care for his fidelity and conscience, would have useful advice for a prince whose affairs Fortune had so arranged that he could establish them once and for all by a single breach and betrayal of his word. But that is not the

---

1 Machiavelli and his disciples.

way it goes. In that sort of bargain you often relapse; you make more than one peace, more than one treaty, in your life. The profit that lures them to the first breach of faith—and nearly always there is profit in it, as in all other wicked deeds; sacrilege, murder, rebellion, treachery, are always undertaken for gain of some sort—this first profit brings after it endless losses, casting this prince out of all dealings and opportunities for negotiation in consequence of this betrayal of trust.

When, during my childhood, Solyman, of the Ottoman race, a race not overly careful about observing promises and pacts, landed his army at Otranto, he learned that Mercurino de' Gratinare and the inhabitants of Castro were held prisoners after having surrendered the place, contrary to the terms of capitulation, and sent word that they should be released; and said that having other great enterprises at hand in that region, such a breach of faith, although it seemed somewhat useful at present, would bring upon him in the future a bad name and a distrust infinitely harmful.

Now for my part I would rather be troublesome and indiscreet than flattering and dissembling. I admit that a touch of pride and stubbornness may enter into keeping me so sincere and open without consideration for others; and it seems to me that I am becoming a little freer, where I ought to be less so, and that I grow heated through opposition to the respect I owe. It may be, too, that I let myself go because of my nature, for lack of the art of tact. When I display to great men the same extreme freedom of tongue and bearing that I exercise in my own house, I feel how much it inclines toward indiscretion and incivility. But besides the fact that I am made that way, I have not a supple enough mind to sidestep a sudden question and escape it by some dodge, or to invent a truth, or a good enough memory to retain it when thus invented, and certainly not enough assurance to maintain it; and I put on a bold face because of weakness. Therefore I give myself up to being candid and always saying what I think, by inclination and by reason, leaving it to Fortune to guide the outcome.

Aristippus said that the chief fruit he had gathered from philosophy was that he spoke freely and openly to everyone.

Memory is a wonderfully useful tool, and without it judgment does its work with difficulty; it is entirely lacking in me. What anyone wants to propound to me must be propounded piecemeal. For it is not in my power to answer a discourse in which there are several different headings. I cannot receive a commission without tablets to note it down. And when I have an important speech to make, if it is of some length, I am reduced to the mean and miserable necessity of learning by heart, word for word, what I have to say; otherwise I would have neither manner nor assurance, being in fear that my memory would play me a bad trick. But this way is no less difficult for me. To learn three lines of poetry I need three hours. And then, in a work of my own, the freedom and authority to change the order and alter a word, ever varying the material, makes it harder to remember.

Now, the more I distrust my memory, the more confused she becomes. She serves me better by chance encounter; I have to solicit her nonchalantly. For if I press her, she is stunned; and once she has begun to totter, the more I probe her, the more she gets mixed up and embarrassed. She serves me at her own time, not at mine.

This thing that I feel in my memory, I feel in several other parts. I shun command, obligation, and constraint. What I do easily and naturally, I cannot do any more if I order myself to do it by strict and express command. Even as regards my body, the parts that have some particular freedom and jurisdiction over themselves sometimes refuse to obey me when I make plans for them and pin them to a certain time and place for compulsory service. These forced and tyrannical advance orders shock them; they curl up from fear or spite and become paralyzed.

Some time ago, being in a place where it is a barbarous discourtesy not to respond to those who invite you to drink, though I was treated with complete freedom, I tried to play the good fellow for the sake of the ladies who were in the party, according to the custom of the country. But what happened was comical; for the threat and anticipation of having to force myself beyond my natural habit stopped up my gullet so that I could not swallow a single drop, and was deprived of drink, even as much as my meal required. I found myself surfeited and my thirst quenched by all the drink that my imagination had anticipated.

This effect is more apparent in those who have a more ardent and powerful imagination; but for all that, it is natural, and there is no one who does not feel it somewhat. An excellent archer, condemned to death, was offered his life if he would show some notable proof of his skill; he refused to try it, fearing that the excessive tension of his will would draw his hand astray, and that instead of saving his life, he would lose the reputation he had acquired for shooting with the bow.

A man whose thoughts are elsewhere will not fail by more than an inch to take always the same number and length of steps in the place where he walks; but if he goes at it attentively, measuring and counting them, he will find that what he did naturally and by chance, he will not do so exactly by design.

My library, which is a handsome one among country libraries, is situated at one corner of my house. If anything enters my fancy that I want to look up or write down there, for fear it may escape me as I merely cross my courtyard, I have to entrust it to someone else. If in speaking I am emboldened to digress however little from my thread, I never fail to lose it; which is the reason why I keep myself constrained, dry, and concise in speaking. I have to call the people who serve me by the name of their job or their province, for it is very hard for me to remember names. To be sure, I will tell you that it has three syllables and a rough sound, that it begins or ends with such and such a letter. And if I were to live a long time, I do not doubt that I would forget my own name, as others have done. Messala Corvinus was two years without any trace of memory, and this is also said of George of Trebizond. And in my own interest I often ruminate about what sort of a life theirs was, and whether without this faculty I shall have enough left to support me with any comfort; and looking at it closely, I fear that this defect, if it is absolute, involves the loss of all the functions of the mind. *It is certain that the memory is the only receptacle, not only of philosophy, but of all that concerns the conduct of life, and of all the arts.* [Cicero]

> *I'm full of cracks, and leak out on all sides.*
> [Terence]

It has happened more than once that I have forgotten the watchword that I had given three hours before, or received from another, and forgotten where I had hidden my purse, in spite of what Cicero says about that. I help myself to lose what I lock up most carefully.

Memory is the receptacle and container of knowledge; mine being so defective, I can hardly complain if I do not know much. I know in general the names of the arts and what they are about, but nothing beyond that. I leaf through books, I do not study them. What I retain of them is something I no longer recognize as anyone else's. It is only the material from which my judgment has gained profit, and the thoughts and ideas with which it has become imbued; the author, the place, the words, and other circumstances, I immediately forget.

And I am so good at forgetting that I forget even my own writings and compositions no less than the rest. People are all the time quoting me to myself without my knowing it. Anyone who would like to know the sources of the verses and examples I have piled up here would put me to great trouble to tell him. And yet I have begged them only at well-known and famous doors, not content with their being rich unless they also came from rich and honorable hands; in them authority and reason concur. It is no great wonder if my book follows the fate of other books, and if my memory lets go of what I write as of what I read, and of what I give as of what I receive.

Besides the defect of my memory I have others which contribute greatly to my ignorance. My mind is slow and dull; the slightest cloud arrests its point, so that, for example, I never offered it any enigma easy enough for it to unravel. There is no subtlety so empty that it will not stump me. Of games in which the mind has a part—chess, cards, draughts, and others—I understand nothing but the barest rudiments.

My apprehension is slow and muddled; but what it once

grasps, it grasps well and embraces most thoroughly, closely, and deeply, for such time as it does grasp it. My sight is long, sound, and perfect, but it is easily tired by work and grows blurred; for that reason I cannot have long sessions with books except by the help of others. The younger Pliny will inform those who have not experienced it how important this delay is to those who devote themselves to this occupation.

There is no mind so puny or brutish as not to reveal some particular faculty shining out; there is none so buried but that some bit of it will burst forth. And how it happens that a mind that is blind and asleep to everything else is lively, clear, and excellent in some particular task, we must inquire of the masters. But the fine minds are the universal minds, open and ready for everything; if not well taught, at least teachable. And I say this to accuse my own; for whether by weakness or nonchalance (and to be nonchalant about what lies at our feet, what we have between our hands, what most concerns our use of life, is something far removed from my principles), there is none as incapable and ignorant as mine of many such ordinary common things of which a man cannot be ignorant without disgrace. I must tell a few examples.

I was born and brought up in the country and in the midst of farming; I have had affairs and management in my hands ever since my predecessors in the possession of the property I enjoy left me their place. Now I cannot reckon, either with counters or with a pen; most of our coins I do not know; nor do I know the difference between one grain and another, either in the ground or in the barn, unless it is too obvious; and I can scarcely distinguish between the cabbages and lettuces in my garden. I do not even understand the names of the chief household implements or the roughest principles of agriculture, which children know. I know still less of the mechanical arts, of trade and merchandise, of the diversity and nature of fruits, wines, and foods; nor how to train a bird or treat a sick horse or dog. And since I must make my shame quite complete, not a month ago I was caught ignorant that leaven was used to make bread, and what was meant by fermenting wine. Once in Athens people conjectured an aptitude for mathematics in a man who was seen cleverly arranging a load of brushwood and making it into faggots. Truly they would draw the very opposite conclusion about me; for if you give me all the equipment of a kitchen, I shall starve.

From these lines of my confession you can imagine others at my expense. But whatever I make myself known to be, provided I make myself known as I am, I am carrying out my plan. And so I do not apologize for daring to put into writing such mean and trivial matters as these. The meanness of my subject forces me to do so. Blame my project if you will, but not my procedure. At all events, I see well enough, without others' telling me, how little all this matters and is worth, and the folly of my plan. It is enough that my judgment is not unshod, of which these are the essays:

> Be nosy as you will, have such a nose
> That Atlas to support it would refuse;
> Latinus' self bewilder with your wit:
> Against my trifles you can say no whit
> More than I've said myself. Why use your teeth
> On teeth? If you'd be full, you must have meat.
> Save up your pains, your sting, for those who so
> Admire themselves; that this is naught, we know.
>
> {Martial}

I am not obliged not to say stupid things, provided I do not fool myself and that I recognize them as such. And to slip up knowingly is so common for me that I scarcely ever slip up in any other way; I never slip up accidentally. It is a small matter to attribute my silly actions to the rashness of my disposition, since I cannot help commonly attributing my vicious actions to it.

One day at Bar-le-Duc I saw King Francis II presented with a portrait that René, King of Sicily, had made of himself, to commend him to his memory. Why is it not permissible in the same way for each man to portray himself with the pen, as he portrayed himself with a pencil?

So I do not want to forget this further scar, very unfit to make public: irresolution, a most harmful failing in negotiating worldly affairs. I do not know which side to take in doubtful enterprises:

> *Nor yes nor no my inmost heart will say.*
> [Petrarch]

I can easily maintain an opinion, but not choose one.

Because in human matters, whatever side we lean to, we find many probabilities to confirm us in it—and the philosopher Chrysippus said that he wanted to learn from Zeno and Cleanthes, his masters, nothing but their tenets, for when it came to proofs and reasons, he would furnish enough by himself—so in whatever direction I turn, I can always provide myself with enough grounds and probabilities to keep me that way. So I keep within me doubt and freedom of choice until the occasion is urgent. And then, to confess the truth, I most often toss a feather to the wind, as they say, and abandon myself to the mercy of fortune. A slight inclination or circumstance carries me away:

> *When the mind doubts, a feather sways it to and fro.*
> [Terence]

The uncertainty of my judgment is so evenly balanced on most occasions that I would willingly submit to the decision of chance and of the dice. And I note, with much reflection on our human weakness, the examples that even sacred history has left us of this custom of entrusting to fortune and chance the determination of choice in doubtful cases: *The lot fell upon Matthias.* [Acts]

Human reason is a two-edged and dangerous sword. And even in the hand of Socrates, its most intimate and familiar friend, see what a many-ended stick it is.

Thus I am fit only to follow, and I let myself be carried away easily by the crowd. I do not trust my own powers enough to undertake to command, to guide; I am very glad to find my steps traced out by others. If I must run the risk of an uncertain choice, I would rather it should be under some man who is more sure of his opinions and wedded to them than I am to mine, whose foundation and grounds I find slippery.

And yet I am not too easy to change, since I perceive a like weakness in the contrary opinions. *The very habit of assenting seems to be dangerous and slippery.* [Cicero] Notably in political matters, there is a fine field open for vacillation and dispute:

> *As when an even scale with equal weights is pressed,*
> *Neither side rises, neither falls; it stays at rest.*
> [Tibullus]

Machiavelli's arguments, for example, were solid enough for the subject, yet it was very easy to combat them; and those who did so left it no less easy to combat theirs. In such an argument there would always be matter for answers, rejoinders, replications, triplications, quadruplications, and that infinite web of disputes that our pettifoggers have spun out as far as they could in favor of lawsuits:

> *We are hard hit, and hit out hard in turn.*
> [Horace]

For the reasons have little other foundation than experience, and the diversity of human events offers us infinite examples in all sorts of forms.

A learned person of our time says that when they say warm in our almanacs, if someone wants to say cold, and wet when they say dry, and always put down the opposite of what they forecast, and if he had to lay a wager on one or the other coming true, he would not care which side he took; except in cases that admit of no uncertainty, such as promising extreme heat at Christmas and the rigors of winter on Midsummer's Day. I have the same opinion about these political arguments: whatever part they give you to play, you have as good a chance as your opponent, provided you do not go against principles that are too plain and obvious. And yet, to my mind, in public affairs there is no course so bad, provided it is old and firmly established, that it is not better than change and commotion. Our morals are extremely corrupt, and incline with remarkable sharpness toward the worse; of our laws and customs, many are barbarous and monstrous; however, because of the difficulty of improving our condition and the danger of everything crumbling into bits, if I could put a spoke in our wheel and stop it at this point, I would do so with all my heart:

Never such shameful, foul examples do we find,
But that still worse, untold, remain behind.

[Juvenal]

The worst thing I find in our state is instability, and the fact that our laws cannot, any more than our clothes, take any enduring form. It is very easy to accuse a government of imperfection, for all mortal things are full of it. It is very easy to engender in a people contempt for their ancient observances; never did a man undertake that without succeeding. But as for establishing a better state in place of the one they have ruined, many of those who had attempted it achieved nothing for their pains.

I give my prudence small share in my conduct; I readily let myself be led by the general way of the world. Happy the people who do what they are commanded better than those who command, without worrying about the reasons, who let themselves roll relaxedly as the heavens roll. Obedience is not pure or tranquil in a man who reasons and argues.

All in all, to return to myself, the only thing that makes me think something of myself is the thing in which no man ever thought himself deficient: my recommendation is vulgar, common, and popular, for who ever thought he lacked sense? That would be a proposition implying its own contradiction. It is a disease that is never where it is perceived; it is indeed tenacious and strong, but it is pierced and dispersed by the first glance from the patient's eye, like a dense fog by a glance from the sun. Self-accusation would be self-excuse in that matter, and self-condemnation would be self-absolution. There never was a street porter or a silly woman who did not think they had enough sense to take care of themselves. We readily acknowledge in others an advantage in courage, in bodily strength, in experience, in alertness, in beauty; but an advantage in judgment we yield to no one. And the arguments that come from simple natural reasoning in others, we think we would have found if we had merely glanced in that direction. Knowledge, style, and such qualities that we see in the works of others, are easily perceived if they surpass our own; but as regards the simple products of the understanding, each man thinks he had it in him to hit upon the very same things, and does not easily perceive their weight and difficulty, unless—and hardly even then—they are at a great distance and beyond comparison. So this is a kind of exercise for which I must hope for very little commendation and praise, and a kind of composition offering little renown.

And then, for whom do you write? The learned men to whom it falls to pass judgment on books know no other value than that of learning, and admit no other procedure for our minds than that of erudition and art. If you have mistaken one of the Scipios for the other, what is there left for you to say that can be worth while? Anyone who does not know Aristotle, according to them, by the same token does not know himself. And common, ordinary minds do not see the grace and the weight of a lofty and subtle speech. Now, these two types fill the world. The third class into whose hands you come, that of minds regulated and strong in themselves, is so rare that for this very reason it has neither name nor rank among us; it is time half wasted to aspire and strive to please this group.

It is commonly said that the fairest division of her favors Nature has given us is that of sense; for there is no one who is not content with the share of it that she has allotted him. Is that not reasonable? If anyone saw beyond, he would see beyond his sight.

I think my opinions are good and sound; but who does not think as much of his? One of the best proofs I have of mine is the little esteem I have for myself; for if these opinions had not been very firm, they would easily have let themselves be fooled by the singular affection I have for myself, being one who concentrates nearly all of it upon himself and does not squander much of it on others. All the affection that others distribute to an infinite multitude of friends and acquaintances, to their glory, to their greatness, I devote entirely to the repose of my mind and to myself. What escapes in other directions is not strictly by command of my reason:

> *Trained to live healthily and for myself.*
> [Lucretius]

Now these opinions of mine are, I find, infinitely bold and constant in condemning my inadequacy. In truth, this too is a subject on which I exercise my judgment as much as on any other. The world always looks straight ahead; as for me, I turn my gaze inwards, I fix it there and keep it busy. Everyone looks in front of him; as for me, I look inside of me; I have no dealing but with myself; I continually observe myself, I take stock of myself, I taste myself. Others always go elsewhere, if they stop to think about it; they always go forward;

> *No man tries to descend into himself;*
> [Persius]

as for me, I roll about in myself.

This capacity for sifting truth, however much or little of it I may have, and this free will not to enslave my belief easily, I owe principally to myself. For the firmest and most general ideas I have are those which, in a manner of speaking, were born with me. They are natural and wholly mine. I produced them crude and simple, boldly and strongly, but a little vaguely and imperfectly. Since then I have established and fortified them by the authority of others and the sound arguments of the ancients, with whom I found my judgment in agreement. These men have given me a firmer grip on my ideas and a fuller enjoyment and possession of them.

The recommendation everyone seeks for liveliness and promptness of wit, I aspire to for orderliness; what they seek for a brilliant and signal deed, or for some particular ability, I aspire to for order, consistency, and tranquillity of opinions and conduct. *Certainly, if anything is becoming, it is uniformity in our whole lives and in our individual actions; which you cannot maintain if, imitating the nature of others, you eliminate your own.* [Cicero]

Here then you see to what extent I feel guilty of what I said was the first part of the vice of presumption. As for the second, which consists in not esteeming others highly enough, I do not know if I can disclaim this as well; for cost what it may, I am determined to tell the facts about it.

Whether it may be that the continual association I have with ancient views, and the idea I have formed of those rich souls of the past, give me a distaste for others and for myself; or whether we are indeed living in a time which produces only very mediocre things; at any rate, I know of nothing worthy of great admiration. Also, I know scarcely any men intimately enough to be able to judge them; and those I come in contact with most commonly through my situation are for the most part men who have little care for the culture of the soul, and to whom one can suggest no other blessing than honor, and no other perfection than valor.

What beauty I see in others I praise and esteem very gladly. Indeed, I often go farther than what I really think of it, and allow myself to lie to that extent. For I am incapable of inventing anything false. I am glad to testify for my friends to the praiseworthy qualities I find in them; and of one foot of value I am likely to make a foot and a half. But as for lending them qualities they do not have, I cannot, nor can I defend them openly for the imperfections they have.

Even to my enemies I frankly render the testimony of honor that is due. My feelings change; my judgment, no. And I do not confuse my criticism with other circumstances that do not enter into it; and I am so jealous of the liberty of my judgment that I can hardly give it up for any passion whatsoever. I do myself more harm by lying than I do to the person I lie about. This laudable and generous custom is observed of the Persian nation, that they speak of their mortal enemies, and wage war to the death against them, honorably and fairly, so far as their valor deserves it.

I know enough men who have various fine qualities, one wit, another courage, another skill, another conscience, another style, one one science, another another. But as for an all-round great man having all these fine parts together, or one part in such excellent degree as to cause astonishment or comparison with the men of the past whom we honor, I have not had the good fortune to find any. And the greatest man I have known in person, I mean for natural qualities of the soul, and the best endowed, was Etienne de la Boétie. He was truly a full soul, handsome from every point of view; a soul of the old stamp, who would have achieved great results if fortune had willed it, for he had added much to this rich nature by learning and study.

But I do not know how it happens—and yet beyond doubt it does happen—that there is as much vanity and weakness of understanding in those who profess to have the greatest capacity, and who meddle with literary occupations and tasks that depend on books, as in any other sort of men; whether because people demand and expect more of them, and cannot excuse ordinary faults in them, or because the thought that they are learned makes them bolder to show off and reveal too much of themselves, whereby they come to grief and give themselves away. Just as an artisan shows his stupidity much better on some rich material he has in his hands, if he arranges and mixes it foolishly and contrary to the rules of his craft, than on some wretched stuff, and as people are more offended at defects in a statue of gold than in one that is of plaster; so do these men when they display things that in themselves, and in their place, would be good; for they use them without discretion, doing honor to their memory at the expense of their intelligence: they do honor to Cicero, Galen, Ulpian, and Saint Jerome, and themselves they make ridiculous.

I gladly return to the subject of the absurdity of our education: its goal has been to make us not good or wise, but learned; it has attained this goal. It has not taught us to follow and embrace virtue and wisdom, but has impressed on us their derivation and etymology. We can give the declension of virtue, if we cannot love it; if we do not know what wisdom is by practice and experience, we know it by jargon and by rote. With our neighbors, we are not content to know their family, their kindred, and their connections; we want to have them as friends and form some association and understanding with them. Education has taught us the definitions, divisions, and partitions of virtue, like the surnames and branches of a genealogy, without any further concern to form between us and virtue any familiar relationship and intimate friendship. It has chosen for our instruction not the books that have the soundest and truest opinions, but those that speak the best Greek and Latin; and amid its beautiful words, it has poured into our minds the most inane ideas of antiquity.

A good education changes your judgment and conduct, as happened to Polemo, that dissipated young Greek, who, having gone by chance to a lesson by Xenocrates, did not notice merely the eloquence and mastery of the teacher, or bring back to his house merely the knowledge of some fine matter, but reaped a more perceptible and solid fruit, which was a sudden change and amendment of his former life. Who has ever experienced such a result from our education?

> *Will you behave like Polemo,*
> *When he reformed, one bygone day? Will you forego*
> *The badges of disease—wraps, anklets, pads,—as he*
> *Tore from his drunken neck, they say, the wreath of glee,*
> *When the undinnered sage addressed him chidingly.*
>
> [Horace]

The least contemptible class of people seems to me to be those who, through their simplicity, occupy the lowest rank; and they seem to show greater regularity in their relations. The morals and the talk of peasants I find usually more obedient to the commands of true philosophy than are those of our philosophers. *The common people are wiser, because they are as wise as they need be.* [Lactantius]

The most notable men I have judged by outward appearances—for to judge them in my own way, I would need a light closer to them—were, in point of war and military ability, the Duke of Guise, who died at Orleans, and the late Marshal Strozzi. As for able men of uncommon virtue, Olivier and L'Hôpital, Chancellors of France. It seems to me that poetry too has flourished in our century. We have a wealth of good craftsmen in that trade: Daurat, Beza, L'Hôpital, Montdoré, Turnebus. As for those writing in French, I think they have raised its poetry to the highest point it will ever reach; and in the respects in which Ronsard and Du Bellay excel, I do not consider them far removed from the perfection of the ancients. Adrianus Turnebus knew more, and knew better what he knew, than any man that lived in his time or for many years before.

The lives of the Duke of Alva, who died recently, and of our Constable de Montmorency, were noble lives with many unusual similarities in fortune. But the glory and beauty of the latter's death, suddenly and in extreme old age, before the eyes of Paris and his king and in their service against his nearest kin, commanding an army victorious through his leadership, deserves, I think, to be placed among the notable events of my time. As also the constant goodness, the gentle conduct, and the conscientious affability of Monsieur de la Noue, amid the injustice of armed factions—true school of treachery, inhumanity, and brigandage—in which this great and very experienced warrior was brought up.

I have taken pleasure in making public in several places the hopes I have for Marie de Gournay le Jars, my covenant daughter, whom I love indeed more than a daughter of my own, and cherish in my solitary retreat as one of the best parts of my own self. She is the only person I still think about in the world. If youthful promise means anything, her soul will some day be capable of the finest things, among others of perfection in that most sacred friendship which, so we read, her sex has not yet been able to attain. The sincerity and soundness of her morals are already sufficient, her affection for me more than superabundant, and in short, such that it leaves nothing to be desired, unless that her apprehension about my end, in view of my fifty-five years when I met her, would not torment her so cruelly. The judgment she made of the first Essays, she a woman, and in this age, and so young, and alone in her district, and the remarkable eagerness with which she loved me and wanted my friendship for a long time, simply through the esteem she formed for me before she had seen me, is a phenomenon very worthy of consideration.[1]

The other virtues are given little or no value nowadays; but valor has become common through our civil wars, and in this respect there are among us souls firm to the point of perfection, and in great numbers, so that selection is impossible.

This is all the extraordinary and uncommon greatness that I have known up to this moment.

---

[1] This paragraph, which does not appear in the "Bordeaux copy" of the *Essays,* is of doubtful authenticity.

Of Giving the Lie [1]

Yes, but someone will tell me that this plan of using oneself as a subject to write about would be excusable in rare and famous men whose reputation had aroused some desire to know them. That is certain; I admit it; and I know full well that an artisan will hardly raise his eyes from his work to see a man of the common sort, while to see a great and conspicuous personage arrive in a city, men leave workshops and stores empty. It ill befits anyone to make himself known save him who has qualities to be imitated, and whose life and opinions may serve as a model. Caesar and Xenophon had something to found and establish their narrative upon, as on a just and solid base: the greatness of their deeds. Desirable therefore would be the journals of Alexander the Great, and the commentaries that Augustus, Cato, Sulla, Brutus, and others left about their deeds. People love and study the figures of such men, even in bronze and stone.

This remonstrance is perfectly sound, but it concerns me only very slightly:

I never recite except to friends, and only on request,
Nor to all men, nor everywhere. But many will not rest,
And keep reciting in the Forum, or the baths infest.
                                    [Horace]

---

[1] Chapter 18.

I am not building here a statue to erect at the town crossroads, or in a church or a public square:

> *I do not aim to swell my page full-blown*
> *With windy trifles. . . .*
> > *We two talk alone.*
> > > [Persius]

This is for a nook in a library, and to amuse a neighbor, a relative, a friend, who may take pleasure in associating and conversing with me again in this form. Others have taken courage to speak of themselves because they found the subject worthy and rich; I, on the contrary, because I have found mine so barren and so meager that no suspicion of ostentation can fall upon my plan.

I willingly judge the actions of others; I give little chance to judge mine because of their nullity. I do not find so much good in myself that I cannot tell it without blushing.

What a satisfaction it would be to me to hear someone tell me, in this way, of the habits, the face, the expression, the favorite remarks, and the fortunes of my ancestors! How attentive I would be! Truly it would spring from a bad nature to be scornful of even the portraits of our friends and forbears, the form of their clothes and their armor. I keep their handwriting, their seal, the breviary and a peculiar sword that they used, and I have not banished from my study some long canes that my father usually carried in his hand. *A father's coat and his ring are the more dear to his children the more they loved him.* [St. Augustine]

However, if my descendants have other tastes, I shall have ample means for revenge: for they could not possibly have less concern about me than I shall have about them by that time.

All the contact I have with the public in this book, is that I borrow their tools of publication, as being swifter and easier. In exchange, perhaps I shall keep some pat of butter from melting in the market place.

> *Lest tunny-fish and olives lack a robe.*
> [Martial]

> *To mackerel I'll often give a shirt.*
> [Catullus]

And if no one reads me, have I wasted my time, entertaining myself for so many idle hours with such useful and agreeable thoughts? In modeling this figure upon myself, I have had to fashion and arrange myself so often to bring myself out, that the model has to some extent grown firm and taken shape of itself. Painting myself for others, I have painted my inward self with colors clearer than my original ones. I have no more made my book than my book has made me—a book consubstantial with its author, concerned with my own self, an integral part of my life; not concerned with some third-hand, extraneous purpose, like all other books. Have I wasted my time by taking stock of myself so continually, so carefully? For those who go over themselves only in their minds and occasionally in words do not penetrate to essentials in their examination as does a man who makes that his study, his work, and his trade, who binds himself to keep an enduring account, as faithfully as he can, as well as he can.

Indeed, the most delightful pleasures are digested inwardly, avoid leaving any traces, and avoid the sight not only of the public but of any other person.

How many times this task has diverted me from annoying cogitations! And all frivolous ones should be counted as annoying. Nature has made us a present of a broad capacity for entertaining ourselves apart, and often invites us to do so, to teach us that we owe ourselves in part to society, but in the best part to ourselves. In order to train my fancy even to dream with some plan and purpose, and in order to keep it from losing its way and straying with the wind, there is nothing like embodying and registering all the little thoughts that come to it. I listen to my reveries because I have to record them. How many times, irritated by some action that civility and reason kept me from reproving openly, have I disgorged it here, not without ideas of instructing the public! And besides, these poetic lashes—

> *One in the eye, one on the snout,*
> *One on the back of the apish lout!*
>
> > [Marot]

—make an even deeper impression on paper than on living flesh. What if I lend a slightly more attentive ear to books, since I have been lying in wait to pilfer something from them to adorn or support my own?

I have not studied one bit to make a book; but I have studied a bit because I had made it, if it is studying a bit to skim over or squeeze, by his head or his feet, now one author, now another; not at all to form my opinions, but certainly to assist, second, and serve those which I formed long ago.

But whom shall we believe when he talks about himself, in so corrupt an age, seeing that there are few or none whom we can believe when they speak of others, with less incentive for lying? The first stage in the corruption of morals is the banishment of truth; for, as Pindar said, truthfulness is the beginning of a great virtue, and is the first item that Plato demands of the governor of his Republic. Our truth of today is not what is, but what others can be convinced of; just as we call "money" not only that which is legal, but also any counterfeit that will pass. Our nation has long been reproached for this vice; for Salvianus of Massilia, who lived in the time of the Emperor Valentinian, says that to the French lying and perjury is not a vice but a manner of speaking. If a man wanted to go this testimony one better, he could say that to them it is now a virtue. Men form and train themselves for it as for an honourable practice; for dissimulation is among the most notable qualities of this century.

Thus I have often pondered what could be the source of that custom, which we observe so religiously, of feeling more bitterly offended when taxed with this vice, which is so common among us, than with any other; and that it should be the worst insult that can be given us in words, to accuse us of lying. My findings on the matter are that it is natural to defend ourselves most for the defects with which we are most tainted. It seems that in resenting the accusation and growing excited about it, we unburden ourselves to some extent of the fault; if we have it in fact, at least we condemn it in appearance.

Would it not also be that this reproach seems to involve cowardice and lack of courage? Is there any more obvious cowardice that to deny what we have said? Worse yet, to deny what we know?

Lying is an ugly vice, which an ancient depicts in most shameful colors when he says that it equals giving evidence of contempt for God, and at the same time of fear of men. It is not possible to represent more vividly the horror, the vileness, and the unhealthiness of it. For what can you imagine uglier than being a coward toward men and brave toward God? Since mutual understanding is brought about solely by way of words, he who breaks his word betrays human society. It is the only instrument by means of which our wills and thoughts communicate, it is the interpreter of our soul. If it fails us, we have no more hold on each other, no more knowledge of each other. If it deceives us, it breaks up all our intercourse and dissolves all the bonds of our government.

Certain nations of the new Indies (there is no use mentioning their names, which are no more; for the desolation of their conquest—a monstrous and unheard-of case—has extended even to the entire abolition of the names and ancient knowledge of the places) offered to their gods human blood, but drawn only from their tongue and ears, in expiation of the sin of falsehood, heard as well as uttered.

That worthy fellow from Greece used to say that children play with knucklebones, men with words.

As for the varied etiquette of giving the lie, and our laws of honor in that matter, and the changes they have undergone, I shall put off till another time telling what I know about that, and shall meanwhile learn, if I can, at what time the custom began of weighing and measuring words so exactly, and attaching our honor to them. For it is easy to see that it did not exist in olden times among the Romans and the Greeks. And it has often seemed to me novel and strange to see them giving each other the lie and insulting each other, without fighting a duel over it. The laws of their duty took some other path than ours. Caesar is called now a robber, now a drunkard, to his face. We see how free are the invectives they use against each other, I mean the greatest war lords of both nations, where words are avenged merely by words, and do not lead to other consequences.

BOOK III

Of Repentance[1]

OTHERS form man; I describe him, and portray a particular one, very ill-formed, whom I should really make very different from what he is if I had to fashion him over again. But now it is done.

Now the lines of my painting do not err, though they change and vary. The world is but a perennial seesaw. All things in it are in constant motion: the earth, the rocks of the Caucasus, the pyramids of Egypt, both with the common motion and with their own. Stability itself is nothing but a more languid motion.

I cannot keep my subject still. It goes along befuddled and staggering, with a natural drunkenness. I take it in this condition, just as it is at the moment I give my attention to it. I do not portray being: I portray passing; not the passing from one age to another, or, as the people say, from seven years to seven years, but from day to day, from minute to minute. My history needs to be adapted to the moment. I may presently change, not only by fortune, but also by intention. This is a record of various changeable occurrences, and of irresolute and, when it so befalls, contradictory ideas: whether I am different myself, or whether I take hold of my

---

[1] Chapter 2.

subjects in different circumstances and aspects. So, all in all, I do indeed contradict myself now and then; but truth, as Demades said, I never contradict. If my mind could gain a firm footing, I would not make essays, I would make decisions; but it is always in apprenticeship and on trial.

I set forth a humble and inglorious life; that does not matter. You can tie up all moral philosophy with a common and private life just as well as with a life of richer stuff: each man bears the entire form of human nature.

Authors communicate with the people by some special extrinsic mark; I am the first to do so by my entire being, as Michel de Montaigne, not as a grammarian or a poet or a jurist. If the world complains that I speak too much of myself, I complain that it does not even think of itself.

But is it reasonable that I, so fond of privacy in actual life, should aspire to publicity in the knowledge of me? Is it reasonable too that I should set forth to the world, where fashioning and art have so much credit and authority, some crude and simple products of nature, and of a very feeble nature at that? Is it not making a wall without stone, or something like that, to construct books without knowledge and without art? Musical fancies are guided by art, mine by chance.

At least I have one thing according to the rules; that no man ever treated a subject he knew and understood better than I do the subject I have undertaken; and that in this I am the most learned man alive. Secondly, that no man ever penetrated more deeply into his material, nor plucked its limbs and consequences cleaner, nor reached more accurately and fully the goal he had set for his work. To accomplish it, I need only bring to it fidelity; and that is in it, as sincere and pure as can be found. I speak the truth, not my fill of it, but as much as I dare speak it; and I dare to do so a little more as I grow old, for it seems that custom allows old age more freedom to prate and more indiscretion in talking about one-self. It cannot happen here as I see it happening often, that the craftsman and his work contradict each other: "Has a man whose conversation is so seemly written such a stupid book?" or "Have such learned writings come from a man whose conversation is so feeble?"

If a man is commonplace in conversation and rare in writing, that means that his capacity is in the place from which he borrows it, and not in himself. A learned man is not learned in all matters; but the capable man is capable in all matters, even in ignorance.

In this case we go hand in hand and at the same pace, my book and I. In other cases one may commend or blame the work apart from the workman; not so here; he who touches the one, touches the other. He who judges it without knowing it will injure himself more than me; he who has known it will completely satisfy me. Happy beyond my deserts if I have just this share of public approval, that I make intelligent people feel that I was capable of profiting by knowledge, if I had had any, and that I deserved better assistance from my memory.

Let me here excuse what I often say, that I rarely repent, and that my conscience is content with itself—not as the conscience of an angel or a horse, but as the conscience of a man; always adding this refrain, not perfunctorily but in sincere and complete submission: that I speak as an ignorant inquirer, leaving the decision purely and simply to the common and authorized beliefs. I do not teach, I tell.

There is no vice truly a vice which is not offensive, and which a sound judgment does not condemn; for its ugliness and painfulness is so apparent that perhaps the people are right who say it is chiefly produced by stupidity and ignorance. So hard it is to imagine anyone knowing it without hating it.

Wickedness sucks up the greater part of its own venom, and poisons itself with it. Vice leaves repentance in the soul, like an ulcer in the flesh, which is always scratching itself and drawing blood. For reason effaces other griefs and sorrows; but it engenders that of repentance, which is all the more grievous because it springs from within, as the cold and heat of fevers is sharper than that which comes from outside. I consider as vices (but each one according to its measure) not only those which reason and nature condemn, but also those that man's opinion has created, even false and erroneous opinion, if it is authorized by laws and custom.

There is likewise no good deed that does not rejoice a well-born nature. Indeed there is a sort of gratification in doing good which makes us rejoice in ourselves, and a generous pride that accompanies a good conscience. A boldly vicious soul may perhaps arm itself with security, but with this complacency and satisfaction it cannot provide itself. It is no slight pleasure to feel oneself preserved from the contagion of so corrupt an age, and to say to oneself: "If anyone should see right into my soul, still he would not find me guilty either of anyone's affliction or ruin, or of vengeance or envy, or of public offense against the laws, or of innovation and disturbance, or of failing in my word; and in spite of what the license of the times allows and teaches each man, still I have not thrust out my hand either to the property or into the purse of any Frenchman, and have lived only on my own, both in war and in peace; nor have I used any man's work without paying his wages." These testimonies of conscience give us pleasure; and this natural rejoicing is a great boon to us, and the only payment that never fails us.

To found the reward for virtuous actions on the approval of others is to choose too uncertain and shaky a foundation. Especially in an age as corrupt and ignorant as this, the good opinion of the people is a dishonor. Whom can you trust to see what is praiseworthy? God keep me from being a worthy man according to the descriptions I see people every day giving of themselves in their own honor. *What had been vices now are moral acts.* [Seneca]

Certain of my friends have sometimes undertaken to call me on the carpet and lecture me unreservedly, either of their own accord or at my invitation, as a service which, to a well-formed soul, surpasses all the services of friendship, not only in usefulness, but also in pleasantness. I have always welcomed it with the wide open arms of courtesy and gratitude. But to speak of it now in all sincerity, I have often found in their blame or praise such false measure that it would hardly have been a sin for me to sin rather than to do good in their fashion.

Those of us especially who live a private life that is on display only to ourselves must have a pattern established within us by which to test our actions, and, according to this pattern, now pat ourselves on the back, now punish ourselves. I have my own laws and court to judge me, and I go to them more than anywhere else. To be sure, I restrain my actions according to others, but I extend them only according to myself. There is no one but yourself who knows whether you are cowardly and cruel, or loyal and devout. Others do not see you, they guess at you by uncertain conjectures; they see not so much your nature as your art. Therefore do not cling to their judgment; cling to your own. *You must use your own judgment. . . . With regard to virtues and vices, your own conscience has great weight: take that away, and everything falls.* [Cicero]

But the saying that repentance follows close upon sin does not seem to consider the sin that is in robes of state, that dwells in us as in its own home. We can disown and retract the vices that take us by surprise, and toward which we are swept by passion; but those which by long habit are rooted and anchored in a strong and vigorous will cannot be denied. Repentance is nothing but a disavowal of our will and an opposition to our fancies, which leads us about in all directions. It makes this man disown his past virtue and his continence:

Why had I not in youth the mind I have today?
Or why, with old desires, have red cheeks flown away?
[Horace]

It is a rare life that remains well-ordered even in private. Any man can play his part in the side show and represent a worthy man on the boards; but to be disciplined within, in his own bosom, where all is permissible, where all is concealed—that's the point. The next step to that is to be so in our own house, in our ordinary actions, for which we need render account to no one, where nothing is studied or artificial. And therefore Bias, depicting an excellent state of family life, says it is one *in which the master is the same within, by his own volition, as he is outside for fear of the law and of what people will say.* And it was a worthy remark of Julius Drusus to the workmen who offered, for three thousand crowns, to arrange his house so that his neighbors would no longer be able to look into it as they could before.

I will give six thousand, he said; *make it so that everyone can see in from all sides.* The practice of Agesilaus is noted with honor, of taking lodging in the churches when traveling, so that the people and the gods themselves might see into his private actions. Men have seemed miraculous to the world, in whom their wives and valets have never seen anything even worth noticing. Few men have been admired by their own households.

No man has been a prophet, not merely in his own house, but in his own country, says the experience of history. Likewise in things of no importance. And in this humble example you may see an image of greater ones. In my region of Gascony they think it a joke to see me in print. The farther from my lair the knowledge of me spreads, the more I am valued. I buy printers in Guienne, elsewhere they buy me. On this phenomenon those people base their hopes who hide themselves while alive and present, to gain favor when dead and gone. I would rather have less of it. And I cast myself on the world only for the share of favor I get now. When I leave it, I shall hold it quits.

The people escort this man back to his door, with awe, from a public function. He drops his part with his gown; the higher he had hoisted himself, the lower he falls back; inside, in his home, everything is wretched and in confusion. Even if there was order there, it takes a keen and select judgment to perceive it in these humble private actions. Besides, order is a dull and somber virtue. To win through a breach, to conduct an embassy, to govern a people, these are dazzling actions. To scold, to laugh, to sell, to pay, to love, to hate, and to deal pleasantly and justly with our household and ourselves, not to let ourselves go, not to be false to ourselves, that is a rarer matter, more difficult and less noticeable.

Therefore retired lives, whatever people may say, accomplish duties as harsh and strenuous as other lives, or more so. And private persons, says Aristotle, render higher and more difficult service to virtue than those who are in authority. We prepare ourselves for eminent occasions more for glory than for conscience. The shortest way to attain glory would be to do for conscience what we do for glory. And Alexander's virtue seems to me to represent much less vigor in his theater than does that of Socrates in his humble and obscure activity. I can easily imagine Socrates in Alexander's place; Alexander in that of Socrates, I cannot. If you ask the former what he knows how to do, he will answer: "Subdue the world"; if you ask the latter, he will say: "Lead the life of man in conformity with its natural condition"; a knowledge much more general, more difficult, and more legitimate.

The value of the soul consists not in flying high, but in an orderly pace. Its greatness is exercised not in greatness, but in mediocrity. As those who judge and touch us inwardly make little fuss over the brilliance of our public acts, and see that these are only thin streams and jets of water spurting from a bottom otherwise muddy and thick; so likewise those who judge us by this brave outward appearance draw similar conclusions about our inner constitution, and cannot associate common faculties, just like their own, with these other faculties that astonish them and are so far beyond their scope. So we give demons wild shapes. And who does not give Tamerlane raised eyebrows, open nostrils, a dreadful face, and immense size, like the size of the imaginary picture of him we have formed from the renown of his name? If I had been able to see Erasmus in other days, it would have been hard for me not to take for adages and maxims everything he said to his valet and his hostess. We imagine much more appropriately an artisan on the toilet seat or on his wife than a great president, venerable by his demeanor and his ability. It seems to us that they do not stoop from their lofty thrones even to live.

As vicious souls are often incited to do good by some extraneous impulse, so are virtuous souls to do evil. Thus we must judge them by their settled state, when they are at home, if ever they are; or at least when they are closest to repose and their natural position.

Natural inclinations gain assistance and strength from education; but they are scarcely to be changed and overcome. A thousand natures, in my time, have escaped toward virtue or toward vice through the lines of a contrary training:

> *As when wild beasts grow tame, shut in a cage,*
> *Forget the woods, and lose their look of rage,*
> *And learn to suffer man; but if they taste*
> *Hot blood, their rage and fury is replaced,*
> *Their reminiscent jaws distend, they burn,*
> *And for their trembling keeper's blood they yearn.*
>
> [Lucan]

We do not root out these original qualities, we cover them up, we conceal them. Latin is like a native tongue to me; I understand it better than French; but for forty years I have not used it at all for speaking or writing. Yet under the stress of sudden and extreme emotions into which I have fallen two or three times in my life—one of them when I saw my father, in perfect health, fall back into my arms in a faint—I have always poured out my first words from the depths of my entrails in Latin; Nature surging forth and expressing herself by force, in the face of long habit. And this experience is told of many others.

Those who in my time have tried to correct the world's morals by new ideas, reform the superficial vices; the essential ones they let alone, if they do not increase them; and increase is to be feared. People are likely to rest from all other well-doing on the strength of these external, arbitrary reforms, which cost us less and bring greater acclaim; and thereby they satisfy at little expense the other natural, consubstantial, and internal vices.

Just consider the evidence of this in our own experience. There is no one who, if he listens to himself, does not discover in himself a pattern all his own, a ruling pattern, which struggles against education and against the tempest of the passions that oppose it. For my part, I do not feel much sudden agitation; I am nearly always in my place, like heavy and inert bodies. If I am not at home, I am always very near it. My excesses do not carry me very far away. There is nothing extreme or strange about them. And besides I have periods of vigorous and healthy reform.

The real condemnation, which applies to the common run of men of today, is that even their retirement is full of corruption and filth; their idea of reformation, blurred; their penitence, almost as diseased and guilty as their sin. Some, either from being glued to vice by a natural attachment, or from long habit, no longer recognize its ugliness. On others (in whose regiment I belong) vice weighs heavily, but they counterbalance it with pleasure or some other consideration, and endure it and lend themselves to it for a certain price; viciously, however, and basely. Yet it might be possible to imagine such an extreme disproportion that a great pleasure might justly excuse a small sin, as we say utility does; not only if the pleasure was incidental and not a part of the sin, as in theft, but if it was in the very exercise of the sin, as in intercourse with women, where the impulse is violent, and, they say, sometimes invincible.

The other day when I was at Armagnac, on the estate of a kinsman of mine, I saw a country fellow whom everyone nicknamed The Thief. He gave this account of his life: That born a beggar, and finding that by earning his bread by the toil of his hands he would never gain sufficient armor against want, he decided to become a thief; and he had spent all his youth at this trade in security, by virtue of his bodily strength. For he reaped his harvest and vintage from other people's lands, but so far away and in such great loads that it was inconceivable that one man could have carried off so much on his shoulders in one night. And he was careful besides to equalize and spread out the damage he did, so that the loss was less insupportable for each individual. He is now, in his old age, rich for a man in his station, thanks to this traffic, which he openly confesses. And to make his peace with God for his acquisitions, he says that he spends his days compensating, by good deeds, the successors of the people he robbed; and that if he does not finish this task (for he cannot do it all at once), he will charge his heirs with it, according to the knowledge, which he alone has, of the amount of wrong he did to each. Judging by this description, whether it is true or false, this man regards theft as a dishonorable action and hates it, but hates it less than poverty; he indeed repents of it in itself, but inasmuch as it was thus counterbalanced and compensated, he does not repent of it. This is not that habit that incorporates us with vice and brings even our understanding into conformity with it, nor is it that impetuous wind that comes in gusts to confuse and blind our soul, and hurls us for the moment headlong, judgment and all, into the power of vice.

I customarily do wholeheartedly whatever I do, and go my way all in one piece. I scarcely make a motion that is hidden and out of sight of my reason, and that is not guided by the consent of nearly all parts of me, without division, without internal sedition. My judgment takes all the blame or all the praise for it; and the blame it once takes, it always keeps, for virtually since its birth it has been one: same inclination, same road, same strength. And in the matter of general opinions, from childhood I established myself in the position where I was to remain.

There are some impetuous, prompt, and sudden sins: let us leave them aside. But as for these other sins so many times repeated, planned, and premeditated, constitutional sins, or even professional or vocational sins, I cannot imagine that they can be implanted so long in one and the same heart, without the reason and conscience of their possessor constantly willing and intending it to be so. And the repentance which he claims comes to him at a certain prescribed moment is a little hard for me to imagine and conceive.

I do not follow the belief of the sect of Pythagoras, that men take on a new soul when they approach the images of the Gods to receive their oracles. Unless he meant just this, that the soul must indeed be foreign, new, and loaned for the occasion, since their own showed so little sign of any purification and cleanness worthy of this office.

They do just the opposite of the Stoic precepts, which indeed order us to correct the imperfections and vices that we recognize in us, but forbid us to be repentant and glum about them. These men make us believe that they feel great regret and remorse within; but of amendment and correction, or interruption, they show us no sign. Yet it is no cure if the disease is not thrown off. If repentance were weighing in the scale of the balance, it would outweigh the sin. I know of no quality so easy to counterfeit as piety, if conduct and life are not made to conform with it. Its essence is abstruse and occult; its semblance, easy and showy.

As for me, I may desire in a general way to be different; I may condemn and dislike my nature as a whole, and implore God to reform me completely and to pardon my natural weakness. But this I ought not to call repentance, it seems to me, any more than my displeasure at being neither an angel nor Cato. My actions are in order and conformity with what I am and with my condition. I can do no better. And repentance does not properly apply to the things that are not in our power; rather does regret. I picture numberless natures loftier and better regulated than mine, but for all that, I do not amend my faculties; just as neither my arm nor my mind becomes more vigorous by imagining another that is so. If imagining and desiring a nobler conduct than ours produced repentance of our own, we should have to repent of our most innocent actions, inasmuch as we rightly judge that in a more excellent nature they would have been performed with greater perfection and dignity, and we should wish to do likewise.

When I consider the behavior of my youth in comparison with that of my old age, I find that I have generally conducted myself in orderly fashion, according to my lights; that is all my resistance can accomplish. I do not flatter myself; in similar circumstances I should always be the same. It is not a spot, it is rather a tincture with which I am stained all over. I know no superficial, halfway, and perfunctory repentance. It must affect me in every part before I will call it so, and must grasp me by the vitals and afflict them as deeply and as completely as God sees into me.

In business matters, several good opportunities have escaped me for want of successful management. However, my counsels have been good, according to the circumstances they were faced with; their way is always to take the easiest and surest course. I find that in my past deliberations, according to my rule, I have proceeded wisely, considering the state of the matter proposed to me, and I should do the same a thousand years from now in similar situations. I am not considering what it is at this moment, but what it was when I was deliberating about it.

The soundness of any plan depends on the time; circumstances and things roll about and change incessantly. I have fallen into some serious and important mistakes in my life, not for lack of good counsel but for lack of good luck. There are secret parts in the matters we handle which cannot be guessed, especially in human nature—mute factors that do not show, sometimes unknown to their possessor himself, which are brought forth and aroused by unexpected occasions. If my prudence has been unable to see into them and predict them, I bear it no ill will; its responsibility is restricted within its limitations. It is the outcome that beats me; and if it favors the counsel I have refused, there is no help for it; I do not blame myself; I accuse my luck, not my work. That is not to be called repentance.

Phocion had given the Athenians some advice that was not followed. When however the affair came out favorably against his opinion, someone said to him: "Well, Phocion, are you glad that the thing is going so well?" "Indeed I am glad," he said, "that it has turned out this way, but I do not repent of having advised that way."

When my friends apply to me for advice, I give it freely and clearly, and without hesitating as nearly everyone else does because, the affair being risky, it may come out contrary to my expectations, wherefore they may reproach me for my advice; that does not worry me. For they will be wrong, and I should not have refused them this service.

I have scarcely any occasion to blame my mistakes or mishaps on anyone but myself. For in practice I rarely ask other people's advice, unless as a compliment and out of politeness, except when I need scientific information or knowledge of the facts. But in things where I have only my judgment to employ, other people's reasons can serve to support me, but seldom to change my course. I listen to them all favorably and decently; but so far as I can remember, I have never up to this moment followed any but my own. If you ask me, they are nothing but flies and atoms that distract my will. I set little value on my own opinions, but I set just as little on those of others. Fortune pays me properly. If I do not take advice, I give still less. Mine is seldom asked, but it is followed even less; and I know of no public or private enterprise that my advice restored to its feet and to the right path. Even the people whom Fortune made somewhat dependent on it have let themselves be managed more readily by anyone else's brains. Being a man who is quite as jealous of the rights of my repose as of the rights of my authority, I prefer it so; by leaving me alone, they treat me according to my professed principle, which is to be wholly contained and established within myself. To me it is a pleasure not to be concerned in other people's affairs and to be free of responsibility for them.

In all affairs, when they are over, however they have turned out, I have little regret. For this idea takes away the worry: that they were bound to happen thus; now they are in the great stream of the universe and in the chain of Stoical causes. Your fancy, by wish or imagination, cannot change a single point without overturning the whole order of things, and the past and the future.

For the rest, I hate that accidental repentance that age brings. The man who said of old that he was obliged to the years for having rid him of sensuality had a different viewpoint from mine; I shall never be grateful to impotence for any good it may do me. *Nor will Providence ever be so hostile to her own work that debility should be ranked among the best things.* [Quintilian] Our appetites are few in old age; a profound satiety seizes us after the act. In that I see no sign of conscience; sourness and weakness imprint on us a cowardly and rheumatic virtue. We must not let ourselves be so carried away by natural changes as to let our judgment degenerate. Youth and pleasure in other days did not make me fail to recognize the face of vice in voluptuousness; nor does the distaste that the years bring me make me fail to recognize the face of voluptuousness in vice. Now that I am no longer in that state, I judge it as though I were in it.

I who shake up my reason sharply and attentively, find that it is the very same I had at a more licentious age, except perhaps in so far as it has grown weaker and worse as it has grown old. And I find that even if it refuses, out of consideration for the interests of my bodily health, to put me in the furnace of this pleasure, it would not refuse to do so, any more than formerly, for my spiritual health. I do not consider it any more valiant for seeing it out of the battle. My temptations are so broken and mortified that they are not worth its opposition. By merely stretching out my hands in front of me, I exorcise them. If my reason was confronted with my former lust, I fear that it would have less strength to resist than it used to have. I do not see that of itself it judges anything differently than it did then, nor that it has gained any new light. Wherefore, if there is any convalescence, it is a deformed convalescence.

Miserable sort of remedy, to owe our health to disease! It is not for our misfortune to do us this service, it is for the good fortune of our judgment. You cannot make me do anything by ills and afflictions except curse them. They are for people who are only awakened by whipping. My reason runs a much freer course in prosperity. It is much more distracted and busy digesting pains than pleasures. I see much more clearly in fair weather. Health admonishes me more cheerfully and so more usefully than sickness. I advanced as far as I could toward reform and a regulated life when I had health to enjoy. I should be ashamed and resentful if the misery and misfortune of my decrepitude were to be thought better than my good, healthy, lively, vigorous years, and if people were to esteem me not for what I have been, but for ceasing to be that.

In my opinion it is living happily, not, as Antisthenes said, dying happily, that constitutes human felicity. I have made no effort to attach, monstrously, the tail of a philosopher to the head and body of a dissipated man; or that this sickly remaining bit should disavow and belie the fairest, longest, and most complete part of my life. I want to present and show myself uniformly throughout. If I had to live over again, I would live as I have lived. I neither complain of the past nor fear the future. And unless I am fooling myself, I have been about the same within as without. It is one of the chief debts I owe to my fortune that the course of my bodily state has been run with each thing in due season. I have seen the grass, the flower, and the fruit, now I see the dryness—happily, since it is naturally. I bear the ills I have much more easily because they are properly timed, and also because they make me remember more pleasantly the long felicity of my past life.

Likewise my wisdom may well have been of the same proportions in one age as in the other; but it was much more dashing and graceful when green, gay, and natural, than it is now, being broken down, peevish, and labored.

Therefore I renounce these casual and sorrowful reformations. God must touch our hearts. Our conscience must reform by itself through the strengthening of our reason, not through the weakening of our appetites. Sensual pleasure is neither pale nor colorless in itself just because we see it through dim and bleary eyes. We should love temperance for itself and out of reverence toward God, who has commanded it, and also chastity; what catarrh lends us, and what I owe to the favor of my colic, is neither chastity nor temperance. We cannot boast of despising and fighting sensual pleasure, if we do not see or know it, and its charms, its powers, and its most alluring beauty.

I know them both; I have a right to speak; but it seems to me that in old age our souls are subject to more troublesome ailments and imperfections than in our youth. I used to say so when I was young; then they taunted me with my beardless chin. I still say so now that my gray hair gives me authority to speak. We call "wisdom" the squeamishness of our humors, our distaste for present things. But in truth we do not so much abandon our vices as change them, and, in my opinion, for the worse. Besides a silly and decrepit pride, a tedious prattle, prickly and unsociable humors, superstition, and a ridiculous concern for riches when we have lost the use of them, I find there more envy, injustice, and malice. Old age puts more wrinkles in our minds than on our faces; and we never, or rarely, see a soul that in growing old does not come to smell sour and musty. Man grows and dwindles in his entirety.

Seeing the wisdom of Socrates and several circumstances of his condemnation, I should venture to believe that he lent himself to it to some extent, purposely, by prevarication, being seventy, and having so soon to suffer an increasing torpor of the rich activity of his mind, and the dimming of its accustomed brightness.

What metamorphoses I see old age producing every day in many of my acquaintances! It is a powerful malady, and it creeps over us naturally and imperceptibly. We need a great provision of study, and great precaution, to avoid the imperfections it loads upon us, or at least to slow up their progress. I feel that, notwithstanding all my retrenchments, it gains on me foot by foot. I stand fast as well as I can. But I do not know where it will lead even me in the end. In any event, I am glad to have people know whence I shall have fallen.

Of Three Kinds
of Association[1]

WE MUST not nail ourselves down so firmly to our humors and dispositions. Our principal talent is the ability to apply ourselves to various practices. It is existing, but not living, to keep ourselves bound and obliged by necessity to a single course. The fairest souls are those that have the most variety and adaptability. Here is an honorable testimony to the elder Cato: *He had a mind so equally versatile for all things that whatever he was doing, you would say that he was born for that one thing alone.* [Livy]

If it was up to me to train myself in my own fashion, there is no way so good that I should want to be fixed in it and unable to break loose. Life is an uneven, irregular, and multiform movement. We are not friends to ourselves, and still less masters, we are slaves, if we follow ourselves incessantly and are so caught in our inclinations that we cannot depart from them or twist them about. I say this now because I cannot easily shake off the importunity of my soul, which cannot ordinarily apply itself unless it becomes wrapped up in a thing, or be employed unless with tension and with its

---

[1] Chapter 3.

whole being. However trivial a subject you give it, it is prone to swell and stretch it to the point where it must work on it with all its strength. For that reason its idleness is a painful occupation for me, and bad for my health. Most minds need foreign matter to arouse and exercise them; mine needs it rather to settle down and rest—*the vices of idleness must be shaken off by occupation* [Seneca]; for its principal and most laborious study is studying itself.

Books are for my mind one of the occupations which entice it away from its study. At the first thoughts that come, it moves about and shows signs of vigor in all directions, practices its touch now for power, now for order and grace, arranges, moderates, and fortifies itself. It has the power to awaken its faculties by itself. Nature has given to it as to all minds enough material of its own for its use, and enough subjects of its own for invention and judgment.

Meditation is a powerful and rich activity for anyone who knows how to examine and exercise himself vigorously: I would rather fashion my mind than furnish it. There is no occupation that is either weaker or stronger, according to the mind involved, than entertaining one's own thoughts. The greatest minds make it their profession, *to whom living is thinking.* [Cicero] Thus nature has favored it with this privilege, that there is nothing we can do so long, nor any action to which we can devote ourselves more commonly and easily. It is the occupation of the Gods, says Aristotle, from which springs their happiness and ours.

Reading serves me particularly to awaken my reason by offering various subjects for meditation, to set my judgment to work, not my memory.

Therefore few conversations hold my interest unless they have vigor and effort. It is true that pleasantness and beauty satisfy and occupy me as much as weight and depth, or more. And inasmuch as I grow sleepy in any other sort of conversation, and lend it only the rind of my attention, it often happens in such abject and feeble sort of talk, small talk, I make feeble and stupid remarks and replies, ridiculous and unworthy of a child, or, still more awkwardly and impolitely, maintain an obstinate silence. I have a dreamy way of withdrawing into myself, and, besides, a dull and childish ignorance of many common things. By these two qualities I have earned the honor that five or six stories can be truthfully told about me, as silly as can be told about any man whatever.

Now to go on with my subject, this fastidious disposition makes me hard to please in dealings with men—I have to pick them by the sorting-board—and makes me ill-fitted for ordinary actions. We live and deal with plain people. If association with them is a burden to us, if we disdain to adjust ourselves to humble and vulgar souls—and the humble and vulgar ones are often as well-regulated as the subtler ones (all wisdom is foolish that does not adapt itself to the common folly)—we should no longer meddle with either our own affairs or those of others: both private and public affairs are worked out with these people.

The least strained and most natural ways of the soul are the most beautiful; the best occupations are the least forced. Lord, what a favor wisdom does for those whose desires she adjusts to their power! There is no more useful knowledge. *According to one's power*, that was the refrain and favorite saying of Socrates, a saying of great substance. We must direct and fix our desires on the easiest and nearest things. Is it not a stupid humor of mine to be out of tune with a thousand to whom I am joined by fortune, whom I cannot

do without, only to cling to one or two, who are not associated with me, or rather to a fantastic desire for something
I cannot recapture? My easygoing ways, opposed to all bitterness and asperity, may very well have relieved me of envy
and hostility; to be loved I will not say, but no man ever gave
more occasion not to be hated. But the coolness of my dealings has rightly robbed me of the good will of many, who
are to be excused for interpreting it in another and worse
sense.

I am very capable of forming and maintaining rare and
choice friendships. Inasmuch as I grasp so hungrily at any
acquaintances that suit my taste, I make advances, I throw
myself at them so avidly, that I hardly fail to attach myself
and to make an impression wherever I land. I have often
made happy proof of this. In ordinary friendships I am
somewhat barren and cool, for my pace is not natural if it is
not under full sail. Besides, my fortune, having accustomed
me from my youth to a single perfect friendship and given
me a taste for it, has given me a certain distaste for the
others; and has imprinted too deeply on my fancy that
friendship is an animal made for company, not for the herd,
as that ancient [1] said. And furthermore, by nature I find it
hard to share myself by halves and moderately, and with that
servile and suspicious prudence that is prescribed to us for
association in these numerous and imperfect friendships; and
it is prescribed to us especially in these times when we cannot
talk about the world except with danger, or falsely.

Yet I see clearly that whoever, like myself, has as his goal
the comforts of life (I mean the essential comforts), should
shun like the plague these fastidious and squeamish humors.

---

[1] Plutarch.

I would admire a soul with different levels, which could both be tense and relax, which would be well off wherever Fortune might take it, which could chat with a neighbor about his building, his hunting, and his lawsuit, and keep up an enjoyable conversation with a carpenter and a gardener. I envy those who know how to be familiar with the humblest of their retinue and carry on a conversation with their own servants.

And I do not like Plato's advice, always to talk to our servants, whether male or female, in masterful terms, without playfulness and without familiarity. For besides the reason I have given, it is inhuman and unjust to make so much of this accidental privilege of fortune. And the households which admit the least disparity between servants and masters seem to me the most equitable.

Others study how to elevate their minds and wind them up tight; I, how to humble mine and lay it to rest. It is defective only when it reaches out:

> *You tell of Aeacus' line*
> *And wars men waged by sacred* **Troy.**
> *How much a cask of Chian wine*
> *Will cost us, or what servant boy*
> *Will heat my bath, or when whose bed*
> *Will keep out cold, you leave unsaid.*
>
> [Horace]

Thus, as the Lacedaemonian valor needed moderation and the soft and gracious notes of the flute to soothe it in war, for fear it should fling itself into recklessness and fury, whereas all other nations ordinarily use shrill and powerful sounds and voices that arouse and inflame the courage of the soldiers to the utmost; similarly it seems to me, contrary to the usual opinion, that in using our minds, we have more need, for the most part, of lead than of wings, of coolness and calm than of heat and agitation. Above all, in my opinion, it is thoroughly playing the fool to act knowing among those who are not, to speak always formally, "to talk on the point of a fork." You must stoop to the level of the people you are with, and sometimes affect ignorance. Lay aside your strength and subtlety; in ordinary practice it is enough to retain order. For the rest, crawl along the ground, if they want.

Learned men are prone to stumble over this stone. They are always parading their mastery and scattering their book learning on all sides. In these days they have poured it so hard into the boudoirs and ears of the ladies, that if they have not retained the substance, at least they have the appearance of it. For every sort of subject and matter, however humble and commonplace, they use a novel and learned manner of speaking and writing:

> *Thus they express their fears, thus they outpour*
> *Anger, joys, secrets of the soul; what more?*
> *They copulate in learned style.*
>
> [Juvenal]

They quote Plato and Saint Thomas in matters where the first comer would make as good a witness. The learning that could not reach their mind remains on their tongue.

If the wellborn ladies will take my advice, they will content themselves with displaying their own natural riches. They conceal and cover up their own beauties under foreign beauties. It is very simple-minded to put out your own light so as to shine by a borrowed light. They are buried and entombed under artifice. *Right out of a bandbox.* [Seneca] The reason is that they do not know themselves well enough. The world has nothing more beautiful; it is for them to do honor to artifice and to decorate decoration. What do they need but to live beloved and honored? They possess and know only too much for this already; they need only arouse a little and rekindle the faculties that are in them. When I see them intent on rhetoric, astrology, logic, and similar drugs, so vain and useless for their needs, I begin to fear that the men who advise them to do this, do so as a means of gaining authority over them under this pretext. For what other excuse could I find for them? Enough that without our help they can adjust the charm of their eyes to gaiety, severity, or sweetness, season a "no" with harshness, uncertainty, or encouragement, and that they need no interpreter for the speeches we make in courting them. With this knowledge they hold the whip hand and master the schoolmasters and the school.

If, however, it vexes them to yield to us in any matter at all, and they want, out of curiosity, to have a share in book learning, poetry is an amusement suited to their needs; it is a wanton and subtle art, in fancy dress, wordy, all pleasure and show, like themselves. They will also derive various benefits from history. In philosophy, from the part that is useful for life, they will take the lessons that will train them to judge our humors and characteristics, to defend themselves against our treacheries, to control the impetuosity of their own desires, to husband their freedom, to prolong the pleasures of life, and to bear humanly the inconstancy of a lover, the rudeness of a husband, and the annoyance of years and wrinkles; and things of that sort. That is the most I should assign to them in the matter of learning.

There are private, retiring, and ingrown natures. My essential pattern is suited to communication and revelation. I am all in the open and in full view, born for company and friendship. The solitude that I love and preach is primarily nothing but leading my feelings and thoughts back to myself, restraining and shortening not my steps, but my desires and my care, abandoning solicitude for outside things, and mortally avoiding servitude and obligation, and not so much the mill of people as the mill of business. Solitude of place, to tell the truth, rather makes me stretch and expand outward; I throw myself into affairs of state and into the world more readily when I am alone. At the Louvre and in the crowd I withdraw and contract into my skin; the crowd drives me back to myself, and I never entertain myself so madly, licentiously, and privately as in places full of respect and ceremonious prudence. Our follies do not make me laugh, our wisdom does.

By nature I am not an enemy to the bustle of courts; I have spent part of my life in them, and I am built to get along cheerfully in large companies, provided it is at intervals and at my own times. But that indolence of taste, that I have been speaking of, attaches me forcibly to solitude, even at home, in the midst of a numerous household and as many visitors as anywhere. I see enough people there, but rarely people with whom I like to converse; and I there reserve, both for myself and for others, an unusual freedom. There we have a truce on ceremony, on escorting people here and away, and other such troublesome prescriptions of our code of manners (oh, what a servile and bothersome practice!); everyone there behaves as he pleases; anyone who wants to, communes with his own thoughts; I remain mute, dreamy, and locked up in my thoughts, without offense to my guests.

The men whose society and intimacy I seek are those who

are called talented gentlemen; the idea of them spoils my taste for the others. It is, if you take it rightly, the rarest type among us, and a type that is chiefly due to Nature. The object of this association is simply intimacy, fellowship, and conversation: exercise of minds, without any other fruit. In our talks all subjects are alike to me. I do not care if there is neither weight nor depth in them; charm and pertinency are always there; everything is imbued with mature and constant good sense, and mingled with kindliness, frankness, gaiety, and friendliness. It is not only on the subject of lineal substitutions or the affairs of kings that our mind shows its beauty and strength; it shows it as much in private confabulations. I know my men even by their silence and their smiles, and perhaps find out more about them at table than in the council chamber. Hippomachus used to say shrewdly that he knew good wrestlers by seeing them just walk in the street.

If learning is pleased to enter our conversation, she will not be turned out; she will not be magisterial, overbearing, and troublesome, as she usually is, but subordinate and docile. We seek only to pass the time; when it is time to be instructed and preached at, we will go and find her on her throne. Let her stoop to our level just for once, if she will; for, useful and desirable as she is, even so I suppose that in a pinch we could perfectly well get along without her completely, and do our work. A wellborn mind that is practiced in dealing with men can make itself thoroughly agreeable by itself. Art is nothing else but the list and record of the productions of such minds.

Another pleasant association for me is that of beautiful and well-bred women: *For we too have practiced eyes.* [Cicero] If the soul has not so much to enjoy here as in the first association, the bodily senses, which conversely take a greater part in this one, bring it to a proportion close to the other, though in my opinion not equal. But it is an association in which we must keep a bit on guard, especially those in whom the body has much power, as in my case. I burned my fingers at it in my youth, and suffered all the furies that the poets say come upon all those who let themselves go after women without restraint and without judgment. It is true that this whiplash has since been a lesson to me:

> *A Greek who from Capharea got away*
> *Into Euboean seas will never stray.*
>
>   [Ovid]

It is madness to fasten all our thoughts upon it and to become involved in a furious and reckless passion. But on the other hand, to go into it without love and without binding our will, like actors, to play the standard role of our age and customs and put into it nothing of our own but the words, that is indeed providing for our safety, but in cowardly fashion, like a man who abandons his honor, his profit, or his pleasure, for fear of danger. For it is certain that from such a relationship those who form it can hope for no fruit that will please or satisfy a noble soul. We must have really desired what we expect to get real pleasure from enjoying. I say this even though Fortune may unjustly reward a passionate mask, as happens often because there is not a woman, however ill-favored she may be, who does not think herself quite attractive, and who does not think well of her youth or her laugh, or her graceful movements. For there are no absolutely ugly women, any more than there are absolutely beautiful ones; and the Brahmin girls who have nothing else to recommend them go to the market place, when the people have been assembled by the public crier for this purpose, and display their matrimonial parts, to see if in this respect at least they are not good enough to get a husband.

Consequently there is not one who does not let herself be easily persuaded by the first vow a man takes to be true to her. Now the necessary outcome of this common and ordinary treachery of the men of today is what experience is already showing us, that they rally and fall back upon themselves or each other to escape us; or else that they too, for their part, fall in line with this example that we give them, play their part in the farce, and lend themselves to this negotiation, without passion, without interest, and without love: *Unsusceptible to passion, whether their own or another's.* [Tacitus] They think, following the argument of Lysias in Plato, that they can devote themselves to us more profitably and conveniently the less we love them. It will turn out as it does in plays: the public will have as much pleasure in it as the comedians, or more.

For my part, I no more recognize Venus without Cupid than maternity without offspring: they are things that lend and owe their essence to each other. Thus this cheating recoils on the man who does it. It does not cost him much, but he gets nothing worth while out of it either. Those who made Venus a goddess regarded her chief beauty as incorporeal and spiritual; but the beauty that these people seek is not so much as human, or even animal. The animals do not want it so gross and so earthy. We see that imagination and desire often heats them and excites them before the body does; we see in both sexes that among the crowd they pick and choose for their affections, and that they have bonds of enduring fondness for each other. Even those to whom old age denies bodily vigor still tremble, neigh, and quiver with love. We see them, before the act, full of hope and ardor, and when the body has played its game, still reveling in the sweetness of this memory; and we see some who swell with pride when they have finished and who, weary and sated, give out songs of glee and triumph at their deed. Anyone who has only to relieve his body of a natural necessity has no interest in involving others with such elaborate preparations; that is no meat for a gross and coarse hunger.

Being one who does not ask to be thought better than I am, I will say this about the errors of my youth. Not only because of the danger to health (and yet I did not manage well enough to escape having two touches of it, slight, however, and incipient), but also out of scorn I did not addict myself much to venal and public intimacies. I wanted to make the pleasure keener by difficulty, by desire, and by a certain glory; and I liked the way of Emperor Tiberius, who in his love affairs was won by modesty and noble birth as much as by any other quality, and the whim of the courtesan Flora, who gave herself to no one less than a dictator or a consul or a censor, and took her delight in the dignity of her lovers. Certainly pearls and brocade add to the pleasure, and titles and retinue.

Moreover, I used to set great store by the mind, but only provided the body was not deficient. For, to answer in all conscience, if beauty of one or the other had necessarily to be lacking, I would have chosen sooner to give up the mental. It has its use in better things; but in the matter of love, a matter which is chiefly concerned with sight and touch, you can do something without the charms of the mind, nothing without the charms of the body.

Beauty is the real advantage of the ladies. It is so much their own that ours, though it demands somewhat different characteristics, is at its best only when indistinguishable from theirs, boyish and beardless. They say that at the court of the Grand Turk the youths that serve him on account of their beauty, whose number is infinite, are dismissed, at the latest, at twenty-two. Reason, wisdom, and the offices of friendship are oftener found among men; therefore they govern the affairs of the world.

These two kinds of association are accidental and dependent on others. One is annoying by its rarity, the other withers with age; thus they would not have provided well enough for the needs of my life. Association with books, which is the third kind, is much more certain and more our own. It yields the other advantages to the first two, but it has for its share the constancy and ease of its service. It is at my side throughout my course, and accompanies me everywhere. It consoles me in old age and in solitude. It relieves me of the weight of a tedious idleness, and releases me at any time from disagreeable company. It dulls the pangs of sorrow, unless they are extreme and overpowering. To be diverted from a troublesome idea, I have only to seek help from books; they easily turn my thoughts to themselves and steal away the others. And yet they do not rebel at seeing that I seek them out only for want of those other pleasures, that are more real, lively, and natural; they always receive me with the same expression.

He may well go on foot, as they say, who leads his horse by the bridle; and our James, King of Naples and Sicily, who, handsome, young, and healthy, had himself carried around the country on a stretcher, lying on a wretched feather pillow, dressed in a gown of gray cloth with a cap to match, meanwhile followed by great regal pomp, litters, hand-led horses of all sorts, gentlemen and officers, showed an austerity still weak and wavering. The sick man is not to be pitied who has his cure up his sleeve. In the practice and application of this maxim, which is very true, lies all the fruit I reap from books. Actually I use them scarcely any more than those who do not know them at all. I enjoy them, as misers enjoy treasures, because I know that I can enjoy them when I please; my soul takes its fill of contentment from this right of possession.

I do not travel without books, either in peace or in war. However, many days will pass, and even some months, without my using them. I'll do it soon, I say, or tomorrow, or when I please. Time flies and is gone, meanwhile, without hurting me. For I cannot tell you what ease and repose I find when I reflect that they are at my side to give me pleasure at my own time, and recognize how much assistance they bring to my life. It is the best provision I have found for this human journey, and I am extremely sorry for men of intelligence who do not have it. I sooner accept any other kind of amusement, however trivial, because this one cannot fail me.

When at home, I turn aside a little more often to my library, from which I easily command a view of my household. I am over the entrance, and see below me my garden, my farmyard, my courtyard, and into most of the parts of my house. There I leaf through now one book, now another, without order and without plan, by disconnected fragments. One moment I muse, another moment I set down or dictate, walking back and forth, these fancies of mine that you see here.

It is on the third floor of a tower; the first is my chapel, the second a bedroom and dressing room, where I often sleep in order to be alone. Above it is a great wardrobe. In the past it was the most useless place in my house. In my library I spend most of the days of my life, and most of the hours of the day. I am never there at night. Adjoining it is a rather elegant little room, in which a fire may be laid in winter, very pleasantly lighted by a window. And if I feared the trouble no more than the expense, the trouble that drives me from all business, I could easily add on to each side a gallery a hundred paces long and twelve wide, on the same level, having found all the walls raised, for another purpose, to the necessary height. Every place of retirement requires a place to walk. My thoughts fall asleep if I make them sit down. My mind will not budge unless my legs move it. Those who study without a book are all in the same boat.

The shape of my library is round, the only flat side being the part needed for my table and chair; and curving round me it presents at a glance all my books, arranged in five rows of shelves on all sides. It offers full and free views in three directions, and sixteen paces of free space in diameter.

In winter I am not there so continually; for my house is perched on a rise, as its name indicates, and contains no room more exposed to the winds than this one, which I like for being a little hard to reach and out of the way, for the benefit of the exercise as much as to keep the crowd away. There is my throne. I try to make my authority over it absolute, and to withdraw this one corner from all society, conjugal, filial, and civil. Everywhere else I have only a verbal authority, which really is divided. Sorry the man, to my mind, who has not in his own home a place to be all by himself, to pay his court privately to himself, to hide! Ambition pays its servants well by keeping them ever on display, like a statue in a market place. *Great fortune is great slavery.* [Seneca] Even their privy is not private. I have found nothing so harsh in the austere life that our monks practice as this that I observe in the orders of these men, a rule to be perpetually in company, and to have numbers of others present for any action whatsoever. I find it measurably more endurable to be always alone than never to be able to be alone.

If anyone tells me that it is degrading the Muses to use them only as a plaything and a pastime, he does not know, as I do, the value of pleasure, play, and pastime. I would almost say that any other aim is ridiculous. I live from day to day, and, with all respect for you, I live only for myself; my purposes go no further.

In my youth I studied for ostentation; later, I studied a little to gain wisdom; now, for recreation; never for gain. I gave up long ago a vain and spendthrift fancy I had for that sort of furnishing, not just to supply my needs, but to go three steps further and cover and adorn myself.

Books have many charming qualities for those who know how to choose them. But no blessing without a drawback: it is a pleasure that is no clearer or purer than the others; it has its disadvantages, and very weighty ones. The mind is exercised in books, but the body, whose care I have not forgotten either, remains meanwhile inactive, droops and grieves. I know of no excess worse for me, nor more to be avoided in my declining years.

Those are my three favorite and particular occupations. I will not speak of those that I owe the world out of civic duty.

Of Vanity [1]

THERE is perhaps no more obvious vanity than to write of it so vainly. What the Deity has so divinely told us about it [2] ought to be carefully and continually meditated by intelligent people.

Who does not see that I have taken a road along which I shall go, without stopping and without effort, as long as there is ink and paper in the world? I cannot keep a record of my life by my actions; fortune places them too low. I keep it by my thoughts. Thus I knew a gentleman who gave knowledge of his life only by the workings of his belly; you would see on display at his home a row of chamber-pots, seven or eight days' worth. That was his study, his conversation; all other talk stank in his nostrils.

Here you have, a little more decently, the excrements of an aged mind, now hard, now loose, and always undigested. And when shall I make an end of describing the continual agitation and changes of my thoughts, whatever subject they light on, since Diomedes filled six thousand books with the sole subject of grammar? What must prattle produce, when

---

[1] Chapter 9.

[2] *Vanity of vanities, saith the Preacher, vanity of vanities; all is vanity.* Ecclesiastes, 1:2.

the stammering and loosening of the tongue smothered the world with such a horrible load of volumes? So many words for the sake of words alone! O Pythagoras, why did you not conjure away this tempest? [1]

One Galba was blamed in the past for living idly. He replied that each man should give account of his actions, not of his leisure. He was wrong; for justice has cognizance and corrective power also over those who are on a holiday.

But there should be some legal restraint aimed against silly and useless writers, as there is against vagabonds and idlers. Both I and a hundred others would be banished from the hands of our people. This is no jest. Scribbling seems to be a sort of symptom of an ungovernable age. When did we write so much as since our dissensions began? When did the Romans write so much as in the time of their downfall? Besides the fact that mental refinement does not mean wiser conduct in a society, this idle occupation arises from the fact that everyone goes about the duties of his office laxly, and takes time off.

The corruption of the age is produced by the individual contribution of each one of us; some contribute treachery, others injustice, irreligion, tyranny, avarice, cruelty, in accordance with their greater power; the weaker ones bring stupidity, vanity, idleness, and I am one of them. It seems to be the season for empty things, when harmful ones weigh upon us. In a time when it is so common to do evil, it is practically praiseworthy to do what is merely useless. I console myself by thinking that I shall be one of the last on whom they will have to lay hands. While they are attending to the

---

[1] Pythagoras is said to have imposed on his disciples a silence of two to five years.

more urgent cases, I shall have leisure to reform. For it seems to me that it would be contrary to reason to prosecute petty offenses when we are infested with great ones. And the physician Philotimus said to a man who gave him his finger to dress, and from whose complexion and breath he recognized an ulcer of the lungs: "My friend, this is not the time to attend to your fingernails."

However, in this connection, I saw some years ago that an important person whose memory I hold in unusual esteem, in the midst of our great disorders when there was neither law, nor justice, nor any magistrate doing his duty, any more than now, publicly suggested some puny reforms or other in dress, cookery, and legal procedure. These are amusements with which they feed a maltreated people, to tell them that they are not completely forgotten. Those others do likewise, who confine themselves to prohibiting insistently certain ways of speaking, and dancing, and games, to a people ruined by all sorts of execrable vices. It is no time to wash and clean up when we are seized with a violent fever. It is for the Spartans alone to start combing and arranging their hair when they are on the point of flinging themselves into some extreme danger to their lives.

As for me, I have this other worse habit, that if I have one shoe on wrong, I also leave my shirt and my cloak on wrong; I scorn to reform halfway. When I am in a bad way, I grow bent on misfortune; I abandon myself in despair, and let myself slip toward the precipice, and, as they say, throw the handle after the ax. I persist in growing worse, and think myself no longer worth my care: either entirely well or entirely ill.

It is a favor for me that the desolation of this state coincides with the desolation of my age; I more willingly endure my ills being increased than I would have endured it if my well-being had been troubled by it. The words I utter in misfortune are words of anger; my courage bristles up instead of lying down. And, in contrast to others, I find myself more devout in good fortune than in bad, following the precept of Xenophon, if not his reason for it; and I am more apt to turn loving eyes to Heaven in thanks than in request. I take more pains to improve my health when it smiles on me than I do to get it back when I have let it get away. Prosperity is discipline and education to me, as are adversities and rods to others. As if good fortune were incompatible with a good conscience, men never become good except in bad fortune. Good fortune to me is a singular spur to moderation and modesty. Prayer wins me, threats repel me; favor makes me bend, fear makes me stiffen.

Among human characteristics, this one is rather common: to be better pleased with other people's things than with our own, and to love movement and change.

> *We only heed the daylight's pleasant course*
> *Because each hour proceeds on a fresh horse.*
> [Petronius]

I have my share of that. Those who go to the other extreme, of taking delight in themselves, of valuing what they have above other things and recognizing nothing as more beautiful than what they see, if they are not wiser than we, are in truth happier. I do not envy their wisdom, but I do their good fortune.

This greedy appetite for new and unknown things helps a lot to foster in me the desire to travel, but enough other circumstances contribute to it. I gladly turn aside from governing my house. There is a certain satisfaction in being in command, were it only of a barn, and in being obeyed by one's people; but it is too monotonous and languid a pleasure. And then it is necessarily mingled with many bothersome thoughts: now the poverty and oppression of your tenants afflicts you, now a quarrel between your neighbors, now their encroachments upon you:

> *It may be vineyards beaten down with hail,*
> *Deceitful soil that makes the harvest fail,*
> *Or trees that blame the rains, the stars that grill*
> *The fields, or winter's devastating chill;*
>
> [Horace]

and the fact that hardly once in six months will God send a spell of weather with which your steward is fully satisfied, and which, if it is good for the vines, does not harm the meadows:

> *The sun above burns with too fierce a glow,*
> *Or sudden showers and icy frosts lay low,*
> *And windstorms harass as they whirl and blow.*
>
> [Lucretius]

Add to that the new and well-shaped shoe of the man of days gone by, which hurts your foot; [1] and the fact that a

---

[1] Plutarch, in his "Life of Aemilius Paulus," tells this story of a Roman who had divorced his wife. "This person being highly blamed by his friends, who demanded, Was she not chaste? was she not fair? was she not fruitful? holding out his shoe, asked them, Whether it was not new? and well made? Yet, added he, none of you can tell where it pinches me. Certain it is, that great and open faults have often led to no separation; while mere petty repeated annoyances, arising from unpleasantness or incongruity of character, have been the occasion of such estrangement as to make it impossible for man and wife to live together with any content."

stranger does not understand how much it costs you and how much you sacrifice to keep up that appearance of order which people see in your family, and that perhaps you buy it too dear.

I was late in taking up the management of a household. Those whom Nature had sent into the world before me relieved me of that burden for a long time. I had already contracted a different bent, more suitable to my disposition. At all events, from what I have seen of it, it is an occupation more bothersome than difficult; whoever is capable of anything else will very easily be capable of this. If I sought to get rich, that way would seem too long to me; I would have served kings, a more productive traffic than any other. Since the only thing I aspire to acquire is the reputation of having acquired nothing, just as I have squandered nothing, in conformity with the rest of my life, unsuited for doing good or doing evil, and since I seek only to pass by, I can do that, thank God, without much attention.

If worst comes to worst, meet poverty halfway by retrenching expenses. That is what I am striving to do, that and to reform before poverty forces me to. Furthermore, I have established enough levels in my soul where I can get along with less than I have; get along contentedly, I mean. *Not by the calculation of your income, but by your manner of living and your culture, is your wealth really to be reckoned.* [Cicero] My real need does not so wholly take up all I have that Fortune does not have something of mine to bite on without biting into the flesh.

My presence, ignorant and uninterested as I am, is very helpful in my domestic affairs. I take part in them, but grudgingly. Besides, there is this about my household, that while I burn the candle privately at my end, the other end is not spared in the least.

Traveling hurts me only by its expense, which is great and beyond my means. Being accustomed to travel not only with the necessary retinue, but with a handsome one, I have to make my trips that much shorter and less frequent; and I use on them only skimmings and reserves, temporizing and postponing until these come to hand. I will not have the pleasure of wandering spoil the pleasure of my repose; on the contrary, I intend that they shall feed and favor each other.

Fortune has helped me in this, that since my principal profession in this life was to live it comfortably, and rather relaxedly than busily, it rid me of the need to multiply my riches to provide for a multitude of heirs. As for the one I have, if she does not have enough with what has been so plentifully enough for me, too bad for her; if she is improvident she will not deserve that I should wish her any more. And each man, according to the example of Phocion, provides adequately for his children who provides for them in so far as they are not unlike himself. I certainly should not concur with the action of Crates. He left his money with a banker, with this condition: that if his children were fools, he should give it to them; if they were clever, he should distribute it to the most simple-minded of the people. As if fools, for being less capable of doing without riches, were more capable of using them.

At all events, the damage resulting from my absence does not seem to merit, as long as I can afford it, my refusing to accept the chances that come up to gain diversion from the vexation of being present. There is always something that goes wrong. The affairs, now of one house, now of another, pester you. You pry into everything too closely; your perspicacity hurts you here, as indeed it does often enough elsewhere. I avoid occasions for vexation, and turn away from the knowledge of things that are going badly; and yet I cannot contrive well enough not to be constantly bumping into something at home that I do not like. And the knaveries that they most hide from me are the ones I know best. There are some that we must ourselves help to conceal, so that they will hurt less. Trivial pinpricks: sometimes trivial, but always pinpricks. The pettiest and slightest nuisances are the most acute; and as small letters hurt and tire the eyes most, so do trifling matters sting us most. The throng of petty troubles pains us more than the violence of a single one, however great it may be. The more crowded and sharp these domestic thorns are, the more sharply and without warning they prick us, easily catching us unawares.

I am no philosopher. Evils crush me according to their weight; and their weight depends on their form as much as on their matter, and often more. I have more experience of them than the common people; so I have more patience. In short, if they do not wound me, they hurt me.

Life is a tender thing and easy to disturb. From the moment I am inclined to bad humor—*for no one resists after yielding to the first impulse* [Seneca]—however stupid the cause that so inclined me, I incite my humor in that direction, and it then feeds and exasperates itself by its own movement; attracting and accumulating matter upon matter to feed on.

> *Small drops of water hollow out a stone.*
> [Lucretius]

These regular drippings gnaw at me. Everyday annoyances are never slight. They are continual and irreparable, especially when they arise from details of household management, which are continual and unavoidable.

When I consider my affairs from a distance and as a whole, I find, possibly because my memory of them is scarcely exact, that they have gotten along until now, and prospered beyond expectations and calculations. It seems to me that I get more out of them than is in them; their success amazes me. But when I am in the midst of the job, and see all these parts in motion,

Then is our soul distraught with countless cares,
[Virgil]

a thousand things fill me with desire and fear. To give them up completely is very easy for me; to become involved in them without worrying, very difficult. It is pitiful to be in a place where everything you see troubles and concerns you. And I seem to enjoy more gaily the pleasures of someone else's house, and to approach them with a purer relish. Diogenes answered in my vein the man who asked him what sort of wine he liked best. "Other people's," he said.

My father loved to build up Montaigne, where he was born; and in all this administration of domestic affairs, I love to follow his example and his rules, and shall bind my successors to them as much as I can. If I could do better for him, I would. I glory in the fact that his will still operates and acts through me. God forbid that I should allow to die in my hands any semblance of life that I could restore to so good a father. Whenever I have taken a hand in completing some bit of old wall and repairing some badly constructed building, it has certainly been more out of regard to his intentions than to my own satisfaction. And I blame my indolence that I have not gone further toward completing the things he began so handsomely in his house; all the more because I have a good chance of being the last of my race to own it, and the last to put a hand to it. For as regards my own personal inclination, neither the pleasure of building, which is said to be so alluring, nor hunting, nor gardens, nor the other pleasures of a retired life, are capable of amusing me very much. That is a thing for which I am annoyed with myself, as I am for all other notions that are a nuisance to me. I do not care so much about their being vigorous and learned, as I care that they be easy and suitable for life; they are true and sound enough if they are useful and pleasing.

Those people make me sick to death who, hearing me declare my incompetence in household occupations, go and whisper in my ears that it is disdain, and that I neglect to learn the implements of farming, its seasons, its order, how my wines are made, how grafting is done, the names and shapes of herbs and fruits, the way to prepare the food I live on, and the names and prices of the materials I wear, because my heart is set on some higher knowledge. That would be foolishness, and rather stupidity than vanity. I would rather be a good horseman than a good logician:

> *Why not make something that will meet a need,*
> *By plaiting wicker and the pliant reed?*
>
> [Virgil]

We entangle our thoughts in generalities, and the causes and conduct of the universe, which get along very well without us, and we neglect our own affairs and Michel, who concerns us even more closely than man in general.

Now I do indeed stay at home most of the time, but I should like to enjoy myself there more than elsewhere:

> *For my old age a haven may it be,*
> *An end of weary trips by land and sea,*
> *And soldiery.*

[Horace]

I don't know whether I shall accomplish this. I wish that instead of some other part of my inheritance from him, my father had turned over to me that passionate love that he had in his old age for his household. He was very fortunate in being able to keep his desires down to his means, and to be pleased with what he had. Political philosophy may condemn, for all I care, the meanness and sterility of my occupation, if only I can acquire a taste for it, as he did. I am of the opinion that the most honorable occupation is to serve the public and to be useful to many. *The greatest fruits of genius, virtue, and all excellence, are received when they are bestowed on some neighbor.* [Cicero] For my part, I stay out of it; partly out of conscience (for in the same way that I see the weight attached to such employments, I see also what little qualifications I have for them; and Plato, a master workman in all political government, nevertheless abstained from it); partly out of laziness. I am content to enjoy the world without being all wrapped up in it, to live a merely excusable life, which will merely be no burden to myself or others.

Never did a man abandon himself more fully and relaxedly to the care and rule of a stranger than I would, if I had someone. One of my wishes at this moment would be to find a son-in-law who could spoon-feed my old age comfortably and put it to sleep, in whose hands I could deposit full sovereignty over the management and use of my possessions, that he might do with them as I do, and gain what I gain instead of me, provided he brought to it a truly grateful and friendly heart. But then, we live in a world where loyalty in our own children is unknown.

Whoever has charge of my purse in my travels, has it absolutely and without control. He could cheat me just as well if I kept accounts; and, unless he is a devil, I oblige him to be honest by such abandoned trust. *Many, by their fear of being cheated, have taught how to cheat, and by their suspicions have justified other men for doing wrong.* [Seneca] The commonest security I take from my people is ignorance. I assume the existence of vices only after having seen them, and I trust the younger ones farther, whom I regard as less corrupted by bad examples. I would rather be told at the end of two months that I have spent four hundred crowns than have my ears drummed every evening with three, five, seven. Yet I have been robbed as little as the next man by this sort of larceny. It is true that I lend a helping hand to my ignorance; I purposely keep my knowledge of my money somewhat hazy and uncertain; up to a certain point I am glad to be able to be in doubt about it. You have to leave a little room for the dishonesty or improvidence of your valet. If we have enough left altogether to play our part, let that surplus of Fortune's liberality run a little more at her mercy: the gleaner's share. After all, I do not prize the fidelity of my people as much as I misprize the damage they do me. Oh, what a vile and stupid study it is to study one's money, to take pleasure in handling it, weighing it, and counting it over and over! That is the way avarice makes its approach.

In the eighteen years that I have been managing an estate, I have not succeeded in prevailing with myself to examine a title deed or my principal affairs, which necessarily have to pass within my knowledge and attention. This is not a philosophical scorn for transitory and mundane things; my taste is not so refined, and I value them at least at their worth; but it certainly is inexcusable and childish laziness and negligence. What would I not do rather than read a contract, rather than go and disturb those dusty masses of papers, a slave to my affairs, or still worse, to those of others, as so many people are for the sake of money? Nothing costs me so dear as care and trouble, and I only seek to grow indifferent and relaxed.

I was, I think, better fitted to live on another man's fortune, if that could be done without obligation and servitude. And at that I do not know, when I look at it closely, whether, given my disposition and my lot, there is not more humiliation, trouble, and bitterness in what I have to endure from business and servants and household, than there would be in serving a man born greater than myself, who would lead me in some sort of comfort. *Servitude is the obedience of a broken and abject mind, lacking free will.* [Cicero] Crates did worse, when he cast himself into the freedom of poverty to get rid of the indignities and cares of a household. That I would not do,—I hate poverty as much as pain—but I certainly would change this sort of life for another less showy and less busy.

Absent from home, I threw off all such thoughts; and I should then feel less the ruin of a tower than I feel, when present, the fall of a tile. My soul easily achieves detachment from a distance, but on the spot it suffers like a vinegrower's.[1] A bridle fixed badly on my horse, a stirrup-leather slapping against my leg, will keep me in a bad humor a whole day. I raise my courage enough to meet annoyances, my eyes I cannot.

The senses, ye gods, the senses!

At home I am responsible for all that goes wrong. Few masters—I am speaking of those of medium condition like mine. and if there are any, they are more fortunate—can rely so much on another that a good part of the load does not remain on their shoulders. That tends to make me less gracious in entertaining visitors (and I may perhaps have kept one or another of them here more by my kitchen than by my graciousness, as bores do), and takes away much of the pleasure I should derive at home from the visits and gatherings of my friends. The stupidest demeanor of a gentleman in his own house is when we see him caught up in the business of housekeeping, whispering in the ear of one servant, threatening another with his eyes; it should flow imperceptibly and seem like a normal process. And I think it ugly to talk to your guests about the way you are treating them, whether to excuse it or boast of it.

I love order and cleanliness—

> *Plate and goblet such that they*
> *Me unto myself display,*
>
> [Horace]

—as much as abundance; and in my house I give careful attention to what is needful, little to ostentation.

---

[1] Montaigne lived in the Bordeaux wine country, and his great-grandfather was a wine merchant.

If a footman starts fighting at another man's house, if a dish is tipped over, you only laugh at it; you sleep, while the master arranges with his butler for your next day's entertainment.

I speak of these things as I see them, generally not failing to appreciate what a pleasant occupation for certain natures is a peaceful, prosperous household, conducted in a determined order; and not wishing to fasten my own errors and shortcomings to the matter, or to give the lie to Plato, who thinks the happiest occupation for each man is to carry on his own affairs without injustice.

When I travel, I have only myself and the use of my money to think about; that is disposed of with a single precept. For amassing it too many qualities are required; I do not know a thing about it. I know something about spending, and making a show of what I spend, which is really its principal use. But I apply myself to it too ambitiously, which makes it uneven and shapeless, and immoderate besides, in both directions. If it makes a show and is useful, I let myself go injudiciously; and I tighten up just as injudiciously if it does not shine and does not please me.

Whatever it is, whether art or nature, that imprints in us this disposition to live with reference to others, it does us much more harm than good. We cheat ourselves out of our own advantages to make appearances conform with public opinion. We do not care so much what we are in ourselves and in reality as what we are in the public mind. Even the joys of the mind, and wisdom, appear fruitless to us, if they are enjoyed by ourselves alone, if they do not shine forth to the sight and approbation of others.

There are men whose gold flows in great streams through underground places, imperceptibly; others beat it all out into sheets and leaf; so that for some, farthings are worth crowns, for the others the reverse, since the world judges expense and means according to the show. All anxious care about riches smells of avarice, as does even spending and liberality, when it is too systematic and artificial. They are not worth painful watchfulness and care. He who tries to make his spending exact makes it pinched and constrained. Saving and spending are in themselves indifferent things, and take on color of good or bad only according to the application of our will.

The other thing that invites me to these excursions is that the present moral state of our country does not suit me. I could easily console myself for this corruption as regards the public interest—

> *Worse than the Iron Age, times for whose shame*
> *Nature herself in vain would find a name,*
> *Or metal symbolizing their ill fame,*
>
> [Juvenal]

—but with regard to my own, no. I in particular suffer from it too much. For in my neighborhood we have now grown old, through the long license of these civil wars, in so riotous a form of government,

> *Where right and wrong are interchanged,*
> [Virgil]

that in truth it is a marvel that it can subsist.

> *In arms they till the soil, and ever their delight*
> *Is to amass new loot, and live by lawless might.*
> [Virgil]

I see at last, from our example, that human society holds and is knit together at any cost whatever. Whatever position you set men in, they pile up and arrange themselves by moving and crowding together, just as dissimilar objects, put in a bag without order, find of themselves a way to unite and fall into place together, often better than they could have been arranged by art. King Philip collected a rabble of the most wicked and incorrigible men he could find, and settled them all in a city he had built for them, which bore their name. I judge that from their very vices they formed a political system among themselves and a workable and regular society.

I see not one action, or three, or a hundred, but morals in common and accepted practice, so monstrous, especially in inhumanity and treachery, that I have not the heart to think of them without horror; and I marvel at them almost as much as I detest them. The practice of these arrant villainies bears the mark of vigor and strength of soul as much as of error and disorder.

Necessity reconciles men and brings them together. This accidental link afterwards takes the form of laws; for there have been some as savage as any human opinion can produce, which have nevertheless maintained their bodily health and long life as well as those of Plato and Aristotle could do.

And indeed all those imaginary, artificial descriptions of a government prove ridiculous and unfit to put into practice. These great lengthy altercations about the best form of society and the rules most suitable to bind us, are altercations fit only for the exercise of our minds; as in the liberal arts there are several subjects whose essence is discussion and dispute, and which have no life apart from that. Such a description of a government would be applicable in a new world, but we take men already bound and formed to certain customs; we do not create them, like Pyrrha or Cadmus. By whatever means we may have power to correct and reform them, we

can hardly twist them out of their accustomed bent without
breaking up everything. Solon was asked whether he had
established the best laws he could for the Athenians. "Yes
indeed," he answered, "the best they would have accepted."

Varro excuses himself in the same way, saying that if he
had to write about religion, if it were new, he would say
what he thinks of it; but since it is already formed and accepted, he will speak of it more according to custom than
according to nature.

Not in theory, but in truth, the best and most excellent
government for each nation is the one under which it has
maintained itself. Its form and essential fitness depend on
habit. We are prone to be discontented with the present state
of things. But I maintain, nevertheless, that to wish for the
government of a few in a democratic state, or another type
of government in a monarchy, is foolish and wrong.

> *Love your own state, and be it what it will.*
> *If it is royal, then love royalty;*
> *If oligarchy or democracy,*
> *God brought you into it, so love it still.*
>
> [Pibrac]

Good Monsieur de Pibrac, whom we have just lost, such a
noble mind, such sound opinions, such gentle character! This
loss, and that of Monsieur de Foix, which we suffered at the
same time, are important losses to our crown. I do not know
if France has another pair left, comparable in sincerity and
ability, to substitute for these two Gascons in the councils of
our kings. They were souls beautiful in different ways, and
certainly rare and beautiful by the standards of our times,
each in his own way. But who placed them in this age, they

who were so out of tune and proportion with our corruption and tempests?

Nothing endangers a state except innovation; change alone lends shape to injustice and tyranny. When some part is dislocated, we can prop it up; we can fight against letting the alteration and corruption natural to all things carry us too far from our beginnings and principles. But to undertake to recast so great a mass, to change the foundations of so great a structure, that is a job for those who wipe out a picture in order to clean it, who want to reform defects of detail by universal confusion and cure illnesses by death, *who desire not so much to change as to overthrow everything.* [Cicero] The world is ill fitted to cure itself; it is so impatient of its affliction that it only aims at getting rid of it, without considering the cost. We see by a thousand examples that it usually cures itself to its own disadvantage. Riddance from a present evil is not cure, unless there is an all-round improvement in condition.

The surgeon's aim is not to kill the diseased flesh; that is only the road to his cure. He looks beyond, to make the natural flesh grow again, and restore the part to its proper condition. Whoever proposes merely to remove what is biting him falls short, for good does not necessarily succeed evil; another evil may succeed it, and a worse one, as happened to Caesar's slayers, who cast the Republic into such a state that they had reason to repent of having meddled with it. To many others since, right down to our own times, the same thing has happened. The French, my contemporaries, could tell you a thing or two about it. All great changes shake the state and throw it into disorder.

Anyone who would aim straight at cure and would reflect

on it before taking any action, would be likely to cool off about setting his hand to it. Pacuvius Calavius corrected the error of this procedure by a signal example. His fellow citizens were in revolt against their magistrates. He, a person of great authority in the city of Capua, one day found means to lock up the senate in the palace, and, calling the people together in the market place, told them that the day had come when with complete freedom they could take vengeance on the tyrants who had so long oppressed them, and whom he held alone and disarmed at his mercy. He advised them that these men should be brought out one by one, by lot, and that they should decide about each one individually, and have their sentence executed on the spot; with this provision also that at the same time they should decide to appoint some honorable man in the place of the condemned man, so that the office should not remain vacant. They had no sooner heard the name of one senator than there arose a cry of general dissatisfaction against him. "I see very well," said Pacuvius, "that we must dismiss this one; he is a wicked man; let us have a good one in exchange." There was a prompt silence, everyone being much at a loss whom to choose. The first bolder man to speak his choice met a still greater unanimity of voices to reject him, and a hundred imperfections and just causes for refusing him. These contradictory humors having grown heated, it fared still worse with the second senator, and the third: as much disagreement about election as agreement about dismissal. Having tired themselves out uselessly in this dispute, they began bit by bit, one here, one there, to steal away from the assembly, each one bearing away this conclusion in his mind, that the oldest and best-known evil is always more bearable than an evil that is new and untried.

Because I see us pitifully agitated (for what have we not done?)—

> Alas, by scars and sins our souls are stained,
>> And brothers' blood. From what have we refrained
> In this hard age? What evil have we fled
>> Or left undone? Whence has our youth in dread
> Of irritated Gods its hands restrained?
>> What altar not profaned?

[Horace]

—I do not immediately jump to the conclusion that

> Though even Safety would
> Preserve this family, henceforth she never could.

[Terence]

Perhaps we are not on our last legs, for all that. The preservation of states is a thing that is probably beyond our understanding. As Plato says, a civil government is a powerful thing and hard to dissolve. It often holds out against mortal internal diseases, against the mischief of unjust laws, against tyranny, against the excesses and ignorance of the magistrates and the license and sedition of the people.

In all our fortunes we compare ourselves with what is above us and look toward those who are better off; let us measure ourselves with what is below: there is no one so ill-starred that he may not find a thousand examples to console him. It is our weakness that we are more unhappy to see people ahead of us than happy to see people behind us. However, Solon used to say that if someone made a pile of all the ills together, there is no one who would not choose rather to take back with him the ills he has than to come to a legitimate division with all other men, and take his rightful share. Our government is in bad health; yet some have been sicker with-

out dying. The gods play handball with us and drive us about
in every way:

> *Truly the Gods play with us as with balls.*
> [Plautus]

The stars fatally destined the state of Rome for an example
of what they can do in this way. In it are comprised all the
forms and vicissitudes that affect a state: all that order can do,
and disorder, and good fortune, and misfortune. What state
ought to despair of its condition, seeing the shocks and commotions by which Rome was disturbed, and which it with-
stood? If extent of dominion is the health of a state (which
I do not at all believe, and I like Isocrates when he instructs
Nicocles not to envy princes who have broad dominions,
but rather those who know how to keep in good condition
the ones that have been handed down to them), the Roman
state was never so healthy as when it was sickest. The worst
of its forms was the most fortunate.

One can hardly distinguish the features of any kind of
government under the first emperors; it was the thickest and
most horrible confusion imaginable. Nevertheless Rome endured it and continued in it, preserving not a monarchy confined within its own bounds, but all those nations, so unlike,
so remote, so ill-disposed, ruled with so little order and
conquered so unjustly:

> *Fortune gives no right*
> *To any nation, to indulge her spite*
> *Against the state that rules o'er land and sea.*
> [Lucan]

All that totters does not fall. The fabric of so great a body
holds together by more than a single nail. It holds together
even by its antiquity, like old buildings the foot of which

has been worn away by age, without cement or mortar, which yet live and support themselves by their own weight:

> *The day it clung to healthy roots is past,*
> *Now its weight makes it fast.*

[Lucan]

Furthermore, it is not a good procedure to reconnoiter only the flank and the moat; to judge the security of a place, we must see from what direction it can be approached, and what is the condition of the attacker. Few ships sink of their own weight and without external violence. Now let us turn our eyes in all directions: everything is crumbling about us; in all the great states that we know, whether in Christendom or elsewhere, take a look: you will find the evident threat of change and ruin:

> *They have their own misfortunes, and have all been*
> *through the storm.*

[Adapted from Virgil]

The astrologers have an easy game when they warn us, as they do, of great and imminent changes and revolutions; their prophecies are present and palpable—we do not need to go to the heavens for that.

We may derive not only consolation from this universal community of evils and menaces, but even some hope for the duration of our state, inasmuch as naturally nothing falls where everything falls. Universal sickness is individual health; conformity is a quality hostile to dissolution. For my part, I do not despair about it, and in it I seem to see ways of saving ourselves:

> *Perhaps a god will yet restore,*
> *By happy change, our bliss of yore.*

[Horace]

Who knows but that God wills it to happen, as with bodies that purge themselves and are restored to better condition by long and grievous maladies, which give them back a clearer and more complete health than they took away from them?

What most weighs me down is that when I count up the symptoms of our trouble, I see as many that are natural and that Heaven sends us from its own stock, as of those that our disorder and human heedlessness contribute. It seems as if the very stars have ordained that we have lasted long enough beyond the ordinary term. And this also troubles me, that the evil that threatens us closest is not an alteration in the entire and solid mass, but its dissipation and disintegration, the worst of our fears.

Also in these ramblings of mine I fear the treachery of my memory, lest inadvertently it may have made me record something twice. I hate to re-examine myself, and never re-read, if I can help it, what has once escaped me. Now I am bringing in here nothing newly learned. These are common ideas; having perhaps thought of them a hundred times, I am afraid I have already set them down. Repetition is boring anywhere, even in Homer; but it is ruinous in things that attract only superficial and passing attention. I dislike inculcation, even of useful things, as in Seneca; and I dislike the practice of his Stoical school of repeating, in connection with every subject, in full length and breadth, the principles and premises for general use, and restating ever anew their common and universal arguments and reasons.

My memory grows cruelly worse every day,

> *As though with thirsty throat I'd quaffed*
> *Some soporific Lethean draught.*

> [Horace]

Henceforth—for thank God, up to now, no serious blunder has resulted—whereas others seek time and opportunity to think over what they have to say, I shall have to avoid any preparation, for fear of binding myself to some obligation on which I should be dependent. To be held and bound puts me off my track, and likewise to depend on so feeble an instrument as my memory.

I never read the following story without indignation, and natural and personal resentment. Lyncestes, accused of conspiracy against Alexander, on the day when he was brought before the army, according to custom, to be heard in his own defense, had in his head a studied oration, of which, all hesitating and stammering, he pronounced a few words. As he was growing more and more confused, struggling with his memory and searching it, the soldiers nearest him charged him and killed him with their pikes, considering him convicted. His confusion and his silence was to them as good as a confession. Having had so much leisure to prepare himself in prison, it was not, in their opinion, his memory that failed him: it was his conscience that tied his tongue and took away his strength. That certainly was good reasoning! The place, the audience, the anticipation, daze a man even when nothing is at stake but the ambition to speak well. What can a man do when it is a speech on which his life depends?

For my part, the very fact of being bound to what I have to say serves to break my grip on it. When I have committed and entrusted myself entirely to my memory, I lean so heavily on it that I overburden it: it takes fright at its load. As long as I rely on it, I place myself outside of myself, till it becomes dangerous for my bearing; and some days I have found myself hard pressed to conceal the slavery in which I was bound, whereas my plan in speaking is to display ex-

treme carelessness and unstudied and unpremeditated gestures, as if they arose from the immediate occasion. For I
would as soon say nothing worth while as show I had come
prepared to be eloquent, an unbecoming thing, especially for
people of my profession, and too binding a thing for a man
who cannot live up to much: the preparation gives more
hope than it fulfills. Often a man stupidly strips to his doublet only to jump no better than he would in a cloak. *There
is nothing so unfavorable to those who wish to please as the
expectation they arouse.* [Cicero]

It is recorded of the orator Curio that when he stated first
the division of his oration into three or four parts, or the
number of his arguments and reasons, it often happened that
he either forgot one, or added one or two extra. I have always
carefully guarded against falling into this predicament, having always hated these promises and prescriptions, not only
out of distrust of my memory, but also because this method
owes too much to artificiality. *A simpler style becomes a
soldier.* [Quintilian] Enough that I have promised myself
henceforth never again to take up the task of speaking on
formal occasions. For, as for reading one's speech, besides
being unnatural, it is a great disadvantage for those who naturally have some power of gesture. And as for throwing
myself on the mercy of my improvisation, that is even less
desirable; mine is sluggish and confused, and could not meet
sudden and important emergencies.

Reader, let this first essay of strength run on, and this
third extension of the other parts of my painting. I add, but
I do not correct. First, because when a man has mortgaged
his work to the world, it seems to me that he has no further
right to it. Let him speak better elsewhere, if he can, and not
adulterate the work he has sold. From such people nothing

should be bought until after their death. Let them think carefully before publishing. Who is hurrying them?

My book is always one. Except that at each new edition, so that the buyer may not come off completely empty-handed, I allow myself to add, since it is only an ill-fitted mosaic, some extra ornaments. These are only overweights, which do not condemn the original form, but give some special value to each of the subsequent ones, by a bit of ambitious subtlety. Thence, however, it may easily happen that some transposition of chronology may slip in, for my stories take their place according to their timeliness, not always according to their age.

Secondly, because, as far as I am concerned, I fear to lose by the change: my understanding does not always go forward, it goes backward too. I distrust my thoughts hardly any less for being second or third than for being first, or for being present than for being past. We often correct ourselves as stupidly as we correct others. My first edition was in the year fifteen hundred and eighty. Since then I have grown older by a long stretch of time; but certainly I have not grown an inch wiser. Myself now and myself a while ago are indeed two; but when better, I simply cannot say. It would be fine to be old if we traveled only toward improvement. It is a drunkard's motion, staggering, dizzy, wobbling, or that of reeds that the wind stirs as it pleases.

Antiochus had written vigorously in favor of the Academy; in his old age he took a different stand. Whichever of the two I followed, should I not still be following Antiochus? After having established the doubtfulness of human opinions, to try to establish their certainty, was that not establishing doubt, not certainty, and promising that if he had been given another age to live he would still be ready for some new change, not so much better as different?

The favor of the public has given me a little more boldness than I expected; but what I fear most is to surfeit my readers: I would rather irritate them than weary them, as a learned man of my time has done. Praise is always pleasing, from whomever and for whatever reason it may come; yet to enjoy it properly, we must be informed of the cause of it. Even imperfections have a way of recommending themselves. Vulgar and popular esteem is seldom happy in its choice; and in my time I am much mistaken if the worst writings are not those which have gotten the best share of the wind of public favor. Certainly I give thanks to well-bred people who deign to take my feeble efforts in good part.

There is no place where the faults of workmanship are so apparent as in material which has nothing in itself to recommend it. Do not blame me, reader, for those that slip in here through the caprice or inadvertency of others: each hand, each workman contributes his own. I do not concern myself with spelling, and simply order them to follow the old style; or with punctuation; I am inexpert in both. When they wholly shatter the sense, I am not much troubled about it, for at least they relieve me of responsibility; but when they substitute a false meaning, as they do so often, and twist me to their view, they ruin me. However, when the thought is not up to my strength, a fair-minded man should reject it as not mine. Anyone who knows how little I like to work, how much I am formed in my own way, will easily believe that I would rather write as many more essays again than subject myself to going over these again for such childish correction.

So I was saying a while ago that being planted in the deep-est mine of this new metal,[1] not only am I deprived of any great familiarity with people of different morals and opin-ions from mine, by which they hold together with a bond that avoids all other bonds; but also I am not free from danger among people to whom everything is equally permissible, and most of whom cannot make their account with the law worse—from which arises the extreme degree of licentious-ness. Counting up all the particular circumstances concern-ing myself, I find no man of our country to whom the defense of laws costs more, both in gains ceasing and in damages ensuing, as the lawyers say, than myself. And cer-tain people make much of their zeal and eagerness who, weighing things justly, do much less than I.

As a house that has always been free, very accessible, and at anyone's service (for I have never let myself be induced to make it an instrument of war, in which I take part most willingly when it is most distant from my neighborhood), my house has deserved considerable popular affection, and it would be very hard to scold me on my own dunghill. And I think it is a wonderful and exemplary masterpiece that it is still virgin of blood and pillage, under so long a storm, with so many changes and disturbances in the neigh-borhood. For, to tell the truth, it was possible for a man of my disposition to escape any one constant and continued form of danger, whatever it might be; but the conflicting invasions and incursions and the alternations and vicissitudes of fortune around me have up to now more exasperated than

---

[1] An allusion to the Juvenal quotation on p. 227, which itself al-ludes to the legend of four ages (gold, silver, bronze, and iron), and suggests that a new metal is needed to represent the new depths to which man has sunk.

mollified the temper of the country, and burden me again and again with insuperable dangers and difficulties. I escape; but I dislike the fact that it is more by good luck, and even by my prudence, than because of justice; and I dislike being outside the protection of the laws and under another safeguard than theirs. As things stand, I live more than half by others' favor, which is a harsh obligation. I do not want to owe my safety either to the kindness and benignity of the great, who approve of my obedience to the laws and my independence, nor to the affable ways of my predecessors and myself. For what if I were different? If my conduct and the frankness of my dealings obligate my neighbors or my kinsmen, it is cruel that they can acquit themselves by letting me live, and say: "We grant him leave to continue to hold the divine service freely in the chapel of his house, all the churches around having been emptied and ruined by us; and we grant him the use of his property, and his life, since he shelters our wives and our cattle in time of need." For a long time we in my house have had a share in the praise given to Lycurgus, the Athenian, who was the general depositary and guardian of his fellow citizens' purses.

Now I hold that we should live by right and authority, not by reward or favor. How many gallant men have chosen rather to lose their lives than to owe them! I avoid subjecting myself to any sort of obligation, but especially any that binds me by a debt of honor. I find nothing so expensive as that which is given me and for which my will remains mortgaged by the claim of gratitude, and I more willingly accept services that are for sale. Rightly so, I think: for the latter I give only money, for the others I give myself. The tie that binds me by the law of honesty seems to me much tighter and more oppressive than is that of legal constraint. A notary ties me down more gently than I do myself. Is it not reasonable that my conscience should be much more firmly bound in matters in which someone relies on it alone? In other cases my fidelity owes nothing, for nothing has been lent it; let them use the trust and security they have taken outside of me. I would much rather break the imprisonment of a wall and of the laws than that of my word. I am scrupulous to the point of superstition in keeping my promises, and I like to make them uncertain and conditional in all matters. To those of no weight I give weight by jealous regard for my rule: it cramps me and burdens me with its own interest. Yes, even in undertakings in which I am alone concerned and wholly free, if I say what I plan to do, it seems to me that I prescribe it for myself, and that to give knowledge of it to another is to impose it upon myself. Thus I seldom air my plans.

The sentence I pass upon myself is sharper and stiffer than that of the judges, who only consider me with respect to common obligation; the grip of my conscience is tighter and more severe. I am lax in following duties to which I should be dragged if I did not go to them. *Even a just action is just only in so far as it is voluntary.* [Cicero] If the action does not have something of the splendor of freedom, it has neither grace nor honor.

> *When I am forced by law, my will gives scant assent.*
> [Terence]

When necessity tugs me, I like to relax my will, *because whatever is exacted by power is ascribed rather to him who commands than to him who executes.* [Valerius Maximus] I know some who follow this mannerism to the point of injustice: who give rather than give back, lend rather than pay.

and do good most stingily to the person they are obliged to. I do not go that far, but I come close to it.

I am so fond of throwing off burdens and obligations that I have sometimes counted as profit the ingratitude, affronts, and indignities that I had received from those to whom, either by nature or by accident, I owed some duty of friendship, taking their offense as an occasion for that much acquittal and discharge of my debt. Although I continue to pay them the external civilities that public interest prescribes, I find it a great saving, all the same, to do for the sake of justice what I used to do for the sake of affection, and to relieve myself a little of the inner tension and solicitude of my will—*It is the part of a wise man to restrain, as he would a chariot, the first impulse of good will* [Cicero]—which is a little too urgent and pressing when I put my heart in a friendship, at least for a man who has no wish to be under pressure. And this economy serves me as some consolation for the imperfections of those in which I am concerned. To be sure, I am sorry that they are worth less for it, but the fact remains that I am also spared in this way something of my diligence and obligation toward them.

I approve of a man who loves his son less for being mangy or hunchbacked, and not only when he is malicious, but also when he is ill-favored and ill-born—God himself has taken off that much from his natural value and estimation—provided he bears himself in his coolness toward him with moderation and exact justice. With me, nearness of kin does not alleviate defects, it rather aggravates them.

After all, as far as I understand the science of benefaction and gratitude, which is a subtle science and of great utility, I see no one freer and less indebted than I am up to this point.

What I owe, I owe to the ordinary natural obligations. There is no one who is more absolutely clear of any others:

> *The gifts of princes are to me unknown.*
> [Adapted from Virgil]

Princes give me much if they take nothing from me, and do me enough good when they do me no harm; that is all I ask of them. Oh, how much I am obliged to God that it was his pleasure I should receive directly from his grace all that I have, and that he has kept all my indebtedness for himself privately! How earnestly I beseech his holy mercy that I may never owe thanks for essential things to anyone! Blessed liberty, which has guided me so far! May it continue to the end!

I try to have no express need of anyone. *All my hope is in myself.* [Imitated from Terence] It is a thing that each man can do for himself, but more easily those whom God has sheltered from natural and urgent necessities. It is very pitiful and hazardous to be dependent on another. We ourselves, who are our most proper and certain protectors, have not made ourselves secure enough. I have nothing of my own but myself, and even there my possession is partly defective and borrowed. I cultivate both my courage, which is the stronger, and also my fortune, to find in them enough to satisfy me if everything else should forsake me.

Hippias of Elis furnished himself not merely with learning, that in the lap of the Muses he might, in case of need, dispense cheerfully with any other company, or with the knowledge of philosophy, to teach his soul to be contented with itself and manfully to do without the comforts that come to it from outside, when Fate so ordains. He was careful enough to learn also to cook, to shave, to make his clothes, his shoes, his rings, so as to be as self-sufficient as he could, and escape from dependence on outside help.

We enjoy borrowed goods much more freely and gaily when the enjoyment is not forced and constrained by need, and when we have, both in our will and in our fortune, the strength and the means to do without them.

I know myself well; but it is hard for me to imagine any such pure liberality coming from anyone, any such free and genuine hospitality, that it would not seem to me ill-favored, tyrannical, and tainted with reproach, if necessity had entangled me in it. As giving is an ambitious quality and a prerogative, so is accepting a quality of submission. Witness the insulting and quarrelsome refusal that Bajazet made of the presents that Tamerlane sent him. And those offered on behalf of Emperor Solyman to the Emperor of Calicut made him so angry that he not only refused them rudely, saying that neither he nor his predecessors were accustomed to take, and that it was their part to give; but besides, he had the ambassadors sent for this purpose thrown into a dungeon.

When Thetis, says Aristotle, flatters Jupiter, when the Lacedaemonians flatter the Athenians, they do not keep refreshing their memory of the good they have done them, which is always odious, but their memory of the benefits they have received from them. Those whom I see so freely using one and all and binding themselves to them, would not do so if they weighed as carefully as a wise man should the bond of an obligation: perhaps sometimes it is paid, but it is never dissolved. Cruel fetters for a man who likes to give his freedom elbowroom in all directions.

Those who know me, both above and below me, know whether they have ever seen a man less demanding of others. If I surpass all modern examples in this respect, it is no great wonder, for so many parts of my character contribute to it: a little natural pride, inability to endure refusal, limitation of desires and plans, incapacity for any kind of business, and my very favorite qualities, idleness and freedom. Through all these I have contracted a mortal hatred of being bound either to another or by another than myself. I employ every power to the utmost to do without, before I employ the kindness of another, however slight or weighty the occasion. My friends bother me strangely when they ask me to ask a favor of a third person. And it seems to me hardly less expensive to release a man who is indebted to me by using him, than to bind myself for them to a man who owes me nothing. Excepting that condition, and this other, that they desire of me nothing involving trouble and care, I am accommodating and approachable for any man's need.

But I have avoided receiving still more than I have sought to give; and indeed that is much easier, according to Aristotle. My fortune has but little allowed me to do good to others, and what little it has allowed me it has assigned to rather meager quarters. If it had brought me into the world to hold some rank among men, I should have been ambitious to make myself loved, not to make myself feared or admired. Shall I express this more insolently? I should have thought as much of giving pleasure as of gaining profit. Cyrus, very wisely, and through the mouth of a very good captain and still better philosopher,[1] esteems his kindness and his good deeds far beyond his valor and his warlike conquests. And the first Scipio, whenever he wants to put his best foot forward, gives more weight to his affability and humanity than to his hardihood and his victories. And he has ever in his

---

[1] Xenophon.

mouth this proud saying: that he left his enemies as good reason to love him as his friends.

I mean to say, then, that if we must thus owe something, it should be by a more legitimate title than the one I am speaking of, to which the law of this miserable war binds me; and not with so great a debt as that of my total preservation: that overwhelms me. I have gone to bed a thousand times in my own home, imagining that someone would betray me and slaughter me that very night, arranging with fortune that it should be without fright and not lingering. And after my Paternoster I have cried out:

Shall a godless soldier possess these well-tilled fields?
[Virgil]

What remedy is there? It is my birthplace and that of most of my ancestors; they set on it their affection and their name.[1] We become hardened to whatever we are accustomed to. And for a wretched condition such as ours, a very favorable gift of Nature is habit, which benumbs our senses to the suffering of many ills. Civil wars are worse in this respect than other wars, that they make us all sentinels in our own houses.

How sad to guard our life with gate and wall,
And scarcely trust the strength of our own hall.
[Ovid]

It is a great extremity to be threatened even in our household and domestic repose. The region where I live is always the

---

[1] Montaigne, appropriately for this chapter, shows here his vanity over his nobility, which is probably intensified by awareness that it is recent. Actually his only ancestor born at Montaigne was his father; and the name came from the estate, not from the family.

first and the last in the battles of our troubled times, and peace never shows her full face there:

> *Even in time of peace, they quake for fear of war.*
> [Ovid]

> *Whenever Fortune stirs unrest,*
> *This is the path of war. I would be better blessed*
> *If Fortune placed me 'neath the sun of Orient,*
> *Or in the frozen North, under a nomad's tent.*
> [Lucan]

I sometimes find in nonchalance and laxity a way of strengthening myself against these considerations; they too, to some extent, lead us toward fortitude. It often happens that I imagine and await mortal dangers with some pleasure: I plunge head down, stupidly, into death, without looking at it and recognizing it, as into a silent and dark abyss which swallows me up at one leap and overwhelms me in an instant with a heavy sleep free from feeling and pain. And in these quick and violent deaths, the consequence that I foresee gives me more comfort than the occurrence gives me fear. They say that as life is not better for being long, so death is better for not being long. I do not so much estrange myself from being dead as I become familiar with dying. I wrap myself and nestle in this storm, which is to blind me and sweep me away furiously with a sudden and insensible attack.

Even so, if it happened, as some gardeners say, that roses and violets spring up more fragrant near garlic and onions, because these draw in and suck up whatever there is that smells bad in the ground—if only these depraved natures likewise absorbed all the venom of my air and climate, and made me so much better and purer by their vicinity that I should not be wholly a loser! That is not the case; but there may be something in this, that goodness is more beautiful and attractive when it is rare; and that contrariety and diversity strengthen well-doing and compress it within itself, and inflame it by jealousy of opposition and love of glory.

Robbers have no particular gratuitous grudge against me. Have I any against them? I should have to hate too many people. Like consciences, under different kinds of fortune, harbor like cruelty, disloyalty, and robbery; and it is all the worse when it is more cowardly, more secure and dark, in the shadow of the laws. I hate open injustice less than treacherous injustice, warlike less than peaceful. Our fever has come upon a body that is hardly the worse for it; the fire was there, it has caught flame; the noise is greater, the evil little greater.

I ordinarily reply to those who ask me the reason for my travels, that I know well what I am fleeing from, but not what I am looking for. If they tell me that among foreigners there may be just as little health, and that their ways are no better than ours, I reply, firstly, that that is not easy,

> *So many are the shapes of crime!*
>
> [Virgil]

Secondly, that it is always a gain to change a bad state for an uncertain one, and that the troubles of others should not sting us like our own.

I do not want to forget this, that I never rebel so much against France as not to regard Paris with a friendly eye; she has had my heart since my childhood. And it has happened to me in this as happens with excellent things: the more other beautiful cities I have seen since, the more the beauty of Paris has power over me and wins my affection. I love her for herself, and more in her own essence than overloaded with foreign pomp. I love her tenderly, even to her warts and her spots. I am a Frenchman only by this great city: great in population, great in the felicity of her situation, but above all great and incomparable in variety and diversity of the good things of life; the glory of France, and one of the noblest ornaments of the world. May God drive our discords far from her! Entire and united, I think she is protected against any other violence. I warn her that of all parties the worst will be the one that throws her into discord. And for her I fear only herself. And I feel certainly as much for her as for any other part of this state. As long as she lasts, I shall not lack a retreat in which to give up the ghost, sufficient to banish my regret for any other retreat.

Not because Socrates said it, but because it is really my feeling, and perhaps excessively so, I consider all men my compatriots, and embrace a Pole as I do a Frenchman, setting this national bond after the universal and common one. I am scarcely infatuated with the sweetness of my native air. Brand-new acquaintances that are wholly of my own choice seem to me to be well worth those other common chance acquaintances of the neighborhood. Friendships purely of our own acquisition usually surpass those to which community of climate or of blood bind us. Nature has put us into the world free and unfettered; we imprison ourselves in certain narrow districts, like the kings of Persia, who bound themselves never to drink any other water than that of the river Choaspes, stupidly gave up their right to use any other waters, and dried up all the rest of the world as far as they were concerned.

What Socrates did near the end of his life, in considering a sentence of exile against him worse than a sentence of death, I shall never, I think, be so broken or so strictly at-

tached to my own country as to do. These divine lives have
enough aspects that I embrace more by esteem than by
affection. And there are also some so lofty and extraordinary
that I cannot embrace them even by esteem, inasmuch as I
cannot understand them. That was a very fastidious attitude
for a man who considered the world his city. It is true that
he disdained peregrination and had scarcely set foot outside
the territory of Attica. What are we to say of his grudging
his friends' money to save his life, and refusing to get out of
prison by the intervention of others, so as not to disobey the
laws, and that at a time when they were so thoroughly corrupt? These examples are of the first type for me. Of the
second type are others that I could find in this same person.
Many of these rare examples exceed my power of performing, but some even exceed my power of judging.

Besides these reasons, travel seems to me a profitable exercise. The mind is continually exercised observing new and
unknown things; and I know no better school, as I have
often said, for forming one's life, than to set before it constantly the diversity of so many other lives, ideas, and customs, and to make it taste such a perpetual variety of forms
of our nature. In it the body is neither idle nor overworked,
and this moderate movement makes it limber.

I stay on horseback, though I have the colic, without dis-
mounting and without pain, for eight or ten hours,

> *Beyond the strength and lot of age.*
> [Virgil]

No season is hostile to me except the fierce heat of a burning
sun; for umbrellas, which Italy has used since the ancient
Romans, burden the arm more than they relieve the head. I
should like to know what device the Persians had so long

ago, in the infancy of luxury, to make themselves a fresh breeze and shade at their pleasure, as Xenophon relates. I love rain and mud like a duck. Change of air and climate has no effect on me; all skies are alike to me. Only the inward troubles that I produce in myself get the better of me, and they attack me less when I travel.

I am hard to set in motion; but once under way, I go as far as anyone wants. I balk as much at little undertakings as at great ones, and at getting equipped for a day's trip and a visit to a neighbor as for a real journey. I have learned to make my day's journeys Spanish fashion, at a single stage: long and sensible stages; and in extreme heat I make them by night, from sunset to sunrise. The other way, of eating your dinner on the way in haste and confusion, is inconvenient, especially on short days. My horses are the better for it. Never has a horse failed me that could make the first day's trip with me. I water them everywhere, and only see to it that they have enough road left to settle their water. My laziness in getting up gives my attendants time to dine at their ease before starting. As for me, it is never too late for me to eat; appetite comes to me as I eat, and not otherwise; I am never at all hungry except at table.

Some people complain of my taking pleasure in continuing this exercise, married and old as I am. They are wrong. It is a better time to leave your family when you have set it on the way to go on without you, when you have left it in an order that will not belie its past arrangement. It is a much greater imprudence to go away, leaving in your house a less faithful guardian, who will have less care to provide for your needs.

The most useful and honorable science and occupation for a woman is the science of housekeeping. I know some that are miserly, very few that are good managers. This is her ruling quality, which a man should seek before any other, as the only dowry that serves to ruin or save our houses. Don't tell me! From what experience has taught me, I require of a married woman, above all other virtues, the virtues of a good housewife. I place my wife in a position to show these, leaving the entire government in her hands by my absence. It irritates me to see in many households Monsieur coming home around noon, fretful and dirty from the mill of business, when Madame is still busy doing her hair and fixing herself up in her boudoir. That is for queens to do; and I'm not even sure about that. It is ridiculous and unfair that the idleness of our wives should be supported by our sweat and toil. No one, if I can help it, shall have readier, quieter, and freer enjoyment of my property than myself. If the husband provides the matter, Nature herself wills that the wife provide the form.

As for the duties of marital love that some people consider injured by absence, I do not believe it. On the contrary, it is a relationship that is readily cooled by too continual association, and harmed by assiduity. Every strange woman seems to us an attractive woman. And every man feels by experience that seeing one another continually cannot match the pleasure of parting and being together again at intervals. These interruptions fill me with a fresh love for my family and give me back a sweeter enjoyment of my home. Alternation warms my appetite for both alternatives.

I know that friendship has arms long enough to hold and join from one end of the world to the other; and especially this kind, in which there is a continual interchange of services, which reawaken the bond and memory of it. The Stoics indeed say that there is so great a tie and fellowship between the sages that the one who dines in France feeds his comrade in Egypt; and that if one merely extends his finger, wherever he is, all the sages on the habitable earth feel help from it.

Enjoyment and possession are principally a matter of imagination. It embraces more warmly what it is in quest of than what we have at hand, and more continually. Count up your daily musings, and you will find that you are most absent from your friend when he is in your company; his presence relaxes your attention and gives your thoughts liberty to absent themselves at any time and for any reason.

From the distance of Rome I keep and control my house and the goods I have left behind there; I see my walls, my trees, and my revenue grow and decrease, within two inches, just as when I am there:

My house appears before my eyes, and forms of places loved.
[Ovid]

If we enjoy only what we touch, farewell to our crowns when they are in our coffers, and our children if they are off hunting. We want them nearer. In the garden—is that far? Half a day away? What about ten leagues—is that far or near? If it is near, what about eleven, twelve, thirteen, and so on, step by step? Truly, if there is a woman who will prescribe to her husband after how many steps ends the near, and with how many steps begins the far, I would advise her to stop him in between:

Let's set an end, and with debate have done . . .
I use my freedom, and subtract your units, one by one,
As bit by bit I might pluck out hairs from a horse's tail,
Till by reduction to the absurd my arguments prevail.
[Horace]

And let them boldly call philosophy to their aid, which someone might accuse—since it sees neither one end nor the other of the joint between too much and too little, long and short, light and heavy, near and far, since it cannot recognize either the beginning or the end of it—of being a very uncertain judge of the middle. *Nature has given us no knowledge of the limits of things.* [Cicero]

Are they not still wives and mistresses of the deceased, who are not at the end of this world, but in the other world? We embrace both those who have been and those who are not yet, not merely the absent. We have not made a bargain, in getting married, to keep continually tied to each other by the tail, like some little animals or other that we see, or like the bewitched people of Karenty, in dog-like fashion. And a woman should not have her eyes so greedily fixed on the front of her husband that she cannot see the back of him, if need be.

But may not this remark of that most excellent painter of their humors be applicable here, to show the cause of their complaints?

If you are late, your wife assumes you're having an affair
With someone, or someone with you, drinking, banishing
     care;
That you alone have all the fun, she all the ills to bear.
                    [Terence]

Or might it not be that opposition and contradiction are in themselves meat and drink to them, and that they are comfortable enough provided they make you uncomfortable?

In true friendship, in which I am expert, I give myself to my friend more than I draw him to me. I not only like better to do him good than to have him do good to me, but also to have him do good to himself than to me; he does me most good when he does himself good. And if absence is pleasant or useful to him, it is much sweeter to me than his presence; and it is not really absence when we have means of communication. In other days I have made use and advantage of our separation. We filled and extended our possession of life better by separating: he lived, he enjoyed, he saw for me, and I for him, as fully as if he had been there. One part of us remained idle when we were together; we were fused into one. Separation in space made the conjunction of our wills richer. This insatiable hunger for bodily presence betrays a certain weakness in the enjoyment of souls.

As for my old age, which they bring up against me, it is, on the contrary, for youth to be enslaved to public opinion and to constrain itself for the sake of others. It can give satisfaction to both, to the public and to itself; we have only too much to do to satisfy ourselves alone. As natural comforts fail us, let us sustain ourselves with artificial ones. It is unjust to excuse youth for following its pleasures and forbid old age to seek any. Young, I covered up my blithe passions with prudence; old, I disperse my sad ones by dissipation. Besides, the Platonic laws prohibit traveling before the age of forty or fifty, to make the travel more useful and instructive. I should more willingly agree to the second article of the same laws, which forbids it after sixty.

"But at such an age you will never return from so long a journey." What do I care? I undertake it neither so as to return from it nor so as to complete it; I undertake only to move about while I like moving. And I walk for the sake of walking. Those who run after a benefice or a hare do not run; they only run who run at prisoner's base and to practice running.

My plan is everywhere divisible; it is not based on great hopes; each day's journey forms an end. And the journey of my life is conducted in the same way. However, I have seen enough distant places where I should have liked to be detained. Why not, if Chrysippus, Cleanthes, Diogenes, Zeno, Antipater, so many sages of the surliest sect, left their country indeed with no cause for complaint about it, and solely for the enjoyment of a different atmosphere? Truly the greatest trouble with my peregrinations is that I cannot bring to them a resolution to fix my abode wherever I please, and that I must always be thinking of coming back, to conform to popular feelings.

If I was afraid to die in any other place than that of my birth, if I thought I would die less comfortably away from my family, I should scarcely go out of France; I should not go out of my parish without terror. I feel death continually clutching me by the throat or the loins. But I am not made that way: death is the same to me anywhere. However, if I had the choice, it would be, I think, rather on horseback than in a bed, and out of my house, away from my people.

There is more heartbreak than consolation in taking leave of our friends. I willingly forget that duty of our courtesy, for of all the duties of friendship that is the only unpleasant one; and I would forget just as willingly to bid that great eternal farewell. If some advantage is derived from this audience, there are a hundred disadvantages. I have seen many dying men pitifully besieged by all this throng: the crowd stifles them. It is contrary to duty, and testimony of scant affection and scant concern, to let you die in peace: one torments your eyes, another your ears, another your tongue; there is not a sense or a part of you that they do not shatter.

Your heart is wrung with pity to hear the laments of your friends, and perhaps with anger to hear other laments that are feigned and counterfeit. A man who has always had fastidious tastes finds them more so when he is in a weakened condition. In such great need he must have a gentle hand, suited to his feelings, to scratch him just where he itches; otherwise he should not be touched at all. If we need a wise woman [1] to bring us into the world, we certainly need a still wiser man to help us out of it. Such a man, and a friend to boot, should be purchased at any price to assist us on such an occasion.

I have not attained that disdainful vigor which finds fortitude in itself, which nothing can either aid or disturb; I am a peg lower. I try to burrow and hide from this passing, not through fear, but through design. It is not my idea to prove or display my fortitude in this act of dying. For whom? Then will end all my right to reputation and my interest in it. I am content with a collected, calm, and solitary death, all my own, in keeping with my retired and private life. In contrast with the Roman superstition, which considered a man unfortunate who died without speaking and who did not have his nearest relatives to close his eyes, I have enough to do to console myself without having to console others, enough thoughts in my head without having circumstances bring me new ones, and enough matter for reflection without borrowing it. Dying is not a role for society; it is the act of one single character. Let us live and laugh among our friends, let us go die and look sour among strangers. You will find, if you pay, someone who will turn your head, rub your feet, who will not trouble you any more than you want, showing

---

[1] *Sage-femme*, literally "wise woman," means midwife.

you an indifferent face, letting you reflect and lament as you like.

Day by day I rid myself by reflection of that childish and inhuman humor that makes us want to arouse compassion and mourning in our friends by our misfortunes. We make more of our troubles than they are worth, to draw their tears. And the firmness in supporting misfortune that we praise in all men, we blame and reproach in our friends when the misfortune is our own. We are not content that they should be aware of our woes, unless they are also afflicted by them.

We should spread joy, but repress sadness as much as we can. He who asks for pity without reason is a man not to be pitied when there is reason. To be always lamenting for ourselves is the way never to be lamented, putting on a pitiful act until we are pitiable to no one. He who acts dead when still alive is subject to be thought alive when dying. I have seen some people get angry to be told that their color was good and their pulse even; I have seen them restrain their laughter because it betrayed their recovery, and hate health because it was not pitiable. What is more, they were not women.

I represent my ailments, at most, just as they are, and avoid words of foreboding and deliberate exclamations. If not cheerfulness, at least a composed countenance is appropriate in people attending a sick sage. Just because he sees himself in the opposite condition, he does not pick a quarrel with health; he likes to contemplate it strong and whole in others, and enjoy it at least by association. Just because he feels himself slipping, he does not utterly reject the thoughts of life, nor avoid ordinary conversation. I want to study sickness when I am healthy; when it is on me, it makes its impression real enough, without the help of my imagination. We prepare ourselves beforehand for the journeys we undertake, and are resolved on them; the time when we are to take horse we leave to our companions and put it off for them.

I feel this unexpected profit from the publication of my behavior, that to some extent it serves me as a rule. Sometimes there comes to me a feeling that I should not betray the story of my life. This public declaration obliges me to keep on my path, and not to give the lie to the picture of my qualities, which are normally less disfigured and contradicted than might be expected from the malice and disease of the judgments of today. The uniformity and simplicity of my behavior indeed produces an appearance easy to interpret, but, because the manner of it is a bit new and unusual, it gives too fine a chance to calumny. Yet the fact is, it seems to me, that to anyone who wants to abuse me fairly I give plenty to bite on in my known and avowed imperfections, and enough to gorge on, without skirmishing with the wind. If it seems to him that by beating him to the accusation and revelation myself I am drawing the teeth of his mordancy, it is reasonable that he exercise his right of amplification and extension (attack has rights beyond justice), that he magnify into trees the vices whose roots I show him in myself, and that he use for this not only those that possess me, but also those that merely threaten me. Harmful vices, both in quality and number; let him beat me with them.

I would frankly follow the example of the philosopher Bion. Antigonus was trying to taunt him on the subject of his origin; he cut him short. "I am," he said, "the son of a slave, a butcher, branded, and of a whore whom my father married because of the baseness of his condition. Both were punished for some misdeed. An orator bought me when I was a child, finding me attractive, and when he died, left me all his possessions. Having transported them to this city of Athens, I devoted myself to philosophy. Let not historians be at a loss in seeking information about me; I will tell them all about it." Free and generous confession takes the edge off reproach and disarms slander.

Yet the fact remains that all in all, it seems to me that I am as often praised as dispraised beyond reason. Even as it seems to me also that from my youth, in rank and degree of honor, I have been given a place rather above than below what I am entitled to.

I should be more at home in a country where these orders of precedence were either regulated or despised. Among men, as soon as an altercation over precedence in walking or sitting goes beyond three replies, it is uncivil. I have no fear of ceding or preceding unfairly to avoid such a bothersome argument; and never did a man covet my right to go first but that I yielded it to him.

Besides this profit that I derive from writing about myself, I hope for this other advantage, that if my humors happen to please and suit some worthy man before I die, he will try to meet me. I give him a big advantage in ground covered; for all that long acquaintance and familiarity could have gained for him in several years, he can see in three days in this record, and more surely and exactly.

Amusing notion: many things that I would not want to tell anyone, I tell the public; and for my most secret knowledge and thoughts I send my most faithful friends to a bookseller's shop.

We bare our hearts to scrutiny.

[Persius]

If by such good signs I knew of a man who was suited to me, truly I would go very far to find him; for the sweetness of harmonious and agreeable company cannot be bought too dearly, in my opinion. Oh, a friend! How true is that old saying, that the enjoyment of one is sweeter and more necessary than that of the elements of water and fire!

To return to my story, there is thus no great hardship in dying far off and alone. Indeed we think it a duty to retire for natural actions less unsightly and less hideous than this. But besides, those who are reduced to dragging out a long, lingering life, ought perhaps not to wish to involve a large family in their misery. Therefore the Indians in a certain province thought it just to kill a man who had fallen into such straits; in another province abandoned him alone to keep alive however he could.

To whom do they not finally make themselves annoying and insupportable? Ordinary duties do not go so far. You teach your best friends perforce to be cruel, hardening both wife and children by long habit not to feel and pity your woes any more. The groans of my colic no longer cause emotion in anyone. And even if we derived some pleasure from their company (which does not always happen, because of the disparity of conditions which easily produces contempt or envy of anyone whatever), is it not too much to take advantage of this for a long period of time? The more I saw them cheerfully restraining themselves for my sake, the more I should be sorry for their pain. We have a right to lean, but not to lie down so heavily, on others, nor to find our support in their ruin. Like the man who had little children's throats cut to use their blood to cure a disease of his own. Or that other, who was furnished with tender young girls to keep his old limbs warm at night, and mingle the sweetness of their breath with the sourness and unpleasantness of his. I should be prone to recommend Venice to myself for retirement in such a feeble condition of life.

Decrepitude is a solitary quality. I am sociable to excess; yet it seems reasonable to me that henceforth I should withdraw my troublesome self from the sight of the world and brood on it by myself, that I should shrink back and withdraw into my shell like a tortoise. I am learning to see men without clinging to them; that would be an outrage in so steep a pass. It is time to turn my back on company.

"But on such a long journey you will be forced to stop miserably in some hovel where you will lack everything." Most of the necessary things I carry around with me. And then, we cannot escape Fortune if she decides to attack us. I need nothing extraordinary when I am sick; what Nature cannot do for me, I do not want to have done by a pill. At the very beginning of my fevers and the maladies that lay me low, while still whole and in the neighborhood of health, I reconcile myself with God by the last Christian offices, and find myself thereby more free and unburdened, feeling all the more triumphant over the sickness. Of notary and counsel I have less need than of physicians. What affairs of mine I shall not have settled when quite well, let no one expect me to settle when sick. What I mean to do for the service of death is always done; I should not dare delay it a single day. And if there is nothing done, that means either that doubt has put off my choice—for sometimes not to choose is to choose well—or that I have quite decided to do nothing.

I write my book for few men and for few years. If it had been durable matter, it would have had to be committed to a more stable language.[1] In view of the continual variation that has prevailed in ours up to now, who can hope that its present form will be in use fifty years from now? It slips out of our hands every day, and has halfway changed since I have been alive. We say that at this moment it is perfected. Every century says as much of its own. I have no mind to think that of it as long as it flees and changes form as it does. It is for the good and useful writings to nail it to themselves, and its credit will go as go the fortunes of our state.

Therefore I do not fear to insert a number of personal items, whose usefulness will not extend beyond this generation, and which touch on things particularly known to some who will see further into them than those of ordinary understanding. After all this I do not want people to go on debating, as I often see them troubling the memory of the dead: "He thought thus, he lived thus; he wanted this; if he had spoken as he was dying, he would have said, he would have given. . . . I knew him better than anyone else." Now, as far as decency allows me, I here make known my inclinations and feelings; but I do so more freely and willingly by word of mouth to anyone who wishes to be informed of them. At all events, in these memoirs, if you look around you will find that I have said everything, or suggested everything. What I cannot express I point to with my finger:

> *But if you have a penetrating mind,*
> *These little tracks will serve the rest to find.*
>
> [Lucretius]

I leave nothing about me to be desired or guessed. If people are to talk about me, I want it to be truly and justly. I would

---

[1] Latin.

willingly come back from the other world to give the lie to any man who portrayed me other than I was, even if it were to honor me. Even the living, I perceive, are spoken of as other than they really are. And if I had not supported with all my strength a friend that I lost, they would have torn him into a thousand contrasting appearances.

To finish telling my feeble humors, I confess that in my travels I hardly ever come to my lodgings without the question passing through my mind whether I could be sick and dying there in comfort. I want to be lodged in a place that I will have all to myself, not noisy, or dirty, or smoky, or stuffy. I try to humor death by these frivolous circumstances, or rather to relieve myself of any other complications, so that I can give my attention exclusively to it, which will easily weigh me down enough without any other load. I want death to have a share in the ease and comfort of my life. It is a great and important part of it, and from this day forth I hope that it will not belie the past.

Death has some shapes that are easier than others, and assumes different characteristics according to each man's fancy. Among natural deaths, that which comes from enfeeblement and stupor seems to me gentle and pleasant. Among violent ones, I picture less comfortably falling from a precipice than being crushed by a falling building, and a piercing sword thrust than a musket shot; and I would rather have drunk the potion of Socrates than stabbed myself like Cato. And, though it is all one, yet my imagination feels as great a difference between throwing myself into a fiery furnace and into the channel of a shallow river, as between death and life. So foolishly does our fear consider the means more than the result! It is only an instant; but it is so important that I would willingly give several days of my life to go through it in my own way.

Since each man's fancy finds differences of more or less in its bitterness, since each man has some choice between forms of dying, let us try a little further to find one that is free from all unpleasantness. Might we not make it even voluptuous, as did the "Partners in Death" of Antony and Cleopatra? I leave aside the harsh and exemplary achievements of philosophy and religion. But among men of little account there have been some, such as a Petronius and a Tigillinus in Rome, who, pledged to kill themselves, put death as it were to sleep by the comfort of their preparations. They made it flow and glide past amid the laxity of their customary pastimes, among wenches and gay companions: no talk of consolation, no mention of a will, no ambitious affectation of constancy, no discourse about their future state, but amidst games, feasting, jests, common and ordinary conversation, music, and amorous verse. Could we not imitate this resoluteness with more decent behavior? Since there are deaths good for fools, deaths good for wise men, let us find some that are good for people in between.

My imagination shows me death in an easy, and, since we must die, a desirable light. The Roman tyrants thought they were giving his life to a criminal when they gave him the choice of his death. But was not Theophrastus, a philosopher so delicate, modest, and wise, forced by reason to speak this line, Latinized by Cicero:

Fortune, not wisdom, rules the life of man.

How Fortune helps the facility of the bargain of my life, having placed it in such a position that henceforth it is neither necessary nor a hindrance to anyone! It is a condition that I would have accepted at any season of my life, but now that it is time to pack up my odds and ends and strap my bags, I take most particular pleasure in giving scarcely any pleasure or displeasure to anyone by dying. It has contrived, by an artful compensation, that those who can hope for some material profit from my death will receive at the same time a material loss from it. Death often weighs heavier on us by its weight on others, and pains us by their pain almost as much as by our own, and sometimes even more.

Among the comforts I seek in lodgings I do not include pomp or grandeur—rather, I hate them—but a certain simple cleanliness which is more often met with in places where there is less art, and which Nature honors with a certain charm that is all her own. *A meal where not abundance but neatness prevails.* [Quoted by Nonius] *More wit than expense.* [C. Nepos]

And then, it is for those whom business drags in winter through the Grisons, to be surprised on the road by this extremity. I, who travel most often for my pleasure, do not direct myself so badly. If it looks ugly on the right, I take the left; if I find myself unfit to ride my horse, I stop. And in so doing I truly see nothing that is not as pleasant and comfortable as my own house. It is true that I find superfluity always superfluous, and feel objections even amid delicacy and abundance. Have I left something unseen behind me? I go back; it is still on my road. I trace no fixed line, either straight or crooked. Do I fail to find what I had been told about, in the place I go? As it often happens that the judgments of others do not agree with mine—and I have found them more often wrong—I do not regret my trouble; I have learned that what they told me about was not there.

I have as adaptable a constitution and as catholic tastes as any man in the world. The divergency in customs from one nation to another affects me only with the pleasure of variety. Each custom has its reason. Let there be plates of tin, wood, or earthenware, boiled meat or roast, butter or nut oil or olive oil, hot or cold food, it is all one to me, and so much one that, as I grow old, I find fault with this liberal capacity, and feel a need that fastidiousness and choice should check the indiscriminateness of my appetite and relieve my stomach from time to time.

When I have been outside of France and people have asked me, out of courtesy, if I wanted to be served in French fashion, I have laughed at the idea and made straight for the tables thickest with foreigners. I am ashamed to see my countrymen besotted with that stupid disposition to shy away from ways contrary to their own; they think they are out of their element when they are out of their village. Wherever they go, they stick to their ways and abominate foreign ones. Do they find a compatriot in Hungary, they celebrate this adventure: see them rally round and join forces, and condemn all the barbarous customs that they see. Why not barbarous, since they are not French? Still, these are the keenest ones, who have noticed them enough to abuse them. Most of them take the trip only for the return. They travel covered and wrapped in a taciturn and incommunicative prudence, defending themselves from the contagion of an unknown atmosphere.

What I am saying about these men reminds me of what I have sometimes observed, in a similar situation, in some of our young courtiers. They stick exclusively with men of their own sort, and look upon us as people from the other world, with contempt or pity. Take away from them their talk of the mysteries of court, and they are out of their field, as green and clumsy to us as we are to them. It is very truly said that a well-bred man is an all-round man.

On the contrary, I travel very fed up with our own ways, not to look for Gascons in Sicily—I have enough of them at home; I rather look for Greeks and Persians; these men I talk to, I study; that is where I lend and apply myself. And what is more, it seems to me that I have encountered hardly any customs that are not as good as ours. I am not risking much, for I have hardly been out of sight of my weather-vanes.

For the rest, most of the chance company you meet on the road is more of a nuisance than a pleasure. I do not stay with it, especially now that old age sets me somewhat alone and apart from the common formalities. You suffer for others, or others for you; both discomforts are painful, but the latter seems to me even harsher. It is rare good fortune, but inestimably comforting, to have a well-bred man, of sound intelligence and ways that conform with yours, who likes to go with you. I have missed such a man extremely on all my travels. But such company must have been chosen and acquired before you leave home.

No pleasure has any savor for me without communication. Not even a merry thought comes to my mind without my being vexed at having produced it alone without anyone to offer it to. *If wisdom were given me on this condition, that I keep it hidden and unuttered, I should reject it.* [Seneca] The other had raised it a tone higher: *If such a life were granted a wise man that, with an abundance of all things pouring in, he could have full leisure to consider and contemplate everything worth knowing, still, if his solitude were such that he could never see a human being, he would abandon life.* [Cicero] I like the idea of Archytas, that it would be unpleasant to be even in heaven and to wander among those great and divine celestial bodies, without the presence of a companion.

But still it is better to be alone than in boring and foolish company. Aristippus liked to live as a stranger everywhere.

> *If fate permitted me my life to guide*
> *As I myself decide,*
>
> [Virgil]

I should choose to spend it with my rear in the saddle:

> *Eager to see*
> *Where the sun's fires hold revelry,*
> *Where clouds and rains sport humidly.*
>
> [Horace]

"Have you no more comfortable pastimes? What do you lack? Is not your house open to fine healthy air, sufficiently furnished, and more than sufficiently capacious? Royal majesty with all its pomp put up there more than once. Are there not more families below yours in orderliness than there are above it in eminence? Is there some local consideration, extraordinary and indigestible, that ulcerates in you?

> *Which, planted in your breast, burns and torments you?*
> [Ennius]

Where do you think you can exist without constraint and without disturbance? *Fortune never grants unmixed favors.* [Q. Curtius] Then realize that you are the only one who constrains you, and that you will follow yourself everywhere, and be sorry for yourself everywhere. For there is no satisfaction here below except for souls either brutish or divine. If a man finds no contentment with such just occasion for it, where does he expect to find it? For how many thousands of men does such a condition as yours constitute the limit of their desires? Reform yourself alone, for in that your power is complete, whereas your only right toward Fortune is patience. *There is no peace and quiet except that which reason has contrived.* [Seneca]"

I see the reasonableness of this admonition, and see it perfectly well; but it would have been quicker and more to the point to tell me in a word: "Be wise." This resolution is beyond wisdom; it is her work and her product. The physician does thus who keeps shouting at a poor languishing patient to be cheerful; he would be advising him a little less stupidly if he told him: "Be well." For my part, I am but a man of the lower sort. A salutary precept, definite, and easy to understand, is: "Be content with what is yours; that is to say, with reason." Yet the execution of it is no more in the power of the wisest men than in mine. It is a popular saying, but terribly far-reaching; what does it not comprehend? All things are subject to distinction and qualification.

I know well that if you take it literally, this pleasure in traveling is a testimony of restlessness and instability. And indeed these are our ruling and predominant qualities. Yes, I confess, I see nothing, even in a dream or a wish, that I could hold myself to; variety alone satisfies me, and the enjoyment of diversity, at least if anything satisfies me. In traveling, my fondness for it is increased by the very fact that I can stop without loss, and that I have a place where I can turn away from it comfortably.

I love a private life because it is by my own choice that I love it, not because of unfitness for public life, which is perhaps just as well suited to my nature. I serve my prince the more gaily because it is by the free choice of my judgment and my reason, without private obligation, and because I am not thrown back on it and constrained to it by being unacceptable and unwelcome to every other party. So with the rest. I hate the morsels that necessity carves for me. Any advantage on which I had to depend exclusively would have me by the throat.

> *Let one oar row in water, the other on the shore.*
> [Propertius]

A single cord never keeps me in place. "There is vanity," you say, "in this amusement." But where is there not? And these fine precepts are vanity, and all wisdom is vanity. *The Lord knoweth the thoughts of the wise, that they are vain.* [Corinthians] These exquisite subtleties are only fit for preaching; they are arguments that would send us all saddled into the other world. Life is a material and corporeal movement, an action which by its very essence is imperfect and irregular; I apply myself to serving it in its own way:

> *We suffer each in his own spirit.*
> [Virgil]

We must so act as not to oppose the universal laws of nature; but, these being safeguarded, let us follow our own nature. [Cicero]

What is the use of these lofty peaks of philosophy on which no human being can sit down, and these rules that exceed our strength and our use? I often see people propose to us patterns of life which neither the proposer nor his hearers have any hope of following, nor, what is more, any desire to follow. From this same sheet of paper on which he has just written the sentence against an adulterer, the judge steals a scrap for a billet-doux to his colleague's wife. The lady you have just been rubbing against in illicit intercourse, will presently, in your very presence, cry out more bitterly against the same fault in her friend than would Portia.[1] And some condemn men to die for crimes that they do not even regard as faults. In my youth I have seen a gentleman offer the public with one hand verses excelling both in beauty and in licentiousness, and with the other at the same moment the most contentious work on theological reform that the world has feasted on for a long time.

This is the way men are. We let laws and precepts go their own way, we take another; not only through dissolute habits, but through a contrary opinion and judgment. Listen to a philosophical lecture: the inventiveness, the eloquence, the pertinence immediately strike your mind and stir you; there is nothing that tickles or pricks your conscience; they are not speaking to her, are they? Yet Aristo used to say that neither a bath nor a lesson is any use unless it cleans and scours. You can linger on the bark, but only after you have extracted the pith; just as after swallowing the wine out of a beautiful cup we examine its engraving and workmanship.

In all the barracks of ancient philosophy you will find this, that the same workman publishes rules of temperance, and publishes at the same time amorous and licentious writings. And Xenophon, in the bosom of Clinias, wrote against Aristippic sensuality. It is not that there is some miraculous conversion stirring them by fits and starts. But it is this: that Solon represents himself now as himself, now in the shape of a lawgiver; now he speaks for the crowd, now for himself;

---

[1] Portia, daughter of Cato, who killed herself on learning of the death of her husband Brutus at Philippi.

and for himself he takes the free and natural rules, feeling sure of firm and complete health.

> *Let great physicians cure the dangerous ills.*
>
> [Juvenal]

Antisthenes permits the sage to love, and to do in his own way whatever he finds opportune, without attention to the laws, inasmuch as he is better advised than they, and has more knowledge of virtue. His disciple Diogenes said to oppose reason to perturbations; to fortune, confidence; to laws, nature.

For delicate stomachs we need strict and artificial diets. Good stomachs simply follow the prescriptions of their natural appetite. So do our doctors, who eat the melon and drink the new wine while they keep their patient tied down to syrups and slops.

"I do not know about their books," said the courtesan Laïs, "or their wisdom, or their philosophy, but those men knock at my door as often as any others." Since our licentiousness always carries us beyond what is lawful and permitted, men have often made the precepts and laws of our life strict beyond universal reason.

> *None thinks he sins enough unless he sins a bit*
> *Further than your permit*
>
> [Juvenal]

It would be desirable that there should be more proportion between the command and the obedience; and a goal that we cannot reach seems unjust. There is no man so good that if he placed all his actions and thoughts under the scrutiny of the laws, he would not deserve hanging ten times in his life even such a man that it would be a very great loss and very unjust to punish and destroy him.

> *Olus, what is it to thee*
> *What he does with his skin, or she?*

[Martial]

And one man might not offend the laws at all, who would not for all that deserve in any degree to be praised as a virtuous man, and whom philosophy would very justly cause to be whipped: so confused and uneven is this relationship.

We have no chance of being good men according to God; we cannot be so according to ourselves. Human wisdom never yet came up to the duties that she herself had prescribed for herself, and, if she had come up to them, she would prescribe herself others beyond, to which she would ever aim and aspire, so hostile to consistency is our condition. Man ordains that he himself shall be necessarily at fault. He is not very clever to cut out his own duty by the pattern of a different nature than his own. To whom does he prescribe what he expects no one to do? Is it wrong of him not to do what it is impossible for him to do? The laws which condemn us not to be able, themselves accuse us for not being able.

At worst, this deformed liberty to present ourselves with two sides out, the actions in one style and the speeches in another, may be permissible for those who tell of things; but it cannot be so for those who tell of themselves, as I do; I must go the same way with my pen as with my feet. Life in society should have some relation to other lives. The virtue of Cato was vigorous beyond the measure of his time; and for a man who undertook to govern others, a man dedicated to the public service, it might be said that it was a justice, if not unjust, at least vain and out of season. Even my own conduct, which deviates by hardly an inch from that which is current, nevertheless makes me somewhat unapproachable and unsociable to my generation. I do not know if I am disgusted without reason with the world I frequent, but I do know well that it would be without reason if I complained that it was more disgusted with me than I am with it.

The virtue assigned to the affairs of the world is a virtue with many bends, angles, and elbows, so as to join and adapt itself to human weakness; mixed and artificial, not straight, clean, constant, or purely innocent. The annals to this day reproach one of our kings for having given in too simply to the conscientious persuasions of his confessor. Affairs of state have bolder precepts:

> *Let him who would be pure from courts retire.*
> [Lucan]

I once tried to employ in the service of public dealings ideas and rules for living as crude, green, unpolished—or unpolluted, as they were born in me or derived from my education, and which I use, if not conveniently, at least surely, in private matters: a scholastic and novice virtue. I found them unsuitable and dangerous. He who walks in the crowd must step aside, keep his elbows in, step back or advance, even leave the straight way, according to what he encounters. He must live not so much according to himself as according to others, not according to what he proposes to himself but according to what others propose to him, according to the time, according to the men, according to the business.

Plato says that whoever escapes with clean breeches from handling the affairs of the world, escapes by a miracle. And he also says that when he ordains his philosopher as head of a government, he does not mean to say this of a corrupted government like that of Athens, and much less like ours, on which wisdom herself would waste her Latin. Just as an herb transplanted to a soil very ill-suited to its nature much rather conforms to it than reforms it to suit itself.

I feel that if I had to train myself thoroughly for such occupations, I should need a great deal of change and reclothing for it. Even if I had enough power over myself to do that (and why could I not, with time and pains?), I should not want to. By the little experience I have had in that profession, I am just that much disgusted with it. I sometimes feel rising in my soul the fumes of certain temptations toward ambition; but I stiffen and hold firm against them:

But thou, Catullus, persevere, persist.
[Catullus]

I am seldom summoned to it, and I offer myself to it just as little. Independence and laziness, which are my ruling qualities, are qualities diametrically opposite to that trade.

We are unable to distinguish the faculties of men; they have divisions and boundaries that are delicate and hard to determine. To conclude from the competence of a man's private life some competence for public service is to conclude badly. One man guides himself well who does not guide others well, and produces Essays, who cannot produce results; another directs a siege well who would direct a battle badly, and talks well in private who would be bad at addressing a crowd or a prince. In fact, to be able to do one is perhaps rather evidence of inability to do the other than otherwise. I find that lofty minds are hardly less adaptable to humble things than are humble minds to lofty things. Was it credible that Socrates should have given the Athenians subject for laughter at his expense because he never could count up the votes of his tribe and make a report on them to the council? Truly, the veneration I have for the perfections of that great man deserves that his fortune should furnish such a magnificent example in excuse of my principal imperfections.

Our ability is cut up into little pieces. Mine has no breadth, and besides, is puny in variety. Saturninus said to those who had conferred on him full command: "Comrades, you have lost a good captain to make a bad general."

Whoever boasts, in a diseased age like this, that he employs a pure and genuine virtue in the service of the world, either does not know what such virtue is, since ideas grow corrupt with conduct (indeed, hear them portray it, hear most of them glorying in their behavior and making their rules; instead of portraying virtue, they portray injustice pure and simple, and vice, and present it thus falsified for the education of princes), or, if he does know it, he boasts wrongly, and, say what he will, does a thousand things of which his conscience accuses him. I would willingly take Seneca's word about the experience he had in such circumstances, provided he was willing to tell me about it candidly. The most honorable mark of goodness in such a predicament is to acknowledge freely our fault and that of others, to resist and hold back with all our power the inclination toward evil, to go down that slope reluctantly, to hope for the better and desire the better.

I perceive that in these dismemberments of France and divisions into which we have fallen, each man labors to defend his cause, but, even the best of them, with dissimulation and lying. Whoever would write about them roundly would write about them rashly and harmfully. The justest party is still a member of a worm-eaten and maggotty body. But in such a body the least diseased member is called healthy; and quite rightly, since our qualities have no titles except by comparison. Civic innocence is measured according to the places and the times.

I should like very much to see in Xenophon a eulogy of Agesilaus in this vein: Being asked by a neighboring prince with whom he had once been at war to let him pass across his territories, he granted this, giving him passage across the Peloponnesus; and not only did he not imprison him or poison him, having him at his mercy, but he welcomed him courteously, without doing him any harm. To natures like his, that would not be saying anything; elsewhere and in other times men will take account of the honesty and magnanimity of such an action. The wretched monkeys in our schools would have laughed at it, so little does Spartan innocence resemble French.

We are not without virtuous men, but only by our standards. Whoever has morals established and regulated above his time, either let him twist or blunt his rules, or, what I rather advise him, let him withdraw apart and have nothing to do with us. What would he gain by it?

If I discern a man in holiness and virtue rare,
To a bi-membered child this freak of nature I compare,
Or to a pregnant mule, or fish found 'neath the plowman's
*   share.*

[Juvenal]

We may regret better times, but not escape the present; we may wish for different magistrates, but we must nevertheless obey these that are here. And perhaps there is more merit in obeying the bad than the good. As long as the image of the ancient and accepted laws of this monarchy shines in some corner, you will find me planted there. If by bad fortune they come to contradict and interfere with each other, and produce two sides dubious and difficult to choose between, my choice will be preferably to steal away and escape from that tempest; in the meantime Nature may lend me a hand, or the hazards of war. Between Caesar and Pompey I should have declared myself openly. But among those three robbers who came after, either I should have had to hide, or follow with the wind; which I consider permissible when Reason no longer guides.

> *Whither do you leave the course?*
>
> [Virgil]

This stuffing is a little out of my subject. I go out of my way, but rather by licentiousness than carelessness. My ideas follow one another, but sometimes it is from a distance, and look at each other, but with a sidelong glance. I have run my eyes over a certain dialogue of Plato,[1] a fantastic motley in two parts, the front part about love, all the lower part about rhetoric. They do not fear these changes, and with wonderful grace they let themselves thus roll in the wind, or seem to. The titles of my chapters do not always embrace their matter; often they only denote it by some sign, like those other titles, *Andria, The Eunuch*,[2] or those other names, Sulla, Cicero, Torquatus. I love the poetic gait, by leaps and bounds. It is an art, as Plato says, light, flighty, supernatural. There are works in Plutarch where he forgets his theme, where the treatment of his subject is found only

---

[1] The *Phaedrus*.
[2] Two comedies of Terence.

incidentally, quite smothered in foreign matter. See his wanderings in "The Daemon of Socrates." Lord, what beauty there is in these lusty sallies and this variation, and more so the more casual and accidental they seem. It is the inattentive reader who loses my subject, not I. Some word about it will always be found off in a corner, which will not fail to be sufficient, though it takes little room. I seek out change indiscriminately and tumultuously. My style and my mind alike go roaming. "A man must be a little mad if he does not want to be even more stupid," say both the precepts of our masters, and even more so their examples.

A thousand poets drag and languish prosaically; but the best ancient prose—and I scatter it here indiscriminately as verse—shines throughout with the vigor and boldness of poetry, and gives the effect of its frenzy. To poetry we must certainly concede mastery and pre-eminence in speech. The poet, says Plato, seated on the tripod of the Muses, pours out in a frenzy whatever comes into his mouth, like the spout of a fountain, without ruminating and weighing it; and from him escape things of different colors, contradictory substance, and an interrupted flow. He himself is utterly poetic, and the old theology is poetry, the scholars say, and the first philosophy. It is the original language of the Gods.

I want the matter to make its own divisions. It shows well enough where it changes, where it concludes, where it begins, where it resumes, without interlacing it with words, with links and connections introduced for the benefit of weak or heedless ears, and without writing glosses on myself. Who is there that would not rather not be read than be read sleepily or in passing? *Nothing is so useful that it can be of value when taken in transit.* [Seneca] If to take up books were to take them in, and if to see them were to consider them. and to run through them were to grasp them, I should be wrong to make myself out quite as ignorant as I say I am.

Since I cannot arrest the attention of the reader by weight, it is all to the good if I chance to arrest it by my embroilment. "True, but he will afterwards repent of having wasted his time over it." That may be, but still he will have wasted his time over it. And then there are natures like that, in whom understanding breeds disdain, who will think the better of me because they will not know what I mean; they will conclude that my meaning is profound from its obscurity, which, to speak in all earnest, I hate very deeply, and I would avoid it if I could avoid myself. Aristotle somewhere boasts of affecting it: blameworthy affectation!

Because such frequent breaks between chapters as I used at the beginning seemed to me to disrupt and dissolve attention before it was aroused, making it disdain to settle and collect for so little, I have begun making them longer, requiring fixed purpose and assigned leisure. In such an occupation, if you will not give a man a single hour, you will not give him anything. And you do nothing for a man for whom you do nothing except while doing something else. Besides, perhaps I have some private obligation to speak only by halves, to speak confusedly, to speak discordantly.

I was about to say that I have no use for that kill-joy reason; and that if those extravagant ambitions that torment our lives, and those wondrously subtle ideas, have any truth in them, I consider it too expensive and inconvenient. On the contrary, I apply myself to make use of vanity itself, and asininity, if it brings me any pleasure, and let myself follow my natural inclinations without examining them too closely.

I have seen elsewhere ruined houses, and statues, and sky,

and earth: it is still men. All that is true; and yet I could not revisit the tomb of that great and mighty city [1] so often that I would not marvel at it and revere it. The care of the dead is recommended to us. Now, I have been brought up from childhood with these dead. I had knowledge of the affairs of Rome long before I had any of those of my own house. I knew the Capitol and its location before I knew the Louvre, and the Tiber before the Seine. I have had the qualities and fortunes of Lucullus, Metellus, and Scipio, more in my head than those of any of our men. They are dead. So indeed is my father, as completely as they; and he has moved as far from me and from life in eighteen years as they have in sixteen hundred. Nevertheless I do not cease to embrace and cherish his memory, his friendship, and his society, in a union that is perfect and very much alive.

Indeed, by inclination I pay greater service to the dead. They can no longer help themselves; therefore they need my help all the more, it seems to me. It is here that gratitude shows in its proper luster. A benefit is less richly bestowed when there is reciprocity and return. Arcesilaus, visiting Ctesibius, who was sick, and finding him badly off, very quietly slipped under his pillow some money he was giving him; and by concealing it from him, gave him also release from gratitude. Those who have deserved friendship and gratitude from me have never lost it through being no longer there; I have paid them better and more carefully in their absence and ignorance. I speak more affectionately of my friends when there is no way left for them to know of it.

Now, I have started a hundred quarrels in defense of Pompey and for the cause of Brutus. This friendship still

---

[1] Rome.

endures between us; even present things we hold only by imagination. Finding myself useless for this age, I throw myself back upon that other, and am so bewitched by it that the state of that ancient Rome, free, just, and flourishing (for I love neither her birth nor her old age), interests me passionately. Therefore I cannot revisit so often the site of their streets and houses and those ruins stretching deep down to the Antipodes, that I do not muse over them. Is it by nature or by an error of the imagination that the sight of the places we know were frequented and inhabited by people whose memory is held in honor, somehow stirs us more than hearing the story of their deeds or reading their writings? *Such is the power of places to bring back memories! And in this city this is infinite; for wherever we walk we set our foot on history.* [Cicero] I like to reflect on their faces, their bearing, and their clothes. I chew over those great names between my teeth and make them resound in my ears. *I venerate them and always rise to honor such great names.* [Seneca] Of things that are in some part great and admirable, I admire even the common parts. I would enjoy seeing them talk, walk, and sup. It would be ingratitude to despise the remains and images of so many worthy and most valiant men, whom I have seen live and die, and who give us so many good instructions by their example, if we only knew how to follow them.

And then, this very Rome that we behold deserves our love, allied for so long and by so many claims to our crown: the only common and universal city. The sovereign magistrate who commands there is acknowledged equally elsewhere. It is the metropolitan city of all Christian nations; the Spaniard and the Frenchman, every man is at home there. To be one of the princes of that state one need only be of Christendom, wherever it may be. There is no place here below that heaven has embraced with such favorable influence and such constancy. Her very ruin is glorious and stately.

> *More precious for her memorable ruins.*
> [Sidonius Apollinaris]

Even in the tomb she retains marks and the picture of empire. *That it may be manifest that in one place Nature rejoiced in her work.* [Pliny]

Some might blame themselves and rebel inwardly at being tickled by so vain a pleasure. Our humors are not too vain if they are pleasant; whatever they may be, if they give constant contentment to a man capable of common sense, I would not have the heart to pity him.

I owe much to Fortune in that up to this point she has done nothing hostile to me, at least not more than I could bear. Might it not be her way to leave in peace those who do not trouble her?

> *The more a man himself denies,*
> *The more to that man Heaven supplies.*
> *Since I am naked, I aspire*
> *To join the men who naught desire . . .*
> *For they lack much who much require.*
> [Horace]

If she continues, she will send me hence well contented and satisfied:

> *For nothing more do I annoy the gods.*
> [Horace]

But beware the crash. There are thousands who are wrecked in port.

I easily console myself for what will happen here when I am here no longer; present things keep me busy enough,

The rest I leave to Fortune.

[Ovid]

Besides, I do not have that strong bond that they say attaches men to the future by the children who bear their name and their honor;[1] and perhaps I ought to desire them all the less, if they are so desirable. I am only too much attached to the world by myself. I am content to be in Fortune's grip by the circumstances strictly necessary to my existence, without extending her jurisdiction over me in other directions; and I have never thought that to be without children was a want that should make life less complete and less contented. The sterile profession has its own advantages too. Children are numbered among the things that have no great reason to be desired, especially at this time when it would be so hard to make them good. *Nothing good can be produced now, so corrupted are the seeds.* [Tertullian] And yet they have just reason to be regretted by anyone who loses them after having had them.

He who left me in charge of my house predicted that I was due to ruin it, considering that I was so little of a home body. He was mistaken; here I am as when I first came into it, if not a little better off; yet without public office and without benefice.

For the rest, if Fortune has done me no violent or extraordinary injury, neither has she done me any great favor. All her gifts that my house enjoys were there more than a hundred years before me. For my own part I enjoy no essential and solid benefit that I owe to her liberality. She has done me

---

[1] Montaigne had one daughter, but no sons.

several windy favors, honorary and titular, without substance, and, in truth, did not grant them, but offered them to
me, Lord knows; to me who am wholly material, whom only
reality satisfies, and who, if I dared confess it, should not
judge avarice much less excusable than ambition, nor pain
less to be avoided than shame, nor health less desirable than
learning, nor riches than nobility.

Among her empty favors there is none that gives so much
pleasure to that silly humor in me which feeds upon it, as an
authentic patent of Roman citizenship, which was granted to
me lately when I was there, pompous in seals and gilt letters,
and granted with all gracious liberality. And because these
patents are granted in various styles, more or less favorable;
and because before I had seen one I would have been very
glad to have been shown their formula, I will, to satisfy some
person, if anyone is sick with the same curiosity as mine,
transcribe it here in due form:

*ON THE REPORT MADE TO THE SENATE BY
ORAZIO MASSIMI, MARZO CECIO, ALESSANDRO
MUTI, CONSERVATORS OF OUR FAIR CITY,
CONCERNING THE RIGHT OF ROMAN CITIZEN-
SHIP TO BE GRANTED TO THE MOST ILLUSTRI-
OUS MICHEL DE MONTAIGNE, KNIGHT OF THE
ORDER OF ST. MICHAEL, AND GENTLEMAN OF
THE CHAMBER IN ORDINARY TO THE MOST
CHRISTIAN KING, THE SENATE AND PEOPLE
OF ROME HAVE DECREED:*

*Considering that, by ancient custom and practice, those
men have ever been adopted among us with ardor and
eagerness, who, distinguished in virtue and nobility, have
been useful and ornamental to our Republic, or might be
so in the future; We, moved by the example and authority*

*of our ancestors, resolve that we should imitate and follow
this noble custom. Wherefore, since the most illustrious
Michel de Montaigne, Knight of the Order of St. Michael,
and Gentleman of the Chamber in ordinary to the Most
Christian King, is most zealous for the Roman name, and,
by the honor and distinction of his family and his own
virtuous merits, most worthy to be admitted to Roman
citizenship by the supreme judgment and will of the Senate
and People of Rome: it has pleased the Senate and People
of Rome that the most illustrious Michel de Montaigne,
adorned with all qualities and very dear to this noble
people, should be inscribed as a Roman citizen, himself
and his posterity, and invested with all the advantages and
honors enjoyed by those who were born Citizens and
Patricians of Rome, or who have been made such by the
best of rights. Wherein the Senate and People of Rome
consider that they do not so much confer the Rights of
Citizenship on him as a gift, as pay them as a debt, nor do
him more benefit than they receive from him, who, in
accepting this Citizenship, gives a singular ornament and
honor to the City itself. Which Senatus-Consultus these
Conservators have caused to be transcribed by the secre-
taries of the Roman Senate and People and deposited in
the archives of the Capitol, and have had this act drawn
up and sealed with the common seal of the City. In the
year 2331 since the foundation of Rome, A. D. 1581, 13th
of March.*

Orazio Fosco,
*Secretary of the Sacred Senate
and of the People of Rome.*
Vincente Martoli,
*Secretary of the Sacred Senate
and of the People of Rome.*[1]

---

[1] Montaigne quotes the entire document in the original Latin.

Being a citizen of no city, I am very pleased to be one of the noblest city that ever was or ever will be. If others examined themselves attentively, as I do, they would find themselves, as I do, full of inanity and nonsense. Get rid of it I cannot without getting rid of myself. We are all steeped in it, one as much as another; but those who are aware of it are a little better off—though I don't know.

This common attitude and habit of looking elsewhere than at ourselves has been very useful for our own business. We are an object that fills us with discontent; we see nothing in us but misery and vanity. In order not to dishearten us, Nature has very appropriately thrown the action of our vision outwards. We go forward with the current, but to turn our course back toward ourselves is a painful movement: thus the sea grows troubled and turbulent when it is tossed back on itself. Look, says everyone, at the movement of the heavens, look at the public, look at that man's quarrel, at this man's pulse, at another man's will; in short, always look high or low, or to one side, or in front, or behind you.

It was a paradoxical command that was given us of old by that God at Delphi: "Look into yourself, know yourself, keep to yourself; withdraw your mind and your will, which are spending themselves elsewhere, into themselves; you are running out, you are scattering yourself; concentrate yourself, resist yourself; you are being betrayed, dispersed, and stolen away from yourself. Do you not see that this world keeps its sight concentrated inward and its eyes open to contemplate itself? It is always vanity for you, within and without; but it is less vanity when it is less extensive. Except for you, O man," said that God, "each thing studies itself first, and, according to its needs, has limits to its labors and desires. There is not a single thing as empty and needy as you, who embrace the universe: you are the investigator without knowledge, the magistrate without jurisdiction, and all in all, the fool of the farce."

Of Experience[1]

THERE is no desire more natural than the desire for knowledge. We try all the ways that can lead us to it. When reason fails us we use experience—

> *Experience, by example led,*
> *By varied trials art has bred,*
>
> [Manilius]

—which is a weaker and less dignified means. But truth is so great a thing that we must not disdain any medium that will lead us to it. Reason has so many shapes that we know not which to lay hold of; experience has no fewer. The inference that we try to draw from the resemblance of events is uncertain, because they are always dissimilar: there is no quality so universal, in this aspect of things, as diversity and variety.

Both the Greeks, and the Latins, and ourselves, use eggs for the most evident example of similarity. However, there have been men, and notably one at Delphi, who recognized signs of difference between eggs, so that he never took one for another; and although there were many hens, he could tell which one the egg came from.

Dissimilarity intrudes by itself into our works; no art can attain similarity. Neither Perrozet nor any other can smooth

---

[1] Chapter 13.

and whiten the backs of his cards so carefully that some gamblers will not distinguish them simply by seeing them slip through another man's hands. Resemblance does not make things as much alike as difference makes them unlike. Nature has committed herself to make nothing separate that was not different.

Therefore I do not much like the opinion of the man who thought by a multiplicity of laws to bridle the authority of judges, cutting up their meat for them. He did not realize that there is as much freedom and latitude in the interpretation of laws as in their creation. And those people must be jesting who think they can diminish and stop our disputes by recalling us to the express words of the Bible. For our mind finds the field no less spacious in registering the meaning of others than in presenting its own. And as if there was less animosity and bitterness in commenting than in inventing!

We see how much he was mistaken. For we have in France more laws than all the rest of the world together, and more than would be needed to rule all the worlds of Epicurus: *As formerly we suffered from crimes, so now we suffer from laws.* [Tacitus] And yet we have left so much room for opinion and decision to our judges, that there never was such a powerful and licentious freedom. What have our legislators gained by selecting a hundred thousand particular cases and actions, and applying a hundred thousand laws to them? This number bears no proportion to the infinite diversity of human actions. Multiplication of our imaginary cases will never equal the variety of the real examples. Add to them a hundred times as many more: it still will not happen that a single future event will find one, in all the many, many thousands of selected and recorded events, that will fit and match it so exactly that some circumstance and

difference will not remain, which will require different consideration in judgment. There is little relation between our
actions, which are in perpetual transformation, and fixed and
immutable laws. The most desirable laws are those that are
rarest, simplest, and most general; and I even think that it
would be better to have none at all than to have them in
such numbers as we have.

Nature always gives us happier laws than those we give
ourselves. Witness the picture of the Golden Age of the
poets, and the state in which we see nations live which have
no other laws. Here are some who use, as the only judges in
their quarrels, the first traveler passing through their mountains. And these others on market day elect one of themselves who decides all their suits on the spot. What would
be the danger if the wisest should settle ours in this way,
according to the circumstances and at sight, without being
bound to precedents, past or future? For every foot its own
shoe. King Ferdinand, when he sent colonists to the Indies,
wisely provided that no students of jurisprudence should be
taken there, for fear that lawsuits might breed in this new
world, it being by nature a science generating altercation and
division; judging, with Plato, that lawyers and doctors are a
bad provision for a country.

Why is it that our common language, so easy for any other
use, becomes obscure and unintelligible in contracts and
wills, and that a man who expresses himself so clearly, whatever he says or writes, finds in this field no way of speaking
his mind that is not subject to doubt and contradiction?
Unless it is that the princes of this art, applying themselves
with particular attention to picking out solemn words and
contriving artificial phrases, have so weighed every syllable,
so minutely examined every sort of combination, that here

they are at last entangled and embroiled in the endless number of figures and in such minute partitions that they can no longer come under any rule or prescription or any sure understanding. *What is broken up into dust becomes confused.* [Seneca]

Who has seen children trying to divide a mass of quick-silver into a certain number of parts? The more they squeeze it and knead it and try to constrain it to their will, the more they provoke the independence of this spirited metal; it escapes their skill and keeps dividing and scattering in little particles beyond all reckoning. This is the same; for by sub-dividing these subtleties they teach men to increase their doubts; they start us stretching and diversifying the difficulties, they lengthen them, they scatter them. By sowing questions and cutting them up, they make the world fructify and teem with uncertainty and quarrels, as the earth is made more fertile the more it is crumbled and deeply plowed. *Learning makes difficulties.* [Quintilian]

We were perplexed over Ulpian, we are still perplexed by Bartolus and Baldus. We should have wiped out the traces of this innumerable diversity of opinions, not wear them as decoration and make them go to the heads of posterity.

I do not know what to say about it, but it is evident from experience that so many interpretations disperse the truth and shatter it. Aristotle wrote to be understood; if he did not succeed, still less will another man, less able, and not treating his own ideas. We open up the matter and dissem-inate it when we water it; of one subject we make a thou-sand, and, multiplying and subdividing, fall back into Epi-curus' infinity of atoms. Never did two men judge alike about the same thing, and it is impossible to find two opin-ions exactly alike, not only in different men, but in the same man at different times. Ordinarily I find subject for doubt in what the commentary has not deigned to mention. I am more apt to trip on flat ground, like certain horses I know who stumble more often on a smooth road.

Who would not say that glosses increase doubts and ignorance, since there is no book to be found, whether human or divine, with which the world busies itself, whose difficulties are cleared up by interpretation? The hundredth commentator hands it on to his successor, thornier and rougher than the first one had found it. When do we agree and say: "There has been enough about this book; henceforth there is nothing more to say concerning it"?

This is best seen in law practice. We give legal authority to numberless doctors, numberless decisions, and as many interpretations. Do we therefore find any end to the need of interpreting? Do we see any progress and advance toward tranquillity? Do we need fewer lawyers and judges than when this mass of law was still in its infancy? On the contrary, we obscure and bury the sense; we no longer find it except at the mercy of so many enclosures and barriers.

Man does not know the natural infirmity of his mind: it does nothing but ferret and quest, and keeps incessantly whirling around, building up and becoming entangled in its own work, like our silkworms, and is suffocated in it. *A mouse in a pitch barrel.* [Latin proverb] It thinks it notices from a distance some sort of glimmer of imaginary light and truth; but while it is running toward it, so many difficulties, obstacles, and new quests cross its path, that they lead it off the road and intoxicate it. Not very different from what happened to Aesop's dogs, who, discovering something that looked like a dead body floating in the sea, and being unable to get near it, attempted to drink up this water and dry up the passage, and choked in the attempt. To which may be joined what a certain Crates said of the writings of Heraclitus, that they needed a good swimmer for a reader, so that the depth and weight of his learning should not sink him or drown him.

It is only personal weakness that makes us content ourselves with what others or ourselves have found out in this hunt for knowledge. An abler man will not rest content with it. There is always room for a successor, yes, and for ourselves, and a road in another direction. There is no end to our researches; our end is in the other world. It is a sign of contraction of the mind when it is content, or of weariness. No spirited mind remains within itself; it is always aspiring and going beyond its strength; it has impulses beyond its powers of achievement. If it does not advance and press forward and come to bay and clash, it is only half alive. Its pursuits are boundless and without form; its food is wonder, the chase, ambiguity. Apollo revealed this clearly enough, always speaking to us equivocally, obscurely, and obliquely, not satisfying us, but keeping our minds interested and busy. It is an irregular, perpetual motion, without model and without aim. Its inventions excite, pursue, and produce one another.

> So in a running stream one wave we see
> After another roll incessantly,
> And line by line, each does eternally
> Pursue the other, each the other flee.
> By this one, that one ever on is sped,
> And this one by the other ever led;
> The water still does into water go,
> Still the same brook, but different waters flow.
>
> [La Boétie]

It is more of a job to interpret the interpretations than to interpret the things, and there are more books about books than about any other subject: we do nothing but write glosses about each other. The world is swarming with commentaries; of authors there is a great scarcity.

Is it not the chief and most reputed learning of our times to learn to understand the learned? Is that not the common and ultimate end of all studies?

Our opinions are grafted upon one another. The first serves as a stock for the second, the second for the third. Thus we scale the ladder, step by step. And thence it happens that he who has climbed highest has often more honor than merit; for he has only climbed one grain higher on the shoulders of the next last.

How often and perhaps how stupidly have I extended my book to make it speak of itself! Stupidly, if only for this reason, that I should have remembered what I say of others who do the same: that these frequent sheep's eyes at their own work testify that their heart thrills with love for it, and that even the disdainful rough blows with which they beat it are only the love-taps and mannerisms of maternal fondness; in keeping with Aristotle, to whom self-appreciation and self-depreciation often spring from the same sort of arrogance. For as for my excuse, that I ought to have more freedom in this than others, precisely because I write of myself and my writings as of my other actions, because my theme turns in upon itself—I do not know whether everyone will accept it.

I have observed in Germany that Luther has left as many divisions and altercations over the uncertainty of his opinions, and more, as he raised about the Holy Scriptures.

Our disputes are purely verbal. I ask what is nature, pleasure, circle, and substitution. The question is one of words, and is answered in the same way. "A stone is a body." But if you insisted: "And what is a body?"—"Substance."—"And what is substance?" and so on, you would finally drive the respondent to the end of his lexicon. We exchange one word for another word, often more unknown. I know better what is man than I know what is animal, or mortal, or rational. To satisfy one doubt, they give me three; it is the Hydra's head.

Socrates asked Meno what virtue was. "There is," said Meno, "the virtue of a man and of a woman, of a magistrate and of a private citizen, of a child and of an old man." "That's fine," exclaimed Socrates; "we were in search of one virtue, and here is a whole swarm of them."

We put one question, they give us back a hive of them. As no event and no shape is entirely like another, so none is entirely different from another; an ingenious mixture on the part of Nature. If our faces were not similar, we could not distinguish man from beast; if they were not dissimilar, we could not distinguish man from man. All things hold together by some similarity; every example is lame, and the comparison that is drawn from experience is always faulty and imperfect; however, we fasten together our comparisons by some corner. Thus the laws serve, and thus adapt themselves to each of our affairs, by some roundabout, forced, and twisted interpretation.

Since the ethical laws, which concern the individual duty of each man in himself, are so hard to frame, as we see they are, it is no wonder if those that govern so many individuals are more so. Consider the form of this justice that governs us: it is a true testimony of human imbecility, so full it is of contradiction and error. What we find to be leniency and severity in justice—and we find so much of them that I doubt if the mean between them is met with as often—are diseased parts and defective members of the very body and essence of justice.

Some peasants have just informed me hastily that a moment ago they left in a wood that belongs to me a man wounded in a hundred places, who is still breathing, and who begged them out of pity for some water and to help him to get up. They say that they did not dare go near him, and ran away, for fear that the officers of the law would catch them there, and, as is done with those who are found near a murdered man, that they might be held accountable for this accident, to their total ruin, having neither ability nor money to defend their innocence. What could I say to them? It is certain that this act of humanity would have got them into trouble.

How many innocent people have we discovered to have been punished—I mean without the fault of the judges; and how many have there been that we have not discovered! Here is something that happened in my time. Certain men are condemned to death for a murder; the sentence, if not pronounced, at least decided and determined. At this point the judges are informed by the officers of an inferior court near by that they have some prisoners who clearly confess this murder and throw a decisive light on the whole business. They deliberate whether because of this they should interrupt and defer the execution of the sentence passed upon the first accused. They consider the novelty of the case and its consequence for suspending judgments; that the sentence has been passed according to law, and that the judges have no right to change their minds. In short, these poor devils are sacrificed to the forms of justice.

Philip, or some other, took care of a similar problem in this manner. He had condemned a man, by a definitive judgment, to pay a heavy fine to another. The truth coming to light some time after, it turned out that he had decided unfairly. On one side were the rights of the case, on the other side the rights of judicial forms. He gave some satisfaction to both, letting the sentence stand and compensating the loss of the condemned man out of his own purse. But he was dealing with a reparable accident; my men were irreparably hanged. How many condemnations I have seen which were more criminal than the crime!

All this reminds me of those ancient notions: That a man is forced to do wrong in detail if he wants to do right in gross, and injustice in little things if he wants to achieve justice in great ones; that human justice is formed on the model of medicine, according to which all that is useful is also just and honest; and what the Stoics maintain, that Nature herself goes against justice in most of her works; and what the Cyrenaics maintain, that there is nothing just in itself, that customs and laws shape justice; and the Theodorians, who consider theft, sacrilege, and every sort of lechery just for a wise man, if he knows that it is profitable for him.

There is no remedy. My position, like that of Alcibiades, is this: I shall never turn myself over, if I can help it, to a man who can dispose of my head, where my honor and my life depend on the skill and care of my attorney more than on my innocence. I would risk a kind of justice that would take into account my good deeds as well as my bad, from which I would have as much to hope as to fear. Lack of punishment is not sufficient pay for a man who does better than not doing wrong. Our justice offers us only one of her hands, and the left at that. Whoever he is, he comes off with a loss.

In China, a kingdom whose government and arts, without dealings with and knowledge of ours, surpass what we have to offer in many branches of excellence, and whose history teaches me how much ampler and more varied the world is than either the ancients or ourselves understand, the officers delegated by the prince to inspect the state of his provinces, even as they punish those who are corrupt in their office, also reward, from pure liberality, those who have conducted themselves better than the average and better than the requirements of their duty. People come before them not merely to defend themselves, but to gain by it, and not simply to be paid, but also to receive presents.

No judge has yet, thank God, spoken to me as a judge in any cause whatever, my own or another man's, criminal or civil. No prison has received me, not even for a visit. Imagination makes the sight of one, even from the outside, unpleasant to me. I am so sick for freedom, that if anyone should forbid me access to some corner of the Indies, I should live distinctly less comfortably. And as long as I find earth or air open elsewhere, I shall not lurk in any place where I have to hide. Lord! how ill could I endure the condition in which I see so many people, nailed down to one section of this kingdom, deprived of the right of entrance to the principal towns and the courts and the use of the public roads, for having quarreled with our laws! If those that I serve threatened even the tip of my finger, I should instantly go and find others, wherever it might be. All my little prudence in these civil wars in which we are now involved is employed to keep them from interrupting my freedom of coming and going.

Now laws remain in credit not because they are just, but because they are laws. That is the mystic foundation of their uthority; they have no other. And that is a good thing for them. They are often made by fools, more often by people who, in their hatred of equality, are wanting in equity; but always by men, vain and irresolute authors.

There is nothing so grossly and widely and ordinarily defective as the laws. Whoever obeys them because they are just, does not obey them for just the right reason. Our French laws, by their irregularity and lack of form, rather lend a hand to the disorder and corruption that is seen in their application and execution. Their commands are so confused and inconsistent that they are some excuse for both disobedience and faulty interpretation, administration, and observance.

Then whatever may be the fruit we can reap from experience, that which we derive from foreign examples will hardly be much use for our education, if we make such little profit from the experience we have of ourselves, which is more familiar to us, and certainly sufficient to inform us of what we need.

I study myself more than any other subject. That is my metaphysics, that is my physics.

> *By what art God our home, the world, controls;*
> *Whence the moon rises, where she sets, how rolls*
> *Her horns together monthly, and again*
> *Grows full; whence come the winds that rule the main;*
> *Where Eurus' blast holds sway; whence springs the rain*
> *That ever fills the clouds; whether some day*
> *The citadels of the world will pass away.*
>
> *Inquire, you who the laboring world survey.*
>   [Propertius and Lucan]

In this universe of things I ignorantly and negligently let

myself be guided by the general law of the world. I shall know it well enough when I feel it. My knowledge could not possibly make it change its path; it will not modify itself for me. It is folly to hope it, and greater folly to be troubled about it, since it is necessarily uniform, common, and public. The goodness and capacity of the governor should free us absolutely and fully from worrying about his government.

Philosophical inquiries and meditations serve only as food for our curiosity. The philosophers with much reason refer us to the rules of Nature; but these have no concern with such sublime knowledge. The philosophers falsify them and show us the face of Nature painted in too high a color, and too sophisticated, whence spring so many varied pictures of so uniform a subject. As she has furnished us with feet to walk with, so she has given us wisdom to guide us in life: a wisdom not so ingenious, robust, and pompous as that of their invention, but correspondingly easy and salutary, performing very well what the other talks about, in a man who has the good fortune to know how to occupy himself simply and in an orderly way, that is to say naturally. The more simply we trust to Nature, the more wisely we trust to her. Oh, what a sweet and soft and healthy pillow is ignorance and incuriosity, to rest a well-made head!

I would rather be an authority on myself than on Cicero. In the experience I have of myself I find enough to make me wise, if I were a good scholar. He who calls back to mind the excess of his past anger, and how far this fever carried him away, sees the ugliness of this passion better than in Aristotle, and conceives a juster hatred for it. He who remembers the evils he has undergone, and those that have threatened him, and the slight causes that have changed him from one state to another, prepares himself in that way for future changes and for recognizing his condition. The life of Caesar has no more to show us than our own; an emperor's or an ordinary man's, it is still a life affected by all human accidents. Let us only listen: we tell ourselves all we most need.

He who remembers having been mistaken so many, many times in his own judgment, is he not a fool if he does not distrust it forever after? When I find myself convicted of a false opinion by another man's reasoning, I do not so much learn what new thing he has told me about this particular ignorance—that would be small gain—as I learn my weakness in general, and the treachery of my understanding; whence I derive the reformation of the whole mass. With all my other errors I do the same, and I feel that this rule is very useful for my life. I do not regard the species and the individual, like a stone I have stumbled on; I learn to mistrust my gait throughout, and I strive to regulate it. To learn that we have said or done a foolish thing, that is nothing; we must learn that we are nothing but fools, a far broader and more important lesson.

The slips that my memory has made so often, even when it reassures me most about itself, are not lost on me; there is no use in her swearing to me now and assuring me, I shake my ears. The first opposition offered to her testimony places me in suspense, and I would not dare trust her in any weighty matter, nor guarantee her in another person's affairs. And were it not that what I do for lack of memory, others do still more often for lack of good faith, I should always accept the truth in matters of fact from another man's mouth rather than from my own.

If each man watched closely the effects and circumstances of the passions that dominate him, as I have done with the ones I have fallen a prey to, he would see them coming and would check their impetuosity and course a bit. They do not always leap at our throats at a single bound; there are threats and degrees.

> *As when a rising wind makes white waves fly,*
> *The sea heaves slowly, raises billows high,*
> *And surges from the depths to meet the sky.*
> [Virgil]

Judgment holds in me a magisterial seat, at least it carefully tries to. It lets my feelings go their way, both hatred and friendship, even the friendship I bear myself, without being changed and corrupted by them. If it cannot reform the other parts according to itself, at least it does not let itself be deformed to match them; it plays its game apart.

The advice to everyone to know himself must have an important effect, since the God of learning and light had it planted on the front of his temple, as comprising all the counsel he had to give us. Plato also says that wisdom is nothing else but the execution of this command, and Socrates, in Xenophon, verifies it in detail.

The difficulties and obscurity in any science are seen only by those who have access to it. For a man needs at least some degree of intelligence to be able to notice that he does not know; and we must push against a door to know that it is closed to us. Whence arises this Platonic subtlety, that neither those who know need inquire, because they know, nor those who do not know, since in order to inquire they must know what they are inquiring about. Thus in this matter of knowing oneself, the fact that everyone is seen to be so cocksure and self-satisfied, that everyone thinks he understands enough about himself, signifies that everyone understands nothing about it, as Socrates teaches Euthydemus in Xenophon.

I, who make no other profession, find in me such infinite depth and variety, that what I have learned bears no other fruit than to make me realize how much I still have to learn. To my weakness, so often recognized, I owe the inclination I have to modesty, obedience to the beliefs that are prescribed me, a constant coolness and moderation in my opinions, and my hatred for that aggressive and quarrelsome arrogance that believes and trusts wholly in itself, a mortal enemy of discipline and truth. Hear them laying down the law: the first stupidities that they advance are in the style in which men establish religions and laws. *Nothing is more discreditable than to have assertion and proof precede knowledge and perception.* [Cicero]

Aristarchus used to say that in former times there were scarcely seven wise men in the world, and that in his time there were scarcely seven ignorant men. Would we not have more reason than he to say that in our time? Affirmation and opinionativeness are express signs of stupidity. This man must have fallen on his nose a hundred times in one day; there he stands on his "ergos," as positive and unshaken as before. You would think that someone had since infused in him some sort of new soul and intellectual vigor, and that he was like that ancient son of the earth, who renewed his courage and strength by his fall:

> *Whose limbs, however tired,*
> *By touching Mother Earth, with energy were fired.*
> [Lucan]

Does not this headstrong incorrigible think that he picks up a new mind by picking up a new argument?

It is from my experience that I affirm human ignorance, which is, in my opinion, the most certain fact in the school of the world. Those who will not conclude their own ignorance from so vain an example as mine, or as theirs, let them recognize it through Socrates, the master of masters. For the philosopher Antisthenes would say to his pupils: "Let us go, you and I, to hear Socrates; there I shall be a pupil with you." And, maintaining this doctrine of the Stoic sect, that virtue was enough to make a life fully happy and free from need of anything whatever, he would add: "Excepting the strength of Socrates."

This long attention that I devote to studying myself trains me also to judge passably of others, and there are few things of which I speak more felicitously and excusably. It often happens that I see and distinguish the characters of my friends more exactly than they do themselves. I have astonished at least one by the pertinency of my description, and have given him information about himself. By having trained myself from my youth to see my own life mirrored in that of others, I have acquired a studious bent in that subject, and when I am thinking about it, I let few things around me escape which are useful for that: countenances, humors, statements. I study everything: what I must flee, what I must follow. So I reveal to my friends, by their outward manifestations, their inward inclinations; not in order to arrange this infinite variety of actions, so diverse and so disconnected, into certain types and categories, and distribute my lots and divisions distinctly into recognized classes and sections:

> *How many kinds there are, their titles manifold,*
> *We are not told.*

[Virgil]

The scholars distinguish and mark off their ideas more specifically and in detail. I, who see no farther into things than practice informs me, without any system, present my ideas in a general way, and tentatively. As in this: I speak my meaning in disjointed parts, as something that cannot be said all at once and in a lump. Relatedness and conformity are not found in low and common minds such as ours. Wisdom is a solid and integral structure, each part of which holds its place and bears its mark. *Wisdom alone is wholly directed toward itself*. [Cicero] I leave it to artists, and I do not know if they will achieve it in a matter so complex, minute, and accidental, to arrange into bands this infinite diversity of aspects, to check our inconsistency and set it down in order. Not only do I find it hard to link our actions with one another, but each one separately I find hard to designate properly by some principal characteristic, so two-sided and motley do they seem in different lights.

What is remarked as rare in Perseus, King of Macedonia, that his mind, sticking to no one condition, kept wandering through every type of life and portraying such a flighty and erratic character that neither he nor anyone else knew what kind of a man he was, seems to me to apply to nearly everybody. And above all men, I have known another of his stature [1] to whom this conclusion would apply still more properly, I think: no middle positions, always being carried away from one extreme to the other by causes impossible to guess; no kind of course without being crossed and changing direction amazingly; no quality unmixed; so that the most likely portrait of him that men will be able to make some

---

[1] Presumably Henry IV of France.

day, will be that he affected and studied to make himself known by being unknowable.

We need very strong ears to hear ourselves judged frankly; and because there are very few who can endure it without its biting, those who venture to undertake this for us show a remarkable act of friendship; for to undertake to wound and offend a man for his own good is to have a healthy love for him. I find it a harsh task to judge a man in whom the bad qualities exceed the good. Plato prescribes three qualities in a man who wants to examine another man's soul: knowledge, good will, boldness.

Sometimes people used to ask me what I would have thought myself good for, if anyone had thought of using me while I was young enough:

> *While better blood gave strength, before the snows*
> *Of envious age were sprinkled on my brows.*
>
> [Virgil]

"For nothing," I said. And I readily excuse myself for not knowing how to do anything that would enslave me to others. But I would have told my master home truths, and watched over his conduct, if he had been willing. Not in general, by schoolmasterly lessons, which I do not know—and I see no true reform spring from them in those who know them—but by observing his conduct step by step, at every opportunity, judging it at sight, piece by piece, simply and naturally, making him see how he stands in public opinion, and opposing his flatterers.

There is not one of us who would not be worse than the kings if he was as continually spoiled as they are by that rabble. How otherwise, if Alexander, that great man both as king and as philosopher, could not defend himself against them?

I should have had enough fidelity, judgment, and independence for that. It would be a nameless office; otherwise it would lose its effect and its grace. And it is a part that cannot be played indiscriminately by anyone. For truth itself does not have the privilege to be used at any time and in any way; its use, noble as it is, has its circumscriptions and limits. It often happens, as the world goes, that people blurt it out into a prince's ear not only fruitlessly, but harmfully, and even unjustly. And no one will make me believe that a righteous remonstrance cannot be applied wrongfully, and that the interest of the substance must not often yield to the interest of the form.

For this occupation I should want a man who is content with his fortune,

> *Who would be what he is, and nothing else prefers,*
> [Martial]

and born to a middle rank; because on the one hand he would have no fear to touch his master's heart deeply and to the quick, at the risk of losing his preferment thereby; and on the other hand, being of middle station, he would have easier communication with all sorts of people. I would have this an office for one man alone, for to spread the privilege of this freedom and intimacy among several would engender a harmful irreverence. And certainly I should require of that man, above all, the fidelity of silence.

A king is not to be believed when he boasts of his constancy in awaiting the shock of the enemy for the sake of his glory, if, for his own good and improvement, he cannot endure the freedom of a friend's words, which have no other power than to sting his ears, the rest of their effect being in his own hands. Now, there is no class of men that has as great need as they of true and frank admonitions. They suffer a public life, and have to suit the opinions of so many spectators, that, since people have formed the habit of concealing from them anything that disturbs their plans, they find themselves, without realizing it, involved in the hatred and detestation of their people, often for reasons that they could have avoided at no sacrifice, even of their pleasures, if they had been advised of it and set right in time. Ordinarily their favorites look out for themselves more than for their master; and this serves them well, for in truth most of the duties of true friendship are hard and dangerous to attempt toward a sovereign; so that there is need, not only of much affection and frankness, but of much courage as well.

In fine, all this fricassee that I am scribbling here is nothing but a record of the essays of my life, which, for spiritual health, is exemplary enough if you take its instruction in reverse. But as for bodily health, no one can furnish more useful experience than I, who offer it pure, not at all corrupted or altered by art or theorizing. Experience is really on its own dunghill in the subject of medicine, where reason yields it the whole field. Tiberius used to say that whoever had lived twenty years should be responsible to himself for the things that were harmful or beneficial to him, and be able to take care of himself without medical aid. And he might have learned this from Socrates, who, advising his disciples, carefully and as a principal study, the study of their health, used to add that it was unlikely that an intelligent man who was careful about his exercise, his drinking, and his eating, should not know better than any doctor what was good or bad for him.

And indeed, medicine professes always to have experience as a touchstone for its workings. So Plato was right in saying that to be a true doctor it would be necessary for the aspirant to have passed through all the illnesses that he wants to cure and all the accidents and circumstances that he is to diagnose. It is reasonable that he should catch the pox if he wants to know how to treat it. Truly I should trust such a man. For the others guide us like the man who paints seas, reefs, and ports while sitting at his table, and sails the model of a ship there in complete safety. Throw him into the real thing, and he does not know how to go about it. They make a description of our diseases like that of a town crier proclaiming a lost horse or dog: such and such a coat, such and such a height, such and such ears; but present it to him, and he does not know it for all that.

For heaven's sake, let medicine some day give me some good perceptible relief, and you will see how I shall cry out in good earnest:

> *At last I yield to an efficient science.*
>
> [Horace]

The arts that promise to keep our bodies in health and our souls in health promise us much; but at the same time there are none that keep their promise less. And in our time those who profess these arts among us show the results of them less than any other men. The most you can say for them is that they sell medicinal drugs; but that they are doctors you cannot say.

I have lived long enough to give an account of the practice that has guided me so far. For anyone who wants to try it I have tasted it like his cupbearer. Here are a few items, as memory supplies me with them. I have no habit that has not varied according to circumstances, but I record here those that I have seen most frequently in action, which have had most hold on me up to this moment.

My way of life is the same in sickness as in health; the same bed, the same hours, the same food serve me, and the same drink. I make no adjustments at all, save for moderating the amount according to my strength and appetite. Health for me is maintaining my accustomed state without disturbance. Do I see that sickness dislodges me in one direction? If I trust the doctors, they will turn me aside in another. Whether by fortune or by art, there I am off my road. I believe nothing with more certainty than this: that I cannot possibly be hurt by the use of things that I have been so long accustomed to.

It is for habit to give form to our life, just as it pleases; it is all-powerful in that; it is Circe's drink, which varies our nature as it sees fit. How many nations, and three steps from us, regard as ridiculous the fear of the night dew, which appears so hurtful to us; and our boatmen and peasants laugh at it. You make a German sick if you put him to bed on a mattress, like an Italian on a feather-bed, and a Frenchman without curtains and a fire. A Spaniard's stomach cannot stand our way of eating, nor ours to drink Swiss fashion.

A German pleased me at Augsburg by attacking the disadvantages of our fireplaces by the same argument we ordinarily use to condemn their stoves. For in truth, that stifling heat and the smell of that heated material they are made of give most of those who are not used to them a headache; not me. But after all, this heat being even, constant, and general, without light, without smoke, without the wind that the opening of our chimneys brings us, it has good grounds in other respects for comparison with ours.

Why do we not imitate the Roman architecture? For they say that in ancient times the fire was made only outside their houses, and at the foot of them; whence the heat entered the entire dwelling by pipes, contrived in the thickness of the walls that surrounded the rooms that were to be warmed. This I have seen clearly indicated, I don't know where, in Seneca.

This German, hearing me praise the comforts and beauties of his city, which certainly deserves it, began to sympathize with me because I had to leave it; and one of the first discomforts he mentioned to me was the heavy-headedness that the fireplaces elsewhere would cause me. He had heard someone make this complaint, and associated it with us, being disabled by habit from noticing it at home.

All heat that comes from fire makes me feel weak and heavy. Yet Evenus said that the best condiment of life was fire. I prefer any other way of escaping from the cold.

We are afraid of the wine at the bottom of the cask; in Portugal its flavor is considered delicious, and it is the drink of princes.

In short, each nation has many customs and habits that are not only unknown, but savage and miraculous to some other nation.

What shall we do with this people that admits none but printed testimony, that does not believe men unless they are in a book, nor truth unless it is of competent age? We dignify our stupidities when we put them in print. It carries very different weight with this people to say "I have read it" than if you say "I have heard it." But I, who do not disbelieve men's mouths any more than their hands, and who know that people write just as injudiciously as they speak, and who esteem this age just like another that is past, I quote a friend of mine as readily as Aulus Gellius or Macrobius, and what I have seen as what they have written. And, as they maintain that virtue is no greater for being of longer standing, likewise I hold that truth is no wiser for being older. I often say that it is pure stupidity that makes us run after foreign and scholarly examples. There is as great an abundance of them in this age as in that of Homer and Plato. But is it not true that we seek rather the honor of quoting than the truth of the argument? As if it were greater to borrow our proofs from the shop of Vascosan or Plantin [1] than from what may be seen in our own village. Or rather, indeed, that we have not the wit to examine and put to use what happens before our eyes, and to judge it keenly enough to make it an example? For if we say we lack authority to gain credence for our testimony, we say so without reason. For in my opinion, from the most ordinary, commonplace, familiar things, if we could put them in their proper light, can be formed the greatest miracles of Nature and the most wondrous examples, especially in the subject of human actions.

Now, in my subject, leaving aside the examples that I know through books, and what Aristotle says about Andro of Argos, that he crossed the arid sands of Libya without drinking, a gentleman, who has acquitted himself worthily in several charges, said in my presence that he had gone from Madrid to Lisbon in midsummer without drinking. He is in vigorous health for his age, and has nothing extraordinary about his way of life except this, that he will go two or three months, even a year, so he told me, without drinking. He feels some thirst, but he lets it pass, and maintains that it is an

---

[1] Two famous printers of Montaigne's day.

appetite that easily grows languid by itself; and he drinks more for caprice than for need or for pleasure.

Here is another. It was not long ago that I found one of the most learned men in France, and a man of no mean fortune, studying in the corner of a hall, which had been partitioned off for him with hangings; and around him an unrestrained hubbub of his servants. He told me, and Seneca said much the same thing of himself, that he derived profit from this racket, as if, battered by this noise, he withdrew and concentrated in himself better for contemplation, and that this storm of voices drove his thoughts inward. While a student at Padua, he had for so long a time a study exposed to the rattle of coaches and the tumult of the square that he trained himself not only to disregard the noise but to use it for the benefit of his studies. Socrates replied to Alcibiades, who wondered how he could endure the perpetual din of his wife's scolding: *Like those who are accustomed to the ordinary sound of wheels drawing water.* I am quite the opposite; my mind is sensitive and ready to take flight; when it is absorbed in itself, the slightest buzz of a fly is the death of it.

Seneca, in his youth, having bitten hard on Sextius' example of eating nothing that had been killed, got along without it for a year with pleasure, as he says. And he left off only so as not to be suspected of borrowing this rule from certain new religions that were disseminating it. At the same time, from the precepts of Attalus he adopted this one, not to sleep any more on yielding mattresses; and continued to use, even in his old age, those which do not yield to the body. What the practice of his time makes him reckon as austerity, ours makes us consider effeminacy.

Look at the difference between the life of my manual

laborers and my own. The Scythians and Indians are in no respect more remote from my powers and ways. I know I have taken boys out of begging into my service, who soon after have left me, my kitchen, and their livery, just to return to their former life. And I found one of them afterwards picking up mussels in the dump heap for his dinner, and neither by entreaties nor by threats could I tear him away from the savor and sweetness he found in indigence. Beggars have their luxuries and sensual pleasures as well as rich men, and, it is said, their political dignities and orders.

These are results of habit. It can shape us not only into whatever form it pleases (therefore, say the sages, we must choose the best form, which habit will promptly make easy for us), but also make us ready for change and variation, which is the noblest and most useful of its teachings. The best of my bodily qualities is that I am flexible and not very stubborn. I have inclinations that are more personal and customary, and more agreeable to me, than others; but with very little effort I turn away from them, and easily slip into the opposite habit. A young man should violate his own rules to arouse his vigor and keep it from growing moldy and lax. And there is no way of life so stupid and feeble as that which is conducted by rules and discipline.

> *If he would drive a mile from town, he looks to bookish*
>   *lore*
> *To set the time; if but a corner of his eye is sore,*
> *He scans his stars, and gets the salve then only, not before.*
>   [Juvenal]

He will even plunge often into excess, if he will take my advice; otherwise the slightest dissipation will ruin him, and he will become awkward and disagreeable in company. The most unsuitable quality for a gentleman is over-fastidiousness and bondage to certain particular ways; and they are particular if they are not pliable and supple. It is shameful for a man to keep from doing what he sees his companions do, because he cannot or dare not. Let such men stick to their kitchens. In anyone else it is unbecoming, but in a military man it is bad and intolerable; he, as Philopoemen said, should get accustomed to every change and vicissitude of life.

Although I was trained as much as possible for freedom and adaptability, yet it is a fact that through carelessness, having lingered more in certain ways as I grow old (my age is past training and henceforth has nothing to consider except holding its own), habit has already so imprinted its stamp upon me imperceptibly in certain things that I call it excess to depart from it. And I cannot, without an effort, sleep by day, or eat between meals, or breakfast, or go to bed without a long interval, of about three full hours, after supper, or beget children except before sleeping, or beget them standing, or endure my sweat, or quench my thirst with pure water or pure wine, or remain bareheaded for long, or have my hair cut after dinner; and I would feel as uncomfortable without my gloves as without my shirt, or without washing when I leave the table or get up in the morning, or without canopy and curtains for my bed, as I would be without really necessary things. I could dine without a tablecloth; but very uncomfortably without a clean napkin, German fashion; I soil them more than they or the Italians do, and make little use of spoon or fork. I am sorry that people have not carried on a fashion that I saw begun, after the example of kings, of changing napkins, like plates, with each course. We are told of that hard-working soldier Marius that as he grew old he grew fastidious in his drinking, and drank only out of one particular cup of his. I too indulge my preference for a glass of a certain shape and do not willingly drink from a common glass, any more than I like to be served by a common hand. I dislike all metal compared with a clear and transparent material. Let my eyes also taste, according to their capacity.

I owe many such squeamish traits to habit. Nature too, for her part, has brought me her share: such as no longer being able to stand two full meals a day without overloading my stomach, nor complete abstinence from one of those meals without filling myself with wind, drying up my mouth, and numbing my appetite; and suffering from too long exposure to the night air. For during the last few years, at war duties, when the whole night passes in them, as commonly happens, after five or six hours my stomach begins to trouble me, as well as violent headaches, and I do not last until daytime without vomiting. As the others are going to breakfast I go to sleep, and after that I am as gay as before.

I had always understood that the evening dew fell only at nightfall, but being long and familiarly associated these past years with a lord who was imbued with the belief that the dew is sharper and more dangerous as the sun is going down, an hour or two before it sets, when he carefully avoids it, despising the night dew, he nearly imprinted me not so much with his opinion as with his feeling.

What shall we say of the fact that even doubt and inquiry strikes our imagination and changes us? Those who yield suddenly to these propensities bring total ruin upon themselves. And I am sorry for several gentlemen who, by the stupidity of their doctors, have made prisoners of themselves, though still young and sound in health. It would still be better to endure a cold than to lose forever through disuse the enjoyment of social life by giving up so general a practice. A troublesome science, that discredits the pleasantest hours of the day. Let us extend our possession to our utmost means. Most often we toughen ourselves if we persist, and correct our constitutions, as Caesar did his epilepsy, by despising it and fighting it. We should apply ourselves to the best rules, but not enslave ourselves to them, unless to those, if any there are, to which bondage and slavery is useful.

Both kings and philosophers defecate, and ladies too. Public lives are owed to ceremony; mine, obscure and private, enjoys every natural dispensation; a soldier and a Gascon, those are also qualities a bit subject to indiscretion. Wherefore I will say this about that action: that we should relegate it to certain prescribed nocturnal hours, and force and subject ourselves to them by habit, as I have done; but not subject ourselves, as I have done as I grew old, to any concern for a particularly comfortable place and seat for this function, and make it a nuisance by slowness and fastidiousness.

And yet in the dirtiest functions is it not somewhat excusable to require more care and cleanliness? *Man is by nature a clean and dainty animal.* [Seneca] Of all natural functions that is the one that I can least willingly endure to have interrupted. I have seen many soldiers inconvenienced by the irregularity of their bowels; mine and I never fail the moment of our rendezvous, which is when I jump out of bed, unless some violent occupation or illness disturbs us.

I have no idea then, as I was saying, where sick men can better find safety than in keeping quietly to the way of life in which they have been brought up and trained. Change of any sort is disturbing and hurtful. Go ahead and believe that chestnuts hurt a native of Périgord or of Lucca, or milk and cheese the mountaineers. They keep prescribing for sick men a way of life not only new, but contrary: a change that a healthy man could not endure. Prescribe water to a seventy-year-old Breton, shut up a seaman in an over-heated room, forbid a Basque footman to take walks. You deprive them of movement, and in the end, of air and light.

> *Is it so great a thing to be alive?*
> [Anonymous]

> *Obliged to wean our souls from things on which they thrive,*
> *We give up living, just to keep alive.*
> *Should they be said to live who cannot breathe free air*
> *Or see the light, without oppressive care?*
> [Maximianus]

If they do no other good, they do at least this, that they prepare their patients early for death, undermining little by little and cutting off their enjoyment of life.

Both in health and in sickness I have readily let myself follow my urgent appetites. I give great authority to my desires and inclinations. I do not like to cure trouble by trouble; I hate remedies that are more of a nuisance than the disease. To be subjected to the stone and subjected to abstaining from the pleasure of eating oysters, those are two troubles for one. The disease pinches us on one side, the rule on the other. Since there is a risk of making a mistake, let us risk it rather in pursuit of pleasure. The world does the opposite, and thinks nothing beneficial that is not painful; it is suspicious of ease.

My appetite, in many cases, has of its own accord suited and adapted itself rather happily to the health of my stomach. Sharpness and pungency in sauces were pleasant to me when I was young; my stomach growing irritated by them since, my taste promptly followed suit. Wine hurts sick people; it is the first thing that my mouth finds distasteful, and with an invincible distaste. Whatever I take with dislike hurts me, and nothing hurts me that I do with hunger and zest; I have never received harm from any action that was really pleasant to me. And yet I have made all the conclusions of medicine, very extensively, give way to my pleasure. And in my youth,

> *When Cupid, flitting round me to and fro*
> *In yellow tunic, shed his radiant glow,*
>
> > [Catullus]

I lent myself as licentiously and thoughtlessly as any other man to the desire that held me in its grip,

> *And fought my battles not without distinction;*
>
> > [Horace]

more, however, in continuation and endurance than in violence:

> *I scarce remember lasting up to six.*
>
> > [Ovid]

It is certainly distressing and miraculous to confess at what a tender age I first chanced to fall under its subjection. It was indeed by chance, for it was long before the age of choice and knowledge. I do not remember about myself so far back. And my lot may be coupled with that of Quartilla, who had no memory of her maidenhood.

> *Hence goatish smells, precocious hair,*
> *A beard to make my mother stare.*
>
> > [Martial]

The physicians ordinarily adjust their rules beneficially to the violence of the sharp cravings that come upon sick people; no great desire can be imagined that is so strange and vicious that nature is not involved in it. And then how much it is to satisfy the imagination! In my opinion that faculty is all-important, at least more important than any other. The most grievous and ordinary troubles are those that fancy loads upon us. I like this Spanish saying from several points of view: *God defend me from myself.* I am sorry, when I am sick, that I do not have some desire that would give me the pleasure of satisfying it; medicine would hardly deter me from it. It is the same when I am well; I see scarcely anything more to hope and wish for. It is pitiful to be languid and enfeebled even in our desires.

The art of medicine is not so fixed that we are without authority, no matter what we do; it changes according to the climates and according to the moons, according to Fernel and according to L'Escale. If your physician does not think it good for you to sleep, to use wine or such and such a food, don't worry: I'll find you another who will not agree with him. The variety of medical arguments and opinions includes all kinds of forms. I saw a wretched patient fainting and dying with thirst in order to be cured, and being laughed at later by another doctor who condemned that advice as harmful. Had he not put his pain to good use? A man of that trade died recently of the stone, who had used extreme abstinence to combat his illness; his colleagues say that on the contrary this fasting had dried him up and baked the gravel in his kidneys.

I have noticed that when I am wounded or sick, talking excites me and hurts me as much as any irregularity I may commit. It is costly and tiring for me to use my voice, for it is loud and strained; so that when I have come to hold the ear of the great with affairs of weight, I have often put them to the trouble of asking me to moderate my voice.

This story deserves a digression: Someone in a certain Greek school was speaking loudly, as I do; the master of ceremonies sent him word to speak lower. "Let him send me," he said, "the tone in which he wants me to speak." The other replied that he should take his tone from the ears of the person he was speaking to. That was well said, provided it is understood to mean: "Speak according to your business with your hearer." For if it means: "Enough that he hear you," or "Be guided by him," I do not think it is right. The tone and movement of the voice is expressive and significant, in my opinion; it is for me to guide it to make myself understood.

There is a voice for instructing, a voice for flattering, or for scolding. I want my voice not only to reach him, but perhaps to strike him and pierce him. When I berate my footman in a sharp and bitter tone, it would be fine if he should say to me: "Master, speak lower, I can hear you." *There is a kind of voice adapted to the hearing, not by its volume, but by its quality.* [Quintilian] Speech belongs half to the speaker, half to the listener. The latter must prepare to receive it according to the motion given it. As among tennis-players, the receiver moves and makes ready according to the motion of the striker and the nature of the stroke.

Experience has further taught me this, that we ruin ourselves by impatience. Troubles have their life and their limits, their illnesses and their health.

The constitution of diseases is patterned after that of animals. They have their destiny, limited from their birth, and their days. He who tries to cut them short imperiously by force, in the midst of their course, prolongs and multiplies them, and stimulates them instead of appeasing them. I agree with **Crantor**, that we must neither obstinately and heedlessly oppose evils nor weakly succumb to them, but give in to them naturally, according to their condition and our own. We should give free passage to diseases; and I find that they do not stay so long with me, who let them go ahead; and I have shaken off some, of those that are considered most stubborn and tenacious, by their own decadence, without help and without art, and against the rules of medicine. Let us give Nature a chance; she knows her business better than we do. "But so and so died of it." So will you, if not of that disease, of some other. And how many have not failed to die of it, with three physicians at their backsides? Example is a hazy mirror, reflecting all things in all ways. If it is a pleasant medicine, take it; it is always that much present gain. I shall never balk at the name or the color, if it is delicious and appetizing. Pleasure is one of the principal kinds of profit.

I have allowed colds, gouty discharges, looseness, palpitations of the heart, headaches, and other ailments to grow old and die a natural death within me; I lost them when I had half trained myself to harbor them. They are conjured better by courtesy than by defiance. We must meekly suffer the laws of our condition. We are born to grow old, to grow weak, to be sick, in spite of all medicine. That is the first lesson that the Mexicans give their children, when, as soon as they come out of their mother's womb, they greet them thus: "Child, you have come into the world to endure; endure, suffer, and keep quiet."

It is unjust to complain that what may happen to anyone has happened to someone. *Complain if anything has been unjustly decreed against you alone.* [Seneca] Look at an old man who is praying God to keep him in complete and **vigorous** health, that is to say, to restore his youth.

> *Fool, why aspire in vain with childish prayers?*
> [Ovid]

Is it not madness? His condition does not allow it. The gout, the stone, indigestion, are symptoms of length of years, as are heat, rains, and winds, of long journeys. Plato does not believe that Aesculapius was at any pains to attempt by treatment to prolong life in a wasted and feeble body, useless to its country, useless to its calling and for producing healthy robust children; and he does not consider such concern consistent with divine justice and forethought, which should guide all things toward utility. My good man, it is all over. No one can put you on your feet again; at most they will plaster and prop you up a bit, and prolong your misery an hour or so:

> *Like one who, wishing to support a while*
> *A tottering building, props the creaking pile,*
> *Until one day the house, the props, and all*
> *Together with a dreadful havoc fall.*
>
> [Maximianus]

We must learn to endure what we cannot avoid. Our life is composed, like the harmony of the world, of contrary things, also of different tones, sweet and harsh, sharp and flat, soft and loud. If a musician liked only one kind, what would he have to say? He must know how to use them together and blend them. And so must we do with good and evil, which are consubstantial with our life. Our existence is impossible without this mixture, and one group is no less necessary for it than the other. To try to kick against nat-

ural necessity is to imitate the folly of Ctesiphon, who undertook a kicking match with his mule.

I do little consulting about the ailments I feel, for these
doctors are domineering when they have you at their mercy.
They scold at your ears with their forebodings. And once,
catching me weakened by illness, they treated me insultingly
with their dogmas and magisterial frowns, threatening me
now with great pains, now with approaching death. I was
not floored by them or dislodged from my position, but I
was bumped and jostled. If my judgment was neither
changed nor confused by them, it was at least bothered. It is
still agitation and struggle.

Now I treat my imagination as gently as I can, and would
relieve it, if I could, of all trouble and conflict. We must
help it and flatter it, and fool it if we can. My mind is suited
to this service; it has no lack of plausible reasons for all
things. If it could convince as well as it preaches, it would
help me out very happily.

Would you like an example? It tells me that it is for my
own good that I have the stone; that buildings of my age
must naturally suffer some leakage. It is time for them to
begin to grow loose and give way. It is a common necessity
—otherwise would it not have been a new miracle in my
favor? Thereby I pay the tribute due to old age, and I could
not get a better bargain.—That the company should console
me, since I have fallen into the commonest ailment of men
of my time of life. On all sides I see them afflicted with the
same type of disease, and their society is honorable for me,
since it preferably attacks the great; it is essentially noble and
dignified.—That of the men who are stricken by it there
are few that get off more cheaply; and at that, they pay the
penalty of an unpleasant diet and the daily taking of loath-

some medicinal drugs, whereas I am indebted solely to my good fortune. For a few ordinary broths of eryngo and rupture-wort that I have swallowed two or three times to please the ladies, who, more graciously than my pain is bitter, offered me half of theirs, seemed to me as easy to take as they were useless in their effect. The others have to pay a thousand vows to Aesculapius, and as many crowns to their doctor, for the easy and abundant outflow of gravel which I often get through the kindness of Nature. Even the propriety of my behavior in ordinary company is not disturbed by it, and I can hold my water ten hours and as long as anyone.

"Fear of this disease," says my mind, "used to terrify you, when it was unknown to you; the cries and despair of those who make it worse by their lack of fortitude engendered in you a horror of it. It is an affliction that punishes those of your members by which you have most sinned. You are a man of conscience:

> *Punishment undeserved gives pain.*

[Ovid]

Consider this chastisement; it is very gentle in comparison with others, and paternally affectionate. Consider its lateness; it only bothers and occupies the season of your life which in any case is henceforth wasted and barren, having yielded, as if by agreement, to the licentiousness and pleasures of your youth.

"The fear and pity that people feel for this illness is a subject of vainglory for you; a quality of which, even if you have purged your judgment and cured your reason of it, your friends still recognize some tincture in your makeup. There is pleasure in hearing people say about you: There indeed is strength, there indeed is fortitude! They see you sweat in agony, turn pale, turn red, tremble, vomit your very blood, suffer strange contractions and convulsions, sometimes shed great tears from your eyes, discharge thick, black, and dreadful urine, or have it stopped up by some sharp rough stone that cruelly pricks and flays the neck of your penis; meanwhile keeping up conversation with your company with a normal countenance, jesting in the intervals with your servants, holding up your end in a sustained conversation, making excuses for your pain and minimizing your suffering.

"Do you remember those men of past times who sought out troubles with such great hunger, to keep their virtue in trim and in practice? Put the case this way, that Nature is bearing and driving you into that glorious school, which you would never have entered of your own free will. If you tell me that it is a dangerous and mortal disease, what others are not? For it is a doctor's trick to except some, which they say do not lead in a straight line to death. What does it matter if they go there by accident and slip and deviate easily toward the road that leads us there?

"But you do not die of being sick, you die of being alive. Death kills you well enough without the help of illness. And illnesses have put off death for some, who have lived longer for thinking that they were on their way out and dying. Furthermore, there are diseases, as there are wounds, that are medicinal and salutary.

"The stone is often no less fond of life than you. We see men in whom it has continued from their childhood up to their extreme old age; and if they had not deserted it, it was ready to accompany them still further. You kill it more often than it kills you; and even if it set before you the picture of imminent death, would it not be a kind service for a man of that age to bring him home to meditations on his death?

"And what is worse, you have no reason left for being cured. In any case, the common fate will call you any day. Consider how artfully and gently she weans you from life and detaches you from the world; not forcing you with tyrannical subjections, like so many other afflictions that you see in old people, which keep them continually fettered and without relief from infirmities and pains, but by warnings and instructions repeated at intervals, alternating with long pauses for rest, as if to give you a chance to meditate and repeat her lesson at your leisure. To give you a chance to form a sound judgment and make up your mind to it like a brave man, she sets before you the condition of your entire lot, both good and bad, and a life that on the same day is now very joyous, now unbearable. If you do not embrace death, at least you shake hands with it once a month. Whereby you have the further hope that it will catch you some day without a threat, and that, being so often led to the port, confident that you are still within the accustomed limits, some morning you and your confidence will have crossed the water unawares. We have no cause for complaint about illnesses that divide the time fairly with health."

I am obliged to fortune for assailing me so often with the same kind of weapons. She fashions and trains me against them by use, hardens and accustoms me. Henceforth I know just about at what cost I shall be quit of them.

For lack of a natural memory I make one of paper, and as some new symptom occurs in my disease, I write it down. Whence it comes about that at the present moment, having passed through virtually every sort of experience, if some grave stroke threatens me, by glancing through these little disconnected notes like the Sibyl's leaves, I never fail to find grounds for comfort in some favorable prognostic from my past experience.

Familiarity also serves to give me better hopes for the future. For this process of evacuation having continued so long, it is probable that Nature will not change this course and that no worse accident will come of it than that which I feel. Besides, the nature of this disease is not ill-suited to my hasty and impetuous disposition. When it assails me mildly it frightens me, for that means for long. But by nature it has vigorous and violent spurts; it shakes me to pieces, for a day or two.

My kidneys lasted an age without weakening; it will soon be another age since their condition changed. Evils have their period like good things; perhaps this ailment is coming to an end. Age weakens the heat of my stomach; its digestion being thereby less perfect, it sends on this crude matter to my kidneys. Why cannot the heat of my kidneys be likewise weakened, at a certain revolution, so that they can no longer petrify my phlegm, and Nature may take steps to find some other way of purgation? The years have evidently made some of my rheums dry up. Why not these excrements that provide material for the gravel?

Furthermore, is there anything sweet in comparison with that sudden change, when from extreme pain, by the ejection of my stone, I come to recover as if by lightning the fair light of health, so free and so full, as happens in our sudden and sharpest attacks of colic? Is there anything in this pain we suffer that can be said to counterbalance the pleasure of such sudden improvement? How much more beautiful health seems to me after the illness, being so near and contiguous that I can recognize them in each other's presence in their highest apparel, when they vie with each other, as if to oppose each other squarely! Just as the Stoics say that vices are brought into the world usefully to give value to virtue and assist it, we can say, with better reason and less bold conjecture, that Nature has lent us pain for the honor and service of pleasure and painlessness. When Socrates, after being relieved of his irons, felt the relish of the itching that their weight had caused in his legs, he rejoiced to consider the close alliance between pain and pleasure, how they are associated by a necessary link, so that they follow and engender each other in turn. And he called out to goodly Aesop that he should have taken from this consideration a subject fit for a fine fable.

The worst thing I see in other maladies is that they are not as serious in their immediate effect as in their consequences. You are a whole year recovering, always full of weakness and fear. There is so much risk and so many steps in returning to safety that it is never over. Before they have rid you of a kerchief, and then of a cap, before they have given you back the enjoyment of air, and wine, and your wife, and melons, it is great good luck if you have not relapsed into some new misery. My sickness has this privilege, that it carries itself clean off, whereas the others always leave some imprint and change for the worse that makes the body susceptible to a new disease, and they lend a hand to one another. Those illnesses are excusable that content themselves with their own possession of us, without extending it and without bringing on their sequels; but courteous and gracious are those whose passage bring us some useful consequence. Since I have had the stone, I have found myself rid of other ailments, more so, it seems to me, than I was before; and I have had no fever since. I argue that the extreme and frequent vomitings that I endure purge me; and, on the other hand, my loss of appetite and the unusual fasts I undergo digest my morbid humors, and Nature evacuates in these stones its superfluous and harmful matter.

Do not tell me that it is a medicine too dearly bought. For what about all the stinking potions, cauteries, incisions, sweatings, setons, diets, and all the methods of cure that often bring us death because we cannot endure their violence and relentlessness? So when I have an attack, I take it as medicine; when I am exempt, I take it as lasting and complete deliverance.

Here is another benefit of my illness, peculiar to it: that it almost plays its game by itself and lets me play mine, unless I lack courage; in its greatest throes I have held out for ten hours on horseback. Just bear it, you need no other regime. Play, dine, run, do this and do that too, if you can; your dissipation will do more good than harm. Say as much to a man with the pox, the gout, or a hernia! Other maladies have more inclusive bonds, hamper our actions far more, disturb our whole order, and involve the entire state of life in consideration of them. Mine only pinches the skin; it leaves your understanding and will at your disposal, and your tongue, and your feet, and your hands; it rather awakens you than puts you to sleep. The soul is smitten by the burning of a fever, and floored by an epileptic fit, and dislocated by a violent headache, and in short stunned by all the ailments that hurt the whole body and the noblest parts. Here, it is not attacked. If it fares badly, it is its own fault; it betrays, abandons, and unhorses itself.

It is only fools that let themselves be persuaded that this hard solid body that is baked in our kidneys can be dissolved by potions. Therefore, once it is in motion, there is nothing to do but give it passage; it will take it anyway.

I notice also this particular convenience, that it is a disease in which we have little to guess about. We are freed from the worry into which other diseases cast us by the uncertainty of their causes and conditions and progress—an infinitely painful worry. We have no concern with doctoral consultations and interpretations; the senses reveal to us what it is, and where it is.

By such arguments, both strong and weak, I try to lull and beguile my imagination and salve its wounds, as Cicero did his disease of old age. If they get worse tomorrow, tomorrow we shall provide other ways out.

Here is proof. Now it has happened again that the slightest movements force the pure blood out of my kidneys. What of it? I do not, just for that, give up moving about as before and pricking after my hounds with youthful and insolent ardor. And I think I come off well from such an important accident when it costs me nothing but a dull weight and uneasiness in that region. It is some big stone that is crushing and consuming the substance of my kidneys, and my life that I am letting out little by little, not without some natural pleasure, as an excrement that is henceforth superfluous and a nuisance. Do I feel something crumbling? Do not expect me to go and amuse myself testing my pulse and my urine so as to take some bothersome precaution; I shall be in plenty of time when I feel the pain, without lengthening it by the pain of fear. He who fears he will suffer, already suffers from his fear.

Besides, the uncertainty and ignorance of those who presume to explain the workings of Nature, and her inner processes, and all the false prognostications of their art, should make us know that she has utterly unknown ways of her own. There is great uncertainty, variety, and obscurity about whether she promises us or threatens us. Except for old age, which is an indubitable sign of the approach of death, in all other ailments I see few signs of the future on which to base our divination.

I judge myself only by actual sensation, not by reasoning. What would be the use, since I intend to apply only waiting and endurance? Do you want to know how much I gain by this? Look at those who do otherwise, and who depend on so many different persuasions and counsels: how often imagination oppresses them, without the body! Many a time, when safe and free from these dangerous afflictions, I have taken pleasure in communicating their symptoms to the doctors as if they were just beginning inside me. I suffered the doom of their horrible conclusions most comfortably, and remained that much more obliged to God for his grace and better informed of the vanity of this art.

There is nothing that should be so highly recommended to youth as activity and vigilance. Our life is nothing but movement. I have trouble getting under way, and am late for everything: getting up, going to bed, at meals. Seven o'clock is early for me, and where I am in charge I do not dine before eleven or sup till after six. In other days I attributed the fevers and illnesses into which I have fallen to the sluggishness and drowsiness that long sleep had brought on me, and I have always repented of going back to sleep in the morning. Plato is more set against excess in sleep than excess in drinking.

I like to sleep hard and alone, even without a woman, in the royal style, rather well covered up. My bed is never warmed, but since I have grown old they give me, when I need them, cloths to warm my feet and stomach. They used to criticize the great Scipio for being such a sleeper, in my opinion for no other reason than that it annoyed men that in him alone there was nothing to criticize. If I am at all particular about my way of life, it is rather about sleeping than anything else; but generally I yield and adapt myself to necessity as much as anyone. Sleeping has taken up a large part of my life, and even at this age I continue to sleep eight or nine hours at a stretch. I am weaning myself profitably from this lazy propensity, and am evidently the better for it. I feel the impact of the change a little, but in three days it is done. And I hardly know anyone who can live with less sleep when necessary, or who stands up better under exercise, or who is bothered less by military duties.

My body is capable of steady but not of vehement or sudden exertion. From now on I avoid violent exercises which put me into a sweat; my limbs grow tired before they grow warm. I can stay on my feet a whole day, and I never weary of walking; but on the pavement, since my early youth, I have never liked to go except on horseback. On foot I get muddy right up to my buttocks; and in our streets small men are subject to being jostled and elbowed, for want of presence. And I have always liked to rest, whether lying or sitting, with my legs as high as my seat or higher.

There is no occupation as pleasant as the military one, an occupation both noble in execution (for the strongest, most generous, and proudest of all virtues is valor) and noble in its cause: there is no more just and universal service than the protection of the peace and greatness of your country. You enjoy the company of so many noble, young, active men, the regular sight of so many tragic spectacles, the freedom of that unstudied relationship, a manly and unceremonious way of life, the variety of a thousand diverse actions, that brave harmony of martial music which fills and warms your ears and your soul, the honor of this exercise, even its severity and hardship, which Plato holds so lightly that in his Republic he makes women and children share them. A volunteer, you invite yourself to particular parts and risks according to your judgment of their brilliance and importance, and you see when life itself may be justifiably devoted to them:

> *I thought how beautiful to die in arms.*
>
> [Virgil]

To fear the common risks that affect so great a throng, not to dare what souls of so many classes dare, that is for a heart immeasurably weak and base. Company reassures even children. If others surpass you in knowledge, in grace, in strength, in fortune, you have external causes to blame for it; but if you yield to them in strength of soul, you have only yourself to blame. Death is more abject, more lingering and distressing in bed than in battle; fevers and catarrhs are as painful and fatal as a musket shot. Whoever is prepared to bear valiantly the accidents of everyday life would not have to swell his courage to become a soldier. *To live, my Lucilius, is to fight.* [Seneca]

I do not remember ever having had the itch; yet scratching is one of the sweetest gratifications of nature, and as ready at hand as any. But repentance follows too annoyingly close at its heels. I mostly scratch my ears, which are sometimes itchy on the inside.

I was born with all my senses sound almost to perfection. My stomach is conveniently good, as is my head and also my wind, and they usually keep up through my fevers. I have recently passed six years beyond the age of fifty, which some nations, not without cause, had prescribed as such a proper limit of life that they allowed no one to exceed it. Yet I still have flashes of recovery so clear, though inconstant and brief, that they fall little short of my youthful health and freedom from pain. I am not speaking of vigor and sprightliness; it is not reasonable that they should follow me beyond their limits:

> *I can endure no longer to remain*
> *Upon a doorstep in the rain.*
>
> > [Horace]

My face immediately betrays me, and my eyes; all my changes begin there, and seem a little worse than they really are. I often move my friends to pity before I feel the reason for it. My mirror does not alarm me, for even in my youth I have more than once found myself thus wearing a muddy complexion and an ill-omened look, without any serious consequences; so that the doctors, finding inside me no cause responsible for this outward change, attributed it to the spirit and to some secret passion gnawing me within. They were wrong. If my body obeyed my orders as well as my soul, we should get along a little more comfortably. My soul was then not only free from disturbance, but also full of satisfaction and glee—as it usually is, half by nature, half by design:

> *Nor does the sickness of my mind infect my limbs.*
>
> > [Ovid]

I hold that this temperateness of my soul has many a time lifted up my body from its falls. My body is often depressed; while if my soul is not jolly, it is at least tranquil and peaceful. I had a quartan fever for four or five months, which had

quite disfigured me; my mind still kept going not only peace-
fully but cheerfully. If the pain is outside of me, the weakness and languor do not distress me much. I know several
bodily infirmities that inspire horror if you merely name
them, which I should fear less than a thousand passions and
agitations of the spirit that I see prevalent. I have made up
my mind to my inability to run any more, it is enough that
I crawl. Nor do I complain of the natural decay that has
hold of me—

> *Who marvels at a goiter in the Alps?*
>
> > [Juvenal]

—any more than I regret that my term of life is not as long
and sound as that of an oak.

I have no cause to complain of my imagination. I have had
few thoughts in my life that have even interrupted the
course of my sleep, unless they have been those of desire,
which awakened me without afflicting me. I seldom dream,
and then it is about fantastic things and chimeras usually
produced by comical thoughts, more ridiculous than sad.
And I hold that it is true that dreams are faithful interpreters
of our inclinations; but there is an art to assorting and understanding them.

> *No wonder dreams repeat whate'er holds waking men in*
> > *sway—*
> *All that they meditate, or care, or see, or do, or say,*
> *Throughout the day.*
>
> > [Accius]

Plato says, moreover, that it is the function of wisdom to
draw from them instructions for divining the future. I see
nothing in that, except for the marvelous experiences that

Socrates, Xenophon, and Aristotle, personages of irreproachable authority, tell of it. Historians say that the Atlantes never dream, and also that they eat nothing that has been killed; which I add because that is perhaps the reason why they do not dream. For Pythagoras prescribed a certain preparation of food to induce appropriate dreams. Mine are gentle and bring on no bodily agitation or vocal utterance. I have known many people of my time to be amazingly agitated by them. Theon, the philosopher, walked in his sleep, and the servant of Pericles on the very tiles and roof of the house.

I make little choice at table, and attack the first and nearest thing, and I change reluctantly from one flavor to another. I dislike a crowd of dishes and courses as much as any other crowd. I am easily satisfied with few dishes, and I hate the notion of Favorinus that at a feast your food should be stolen from you just as you are gaining appetite, and a new dish always substituted, and that it is a wretched supper if the guests have not been glutted with various birds' rumps, and that the beccafico alone deserves to be eaten whole.

I often eat salt meats; however, I prefer bread without salt, and my baker at home serves no other at my table, contrary to the custom of the country. In my childhood they had principally to correct my refusal of things that people ordinarily like best at that age: sugar candies, preserves, pastry. My tutor fought this hatred of dainty foods as being a sort of daintiness. And indeed it is nothing else but fastidious taste, whatever it applies to. Whoever rids a child of some particular and obstinate fondness for brown bread, bacon, or garlic, rids him of finical taste. There are some who act like patient sufferers if they do without beef and ham amid partridges. They have a good time; that is the daintiness of the dainty; it is the taste of a soft existence that is cloyed with the ordinary and accustomed things, *by which luxury beguiles the tedium of wealth.* [Seneca] Not to make good cheer with what another does, to take particular care of what you eat and drink, is the essence of this vice:

If you fear a meal of greens upon a modest plate.
[Horace]

True enough, there is this difference, that it is better to enslave your desire to the things easiest to obtain; but it is always a vice to enslave yourself. I once called a relative of mine fastidious, who in our galleys had lost the ability to use our beds and to get undressed for sleep.

If I had any male children, I should cordially wish them my own fortune. The good father that God gave me (who has no return from me except gratitude for his goodness, but certainly a very hearty gratitude) sent me from the cradle to be brought up in a poor village of his, and kept me there as long as I was nursing, and even longer, training me to the humblest and commonest way of life. *A well-behaved stomach is a great part of liberty.* [Seneca] Never take on, and still less give to your wives, the charge of their upbringing. Let them be formed by Fortune under the laws of the common people and of Nature; leave it to custom to train them to frugality and austerity, so that they may have rather to come down from rigorousness than climb toward it. His notion aimed at still another goal, to ally me with the people and that class of men that needs our help; and he considered that I was duty bound to look rather to the man who extends his arms to me than to the one who turns his back on me. And this was the reason why he also had me held over the baptismal font by people of the lowliest class, to bind and attach me to them.

His plan has succeeded not at all badly. I am prone to devote myself to the little people, whether because there is more vainglory in it, or through natural compassion, which has infinite power over me. The side I condemn in our wars I will condemn more harshly when it is flourishing and prosperous; I will be somewhat reconciled to it when I see it miserable and crushed. How I enjoy considering the fine spirit of Chelonis, daughter and wife of kings of Sparta! While her husband Cleombrotus had the advantage over her father Leonidas in the conflicts within her city, she was the good daughter and rallied to her father in his exile, in his misery, opposing the victor. Did Fortune chance to turn? There she is, her will changed with Fortune's, courageously taking the side of her husband, whom she followed everywhere his ruin led him, having apparently no choice but to rush to the side where she was most needed and where she could best show her compassion. I am more naturally inclined to follow the example of Flaminius, who lent himself to those who needed him more than to those who could benefit him, than that of Pyrrhus, who was prone to cringe before the great and be arrogant with the weak.

Long sessions at table annoy me and disagree with me; for, perhaps because I formed the habit as a boy, for lack of better self-control, I eat as long as I am there. Therefore at home, though the meals are on the short side, I like to sit down a little after the others, in the manner of Augustus; but I do not imitate him in also leaving the table before the others. On the contrary, I like to rest a long time after and listen to stories, provided I do not take part, for it tires me and disagrees with me to talk on a full stomach, whereas I find it a very healthy and pleasant exercise to shout and argue before a meal. The ancient Greeks and Romans had more sense than we, to assign to eating, which is one of the principal actions of life, several hours and the best part of the night, if some other unusual occupation did not interfere, eating and drinking less hastily than we, who perform all our actions on the run, and prolonging this natural pleasure with greater leisure and enjoyment, interspersing it with various useful and agreeable duties of society.

Those who must take care of me could easily deprive me of what they think harmful to me; for in such matters I never desire or find wanting what I do not see. But likewise they waste their time preaching me abstinence from the things that are set before me. So that when I want to fast, I have to be set apart from the supper table, and to have put before me just so much as is necessary for the prescribed collation; for if I sit down to table I forget my resolution. When I order a change in the preparation of some meat, my servants know that it means that my appetite is weakened and that I will not touch it.

All meats that can endure it I like rare, and I like them high, even to the point of smelling bad in many cases. There is nothing but toughness that annoys me as a rule (toward any other quality I am as indifferent and tolerant as any man I have known), so that, contrary to the common humor, even among fish I sometimes find some too fresh and too firm. It is not the fault of my teeth, which have always been good, even excellent, and which only just now are beginning to be threatened by old age. I learned from childhood to rub them with my napkin both in the morning and before and after meals.

God is merciful to those whose life he takes away bit by

bit; that is the only benefit of old age. The last death will be all the less complete and painful; by then it will kill only a half or a quarter of a man. Here is a tooth that has just fallen out, without pain, without effort; that was the natural term of its duration. Both that part of my being and several others are already dead, others half dead, even some of the most active, which held the highest rank during the vigor of my prime. Thus do I melt and slip away from myself. What folly it would be on the part of my intelligence to feel the height of this fall, already so far advanced, just as if it were complete! I hope I shall not.

In truth, I have one principal comfort in thinking about my death, that it will be normal and natural, and that henceforth in this matter I cannot demand or hope for any but illegitimate favor from destiny. Men enjoy a fond belief that in other days their lives were longer, as their stature was greater. But Solon, who belongs to those old days, nevertheless limits the extreme duration of life to seventy years. Shall I, who in all matters have so worshipped that *golden mean* of the past, and have regarded the moderate measure as the most perfect, aspire to an immoderate and unnatural old age? Whatever happens contrary to the course of Nature may be disagreeable, but what happens according to her should always be pleasant. *Everything that happens according to Nature should be considered good.* [Cicero] Thus, says Plato, the death that is brought on by wounds or maladies may be called violent, but that which takes us by surprise as old age guides us to it is the easiest of all and in a way delightful. *Young men lose their lives by violence, old men by ripeness.* [Cicero]

Death mingles and fuses with our life throughout. Decline anticipates death's hour and intrudes even into the course of our progress. I have portraits of myself at twenty-five and thirty-five; I compare them with one of the present: how irrevocably it is no longer myself! How much farther is my present picture from those than from that of my death! We abuse Nature too much by pestering her so far that she is constrained to leave us and abandon our guidance—our eyes, our teeth, our legs, and the rest—to the mercy of foreign assistance that we have begged, and to resign us to the hands of art, weary of following us.

I am not excessively fond of either salads or fruits, except melons. My father hated all kinds of sauces; I love them all. Eating too much bothers me; but I have as yet no really certain knowledge that any kind of food intrinsically disagrees with me; even as I do not distinguish a full or a waning moon, nor autumn from spring. There are changes that take place in us, irregular and unknown. For radishes, for example, I first found to agree with me, then to disagree, now to agree again. In several respects I feel my stomach and appetite vary that way: I have changed back from white wine to claret, and then from claret to white. I am very fond of fish, and have my fat days on the lean days, and my feasts on the fast days. I believe what some say, that it is easier to digest than meat. As it goes against my conscience to eat meat on fish days, so it goes against my taste to mix fish with meat; the difference between them seems to me too great.

Ever since my youth I have occasionally skipped a meal; either to sharpen my appetite for the next day, for, as Epicurus used to fast and make lean meals to accustom his appetite to do without abundance, I do so, on the contrary, to train my appetite to profit better from abundance and use it more joyfully; or I fasted to conserve my vigor for the sake of some action of body or mind, for in me both of these grow cruelly lazy through repletion, and I hate above all things the stupid coupling of so healthy and sprightly a goddess with that little belching god of indigestion, all bloated with the fumes of his liquor;[1] or to cure my sick stomach; or for want of proper company, for I say, like that same Epicurus, that we should not so much consider what we eat as with whom we eat, and I commend Chilo because he would not promise to be at Periander's feast until he was informed who were the other guests. There is no preparation so sweet to me, nor sauce so appetizing, as that which is derived from society.

I think it is healthier to eat more slowly and less, and to eat more often. But I want to make the most of appetite and hunger; I would take no pleasure in dragging out three or four puny meals a day, thus restricted, like a doctor's regime. Who would assure me that I would find again at supper the wide-open appetite I had in the morning? Let us take—old men especially—let us take the first opportune time that comes our way. Let us leave the daily diets to the almanac-makers and the doctors.

The greatest benefit that good health gives me is sensual pleasure; let us stick to the first pleasure that is present and known. I avoid consistency in these laws of fasting. He who wants to make the most of a habit, let him avoid continuing it; we grow hardened to it, our powers go to sleep in it; six months later you will have so debased your stomach to it that your only profit will be to have lost the freedom to treat it otherwise without damage.

I do not keep my legs and thighs any more covered in winter than in summer: just silk hose alone. For the relief

---

[1] Venus and Bacchus.

of my colds I have allowed myself to keep my head warmer, and my stomach because of my stone; my ailments became accustomed to it in a few days and disdained my ordinary precautions. I had risen from a cap to a kerchief, and from a bonnet to a lined hat. The padding of my doublet serves now only for ornament; it is no good unless I add a hare's skin or a vulture's, and a skullcap for my head. Follow these steps and you will go a long way. I will do nothing of the sort, and would gladly disown the start I have made, if I dared. Are you falling into some new ailment? This reform is of no more use to you; you are accustomed to it; look for another. Thus men ruin themselves when they let themselves be entangled in confined regimes, and tie themselves down to them superstitiously. They still need more, and still more after that; it is never done.

For the sake of our occupations and pleasure, it is much more convenient to skip our dinner, as the ancients did, and put off making good cheer till the hour of retirement and rest, without breaking up the day; thus I formerly used to do. For the sake of health, on the contrary, I have since found by experience that it is better to dine, and that digestion is better performed awake.

I am not much subject to thirst, either in health or sickness. To be sure, in the latter case I am apt to have a dry mouth, but without thirst. Normally I only drink from the desire for it that comes to me in eating, and far along in the meal. I drink pretty well for a man of ordinary build; in summer and at an appetizing meal, I not only exceed the limits of Augustus, who drank no more than precisely three times, but, so as not to violate the rule of Democritus, who forbade stopping at four as an unlucky number, I slip on at a pinch to five, about three half-pints; for the little glasses are my favorites, and I enjoy draining them, which others avoid as unbecoming. I mix my wine most often with a half, sometimes with a third of water. And when I am at home, by an ancient practice that my father's doctor prescribed for him and for himself, they mix what I need in the wine cellar two or three hours before serving. They say that Cranaus, King of the Athenians, was the inventor of this practice of mixing wine with water; whether for better or for worse, I have heard it argued. I think it more fitting and healthy for children not to use it until they are sixteen or eighteen. The most usual and common behavior is the best; all peculiarities seem to me things to be avoided; and I should hate as much to see a German putting water in his wine as a Frenchman drinking it pure. Public usage lays down the law in such matters.

I fear a stuffy atmosphere and mortally avoid smoke; the first repairs I hurried to make in my house were in the chimneys and the privies, a common and unbearable defect in old buildings; and among the hardships of war I reckon those thick clouds of dust in which they keep us buried in the hot season for a whole day's journey. My breathing is free and easy, and my colds most often pass off without a cough and without damage to my lungs.

The rigor of summer is more of an enemy to me than that of winter; for besides the discomfort of heat, less easily remedied than that of cold, and besides the beating of the sunbeams on my head, my eyes are hurt by any dazzling light. Right now I could not eat dinner seated opposite a blazing, bright fire. To deaden the whiteness of paper, in the time when I was more in the habit of reading, I used to lay a piece of glass on my book, and found much relief in it. To this moment I am ignorant of the use of spectacles, and I see just as far as I ever did, and as any man. It is true that at the decline of day I begin to feel blurring and weakness in reading, an exercise that has always pained my eyes, but especially at night. Here is a step backward, just barely perceptible. I shall draw back another step, from the second to the third, from the third to the fourth, so quietly that I shall have to be a confirmed blind man before I feel the decadence and old age of my sight. So artfully do the Fates untwist the thread of our life. And so I doubt that my hearing is on the verge of growing dull, and you will see that when I have half lost it I shall still be blaming the voices of those who are speaking to me. We must really strain our soul to make it feel how it is ebbing away.

My walk is quick and firm; and I know not which of the two, my mind or my body, I have had more difficulty in keeping in one place. That preacher is indeed a friend of mine who holds my attention through a whole sermon. In solemn places, where everyone has such a strained expression, where I have seen the ladies keep even their eyes so steady, I have never succeeded in keeping some part of me from always wandering; even though I may be seated there, I am hardly settled there. As the chambermaid of the philosopher Chrysippus said of her master that he was only drunk in his legs—for he had the habit of moving them about, whatever position he was in, and she would say it when wine befuddled the others and he felt no effect from it—so people might have said of me from my childhood that I was crazy in the feet, or had quicksilver in them, so fidgety and restless are they, wherever I place them.

It is bad manners, besides being harmful to health and even to pleasure, to eat greedily, as I do. I often bite my tongue and sometimes my fingers, in my haste. Diogenes, coming upon a boy who was eating that way, gave his tutor a box on the ear for it. There were men at Rome who taught people to chew, as well as to walk, gracefully. By this I lose the leisure for talking, which is such a sweet seasoning for the dinner table, provided the remarks are appropriate, pleasant, and brief.

There is jealousy and envy between our pleasures; they clash and interfere with each other. Alcibiades, a connoisseur in making good cheer, banished even music from the table, so that it should not blur the pleasure of conversation, for the reason that Plato ascribes to him, that it is a practice of vulgar men to call in instrumentalists and singers to their feasts, for lack of good talk and enjoyable remarks, with which intelligent men know how to entertain each other. Varro asks this of a banquet: a gathering of people of handsome presence and agreeable conversation, who are neither mute nor garrulous; cleanliness and delicacy in the food and the place; and fair weather. A well-planned dinner is no small art, nor small pleasure; neither the great generals nor the great philosophers have spurned the practice and science of it. My imagination has entrusted three dinners to the keeping of my memory, which Fortune rendered outstandingly pleasant to me at different times in my more flourishing days. For each of the guests himself brings the principal charm, according to the good temper of body and soul in which he happens to be. My present condition excludes me from this.

I, who always stick close to the ground, hate that inhuman wisdom that would make us disdainful enemies of the cultivation of the body. I consider it equal injustice to set our hearts against pleasures and to set our hearts too much on them. Xerxes was a fool, who, wrapped in all human pleasures, went and offered a reward to anyone who would find him others. But hardly less of a fool is the man who cuts off those that Nature has found for him. We should neither pursue them nor flee them, we should accept them. I accept them a little more plumply and graciously, and more willingly let myself follow a natural inclination. We have no need to exaggerate their inanity; it makes itself felt enough and evident enough. Much thanks to our sickly, kill-joy mind, which disgusts us with them as well as with itself. It treats both itself and all that it takes in, now better, now worse, according to its insatiable, erratic, and versatile nature.

Unless the vessel's pure, all you pour in turns sour.
                                                    [Horace]

I, who boast of embracing the pleasures of life so assiduously and so particularly, find in them, when I look at them thus minutely, virtually nothing but wind. But what of it? We are all wind. And even the wind, more wisely than we, loves to make a noise and move about, and is content with its own functions, without wishing for stability and solidity, qualities that do not belong to it.

The pure pleasures of imagination, as well as the pains, some say, are the greatest, as the scales of Critolaus expressed it. It is no wonder; it composes them to its liking and cuts them out of whole cloth. I see signal, and perhaps desirable, examples of this every day. But I, who am of a mixed and coarse constitution, cannot bite so completely at this single and simple object that I do not let myself go quite grossly after the present pleasures of the general human law, intellectually sensual, sensually intellectual. The Cyrenaic philosophers hold that the bodily pleasures, like the pains, are more powerful, as being both twofold and more appropriate.

There are some who from savage stupidity, as Aristotle says, are disgusted with them; I know some who are that way from ambition. Why do they not also give up breathing? Why do they not live on their own air, and refuse light, because it is **free and** costs them neither invention nor vigor? Let Mars, or Pallas, or Mercury give them sustenance, instead of Venus, Ceres, and Bacchus, just to see what happens. Won't they try to square the circle while perched on their wives! I hate to have people order us to keep our minds in the clouds while our bodies are at table. I would not have the mind nailed down to it nor wallowing at it, but attending to it; sitting at it, not lying down at it.

Aristippus defended the body alone, as if we had no soul; Zeno embraced only the soul, as if we had no body. Both were wrong. Pythagoras, they say, followed a philosophy that was all contemplation, Socrates one that was all conduct and action; Plato found the balance between the two. But they say so to make a good story, and the real balance is found in Socrates, and Plato is much more Socratic than Pythagorean, and it becomes him better.

When I dance, I dance; when I sleep, I sleep; yes, and when I walk alone in a beautiful orchard, if my thoughts have been dwelling on extraneous incidents for some part of the time, for some other part I bring them back to the walk, to the orchard, to the sweetness of this solitude, and to me. Nature has observed this principle like a mother, that the actions she has enjoined on us for our need should also give us pleasure; and she invites us to them not only through reason, but also through appetite. It is unjust to infringe her laws.

When I see both Caesar and Alexander, in the thick of their great tasks, so fully enjoying natural and therefore necessary and just pleasures, I do not say that that is relaxing their minds, I say that it is toughening them, subordinating these violent occupations and laborious thoughts, by the vigor of their spirits, to the practice of everyday life—wise, if they had believed that this was their ordinary occupation, the other the extraordinary.

We are great fools. "He has spent his life in idleness," we say; "I have done nothing today." What, have you not lived? That is not only the fundamental but the most illustrious of your occupations. "If I had been placed in a position to manage great affairs, I would have shown what I could do." Have you been able to think out and manage your own life? You have done the greatest task of all. To show and exploit her resources Nature has no need of fortune; she shows herself equally on all levels and behind a curtain as well as without one. To compose our character is our duty, not to compose books, and to win, not battles and provinces, but order and tranquillity in our conduct. Our great and glorious masterpiece is to live appropriately. All other things, ruling, hoarding, building, are only little appendices and props, at most.

I take pleasure in seeing an army general, at the foot of a breach that he means to attack presently, lending himself wholly and freely to his dinner and his conversation, among his friends; and Brutus, with heaven and earth conspiring against him and Roman liberty, stealing some hour of night from his rounds to read and annotate Polybius with complete assurance. It is for little souls, buried under the weight of business, to be unable to detach themselves cleanly from it, or to leave it and pick it up again:

> *Brave men, who have endured with me*
> *Worse things, now banish cares with wine and glee;*
> *Tomorrow we shall sail the mighty sea.*

[Horace]

Whether it is in jest or in earnest that the theological and Sorbonical wine has become a proverb, and their banquets too, I think that it is right that they should dine all the more comfortably and gaily for having used the morning profitably and seriously in the work of their school. The consciousness of having spent the other hours well is a proper and savory sauce for the dinner table. Thus did the sages live. And that inimitable straining for virtue that astounds us in both Catos, that disposition, severe to the point of being troublesome, submitted meekly and contentedly to the laws of human nature, and of Venus and Bacchus, in accordance with the precepts of their sect, which require the perfect sage to be as expert and versed in the enjoyment of the natural pleasures as in any other duty of life. *A wise palate should go with a wise heart.* [Cicero]

Relaxation and affability, it seems to me, is marvelously honorable and most becoming to a strong and generous soul. Epaminondas did not think that to mingle with the dance of the boys of his city, to sing, to play music, and to concentrate attentively on these things, was at all derogatory to the honor of his glorious victories and the perfect purity of character that was his. And among all the admirable actions of Scipio the grandfather, a personage worthy of the reputation of celestial descent, there is nothing that lends him more charm than to see him playing nonchalantly and childishly at picking up and selecting shells and running potato-races by the sea with Laelius, and in bad weather amusing and tickling his fancy by writing comedies portraying the meanest and most vulgar actions of men; and his head full of that wonderful campaign against Hannibal and Africa, visiting the schools in Sicily, and attending lectures on philosophy until he armed to the teeth the blind envy of his enemies in Rome. Nor is there anything more remarkable in Socrates than the fact that in his old age he finds time to take lessons in dancing and playing instruments, and considers it well spent.

This same man was once seen standing in a trance, an entire day and night, in the presence of the whole Greek army, overtaken and enraptured by some deep thought. He was seen, the first among so many valiant men of the army, to run to the aid of Alcibiades, who was overwhelmed by enemies, to cover him with his body, and to extricate him from the mill by sheer force of arms; and the first among all the people of Athens, outraged like him at such a shameful sight, to come forward to rescue Theramenes, whom the Thirty Tyrants were having led to his death by their satellites; and he only desisted from this bold undertaking at the remonstrance of Theramenes himself, though he was followed by only two men all told. He was seen, when courted by a beauty with whom he was in love, to maintain strict chastity when necessary. He was seen, in the battle of Delium, to pick up and save Xenophon, who had been thrown from his horse. He was constantly seen to march to war and walk the ice barefoot, to wear the same gown in winter and in summer, to surpass all his companions in enduring toil, to eat no differently at a feast than ordinarily.

He was seen for twenty-seven years to endure with the same countenance hunger, poverty, the indocility of his children, the claws of his wife; and in the end calumny, tyranny, prison, irons, and poison. But if that man was summoned to a drinking bout by the duty of civility, he was also the one who did the best in the whole army. And he never refused to play at nuts with children, or to ride a hobbyhorse with them, and he did so gracefully; for all actions, says philosophy, are equally becoming and honorable in a wise man. We have material enough, and we should never tire of presenting the picture of this great man as a pattern and ideal of all sorts of perfection. There are very few full and pure examples of life, and they are unfair to our education when they set before us every day feeble and defective models, hardly good in a single vein, which rather pull us backward, corrupters rather than correctors.

Popular opinion is wrong: it is much easier to go along the sides, where the outer edge serves as a limit and a guide, than by the middle way, wide and open, and to go by art than by Nature; but it is also much less noble and less commendable. Greatness of soul is not so much pressing upward and forward as knowing how to set oneself in order and limit oneself. It regards as great whatever is adequate, and shows its elevation by liking moderate things better than eminent ones. There is nothing so beautiful and legitimate as to play the man well and properly, nor any knowledge so arduous as knowing how to live this life well and naturally; and the most barbarous of our maladies is to despise our being.

He who wants to detach his soul, let him do it boldly, if he can, when his body is ill, to free it from the contagion; otherwise, on the contrary, let the soul assist and favor the body and not refuse to take part in its natural pleasures and enjoy them conjugally, bringing to them moderation, if it is the wiser of the two, for fear that through lack of discretion they may merge into pain. Intemperance is the plague of sensual pleasure; and temperance is not its scourge, it is its seasoning. Eudoxus, who made it the supreme good, and his fellows, who raised it to such high value, savored it in its most charming sweetness by means of temperance, which they possessed in singular and exemplary degree.

I order my soul to look upon both pain and pleasure with a gaze equally self-controlled—*for effusiveness of the soul in joy is as wrong as its contraction in sorrow* [Cicero]—and equally firm, but gaily at the one, at the other severely, and, according to its ability, as anxious to extinguish the one as to extend the other. Viewing good things sanely implies viewing bad things sanely. And pain has something not to be avoided in its mild beginning, and pleasure something to be avoided in its excessive ending. Plato couples them together and claims that it is equally the function of fortitude to fight against pain and against the immoderate and bewitching blandishments of pleasure. They are two fountains from which whoever draws the right amount from the right source at the right time, whether city, man, or beast, he is very fortunate. The first we must take as medicine and through necessity, more sparingly; the other through thirst, but not to the point of drunkenness. Pain, pleasure, love, hatred, are the first things a child feels; if when reason comes they cling to her, that is virtue.

I have a vocabulary all my own. I "pass the time," when it is rainy and disagreeable; when it is good, I do not want to pass it; I savor it, I cling to it. We must run through the bad and settle on the good. This ordinary expression "pastime" or "pass the time" represents the habit of those wise folk who think they can make no better use of their life than to let it slip by and escape it, pass it by, side-step it, and, as far as in them lies, ignore it and run away from it, as something irksome and contemptible. But I know it is other-wise, and find it both agreeable and worth prizing, even in its last decline, in which I now possess it; and Nature has placed it in our hands adorned with such favorable conditions that we have only ourselves to blame if it weighs on us and if it escapes us unprofitably. *The life of the fool is joyless, full of trepidation, given over wholly to the future.* [Seneca] However, I am composing myself to lose it, without regret, but as something that by its nature must be lost; not as some-thing annoying and troublesome. Then too, not to dislike dying is properly becoming only to those who like living. It takes management to enjoy it. I enjoy it twice as much as others, for the measure of enjoyment depends on whether we lend it more or less attention. Especially at this moment when I perceive that mine is so brief in time, I try to increase it in weight; I try to arrest the speed of its flight by the speed with which I grasp it, and by my vigor in using it to com-pensate for the haste of its ebb. The shorter my possession of life, the deeper and fuller I must make it.

Others feel the sweetness of some satisfaction and of pros-perity; I feel it as they do, but it is not in passing and slipping by. Instead we must study it, savor it, and ruminate it, to give proper thanks for it to him who grants it to us. They enjoy the other pleasures as they do that of sleep, without being conscious of them. To the end that sleep itself should not escape me thus stupidly, at one time I saw fit to have mine disturbed, so that I should gain a glimpse of it. I medi-tate on any satisfaction; I do not skim over it, I sound it, and bend my reason, now grown peevish and hard to please, to

welcome it. Do I find myself in some tranquil state? Is there
some voluptuous pleasure that tickles me? I do not let my
senses pilfer it, I bring my soul into it, not to implicate herself, but to enjoy herself, not to lose herself but to find herself, in it. And I set her, for her part, to admire herself in this
prosperous state, to weigh and appreciate and amplify the
happiness of it. She measures the extent of her debt to God
for being at peace with her conscience and from other inner
passions, for having her body in its natural condition, enjoying tranquilly and adequately the agreeable and pleasant
functions with which he is pleased to compensate by his
grace for the pains with which his justice chastises us in its
turn; how much it is worth to her to be lodged at such a
point that wherever she casts her eyes, the sky is serene
around her: no desire, no fear or doubt to disturb the air for
her, no difficulty, past, present, or future, over which her
imagination may not pass without hurt.

This consideration gains great luster by comparison between my condition and that of others. Thus I set before me
in a thousand forms those who are carried away and tossed
about by fortune or their own error, and also those, closer
to my way, who accept their good fortune so languidly and
indifferently. They are the people who really "pass their
time"; they pass over the present and what they possess, to
be the slaves of hope, and for shadows and vain pictures that
imagination dangles before them—

> *Like ghosts that after death are said to flit,*
> *Or visions that delude the slumbering wit,*
>
> [Virgil]

—which hasten and prolong their flight the more they are

pursued. The fruit and goal of their pursuit is to pursue, as Alexander said that the purpose of his work was to work,

> *Believing nothing done while aught was left to do.*
> [Lucan]

As for me then, I love life and cultivate it just as God has been pleased to grant it to us. I do not go about wishing that it should lack the need to eat and drink, and it would seem to me no less excusable a failing to wish that need to be doubled. *The wise man is the keenest searcher for natural treasures.* [Seneca] Nor that we should sustain ourselves by merely putting into our mouths a little of that drug by which Epimenides took away his appetite and kept himself alive; nor that we should beget children insensibly with our fingers or our heels, but rather, with due respect, that we could also beget them voluptuously with our fingers and heels; nor that the body should be without desire and without titillation. Those are ungrateful and unfair complaints. I accept with all my heart and with gratitude what Nature has done for me, and I am pleased with myself and proud of myself that I do. We wrong that great and all-powerful Giver by refusing his gift, nullifying it, and disfiguring it. Himself all good, he has made all things good. *All things that are according to nature are worthy of esteem.* [Cicero]

Of the opinions of philosophy I most gladly embrace those that are most solid, that is to say, most human and most our own; my opinions, in conformity with my conduct, are low and humble. Philosophy is very childish, to my mind, when she puffs herself up and preaches to us that it is a barbarous alliance to marry the divine with the earthly, the reasonable with the unreasonable, the severe with the indulgent, the honorable with the dishonorable; that sensual pleasure is a brutish thing unworthy of being enjoyed by the wise man; that the only pleasure he derives from the enjoyment of a beautiful young wife is the pleasure of his consciousness of doing the right thing, like putting on his boots for a useful ride. May her followers have no more right and sinews and sap in deflowering their wives than her lessons have!

That is not what Socrates says, her tutor and ours. He prizes bodily pleasure as he should, but he prefers that of the mind, as having more power, constancy, ease, variety, and dignity. The latter by no means goes alone, according to him —he is not so fantastic—but only comes first. For him temperance is the moderator, not the adversary of pleasures.

Nature is a gentle guide, but no more gentle than wise and just. *We must penetrate into the nature of things and clearly see exactly what it demands.* [Cicero] I seek her footprints everywhere. We have confused them with artificial tracks, and for that reason the sovereign good of the Academics and the Peripatetics, which is "to live according to her," becomes hard to limit and express; also that of the Stoics, a neighbor to the other, which is "to consent to Nature."

Is it not an error to consider some actions less worthy because they are necessary? No, they will not knock it out of my head that the marriage of pleasure with necessity, with whom, says an ancient, the Gods always conspire, is a very suitable one. To what purpose do we dismember by divorce a structure made up of such close and brotherly correspondence? On the contrary, let us bind it together again by mutual services. Let the mind arouse and quicken the heaviness of the body, and the body check and make fast the lightness of the mind. *He who praises the nature of the soul as the sovereign good and condemns the nature of the flesh as evil, truly both carnally desires the soul and carnally shuns the flesh; for his feeling is inspired by human vanity, not by divine truth.* [St. Augustine]

There is no part unworthy of our care in this gift that God has given us; we are accountable for it even to a single hair. And it is not a perfunctory charge to man to guide man according to his nature; it is express, simple, and of prime importance, and the Creator has given it to us seriously and sternly. Authority alone has power over common intelligences, and has more weight in a foreign language. Let us renew the charge here. *Who would not say that it is the essence of folly to do lazily and rebelliously what has to be done, to impel the body one way and the soul another, to be split between the most conflicting motions?* [Seneca]

Come on now, just to see, some day get some man to tell you the absorbing thoughts and fancies that he takes into his head, and for sake of which he turns his mind from a good meal and laments the time he spends on feeding himself. You will find there is nothing so insipid in all the dishes on your table as this fine entertainment of his mind (most of the time we should do better to go to sleep completely than to stay awake for what we do stay awake for); and you will find that his ideas and aspirations are not worth your stew. Even if they were the transports of Archimedes himself, what of it? I am not here touching on, or mixing up with that brattish rabble of men that we are, or with the vanity of the desires and musings that distract us, those venerable souls, exalted by ardent piety and religion to constant and conscientious meditation on divine things, who, anticipating, by dint of keen and vehement hope, the enjoyment of eternal food, final goal and ultimate limit of Christian desires, sole constant and incorruptible pleasure, scorn to give their attention to our beggarly, watery, and ambiguous comforts, and readily resign to the body the concern and enjoyment of sensual and temporary fodder. That is a privileged study. Between ourselves, these are two things that I have always observed to be in singular accord: supercelestial thoughts and subterranean conduct.

Aesop, that great man, saw his master pissing as he walked. "What then," he said, "shall we have to defecate as we run?" Let us manage our time; we shall still have a lot left idle and ill spent. Our mind probably has not enough other times to do its business, without dissociating itself from the body for that little space it must have for its needs.

They want to get out of themselves and escape from the man. That is madness: instead of changing into angels, they change into beasts; instead of raising themselves, they lower themselves. These transcendental humors frighten me, like lofty and inaccessible places; and nothing is so hard for me to stomach in the life of Socrates as his ecstasies and possessions by his daemon, nothing is so human in Plato as the reason why they say he is called divine. And of our sciences, those seem to me most terrestrial and low which have flown the highest. And I find nothing so humble and so mortal in the life of Alexander as his fancies about his immortalization. Philotas stung him wittily by his answer. He congratulated him by letter on the oracle of Jupiter Ammon which had lodged him among the Gods: *As far as you are concerned, I am very glad of it; but there is reason to pity the men who will have to live with and obey a man who exceeds and is not content with a man's proportions.*

Since you obey the gods, you rule the world.
[Horace]

The nice inscription with which the Athenians honored the entry of Pompey into their city is in accord with my meaning.

> *You are as much a God as you will own*
> *That you are nothing but a man alone.*

[Plutarch]

It is an absolute perfection and virtually divine to know how to enjoy our being lawfully. We seek other conditions because we do not understand the use of our own, and go outside of ourselves because we do not know what it is like inside. Yet there is no use our mounting on stilts, for on stilts we must still walk on our own legs. And on the loftiest throne in the world we are still sitting only on our own rear.

The most beautiful lives, to my mind, are those that conform to the common human pattern, with order, but without miracle and without eccentricity. Now old age needs to be treated a little more tenderly. Let us commend it to that God who is the protector of health and wisdom, but gay and sociable wisdom:

> *Grant me but health, Latona's son,*
> *And to enjoy the wealth I've won,*
> *And honored age, with mind entire*
> *And not unsolaced by the lyre.*

[Horace]